TRUTH TALK

TRUTH
TALK

Telling Yourself and Each Other the Truth

William Backus and Marie Chapian

Inspirational Press . New York

First Inspirational Press edition published in 1995.

Inspirational Press
A division of Budget Book Service, Inc.
386 Park Avenue South
New York, NY 10016

Inspirational Press is a registered trademark of
Budget Book Service, Inc.
Published by arrangement with Bethany House Publishers,
a division of Bethany Fellowship, Inc.
Library of Congress Catalog Card Number 94-74486

ISBN: 0-88486-117-1

Printed in the United States of America.

Table of Contents

TELLING YOURSELF THE TRUTH

Table of Contents

Introduction

This book has been written to help you live with the one person you must live with for life—you. The precepts set forth here are not new; in fact, they've been around since the time of King Solomon and before. People become happy and contented by learning how to practice the habits this book describes.

The current writings of the cognitive therapists such as Albert Ellis, A. T. Beck, M. J. Mahoney, D. Meichenbaum and Arnold Lazarus and their scientific points of view, the writings of philosophers such as Titus and Marcus Aurelius, the findings of psychological researchers as well as the probings of the greatest minds of history bring us to the truths set forth in the Holy Scriptures and the principles we share here with you. These principles are so practical and time-tested—in fact, God's own method for destroying the strongholds of evil in the minds of men and women—that it is amazing the average reader has never heard of such things!

Most of us want to be honest-to-goodness happy human beings who can handle life well and manage to feel good in spite of ever-increasing odds against us. Ironically, we use methods of achieving happiness that make us *unhappy*. We work at and strive for something that we can't quite catch hold of.

What does it mean to be happy? We could define it as a continuing sense of well-being, a state of feeling good about life, others, and self. We could also define happiness as the absence of mental and emotional discomfort and pain. The Bible calls happy "blessed."

> *Blessed*—happy, *fortunate, prosperous and enviable—is the man who walks and lives not in the counsel of the ungodly. . . . But his delight and desire are in the law of the Lord, and on His law—the precepts, the instructions, the teachings of God—.*[1]

In the Sermon on the Mount, Jesus names those who are blessed, or happy. They are people who are "spiritually prosperous [that is, with life-joy and satisfaction in God's favor and salvation, regardless of their outward conditions]."[2]

What is your definition of happiness? After you answer that question, we want you to know that it's possible to be happy, really happy in the deepest corners of your being, and to stay that way. You don't have to be a victim of circumstances, events, relationships. You don't have to be trapped by persistent painful emotions.

This book is written to help you possess the happiness you desire and to be the person you'd like to be. You can live happily ever after with the person you are and make a profound affect on those around you because of it.

"Misbelief Therapy," as we have called our *modus operandi*, involves putting the truth into our value systems, philosophies, demands, expectations, moralistic and emotional assumptions, as well as into the words we tell ourselves. The Bible says it is the *truth* that sets man free. Jesus Christ is the living Truth. When we inject the truth into our every thought, taking a therapeutic broom and sweeping away the lies and misbeliefs which have enslaved us, we find our lives radically changed for the happier better.

It is our hope that other professionals will join us in the exciting discovery that truth as it is in Jesus is a teachable way of life which leads to wholeness, restored functioning, and freedom from neurosis.

We ask the indulgence of our professionally trained readers who will find little scientific terminology in this book. We have purposely eschewed "psychologese" in order that all of our readers will feel comfortable with us.

Recently we completed a research project which involved follow-up calls to every client seen at the Center for Christian Psychological Services in a six-month period. The purpose was to ascertain how well Misbelief Therapy, as we call it, had actually worked in the lives of the clients. The results were gratifying. Ninety-five percent of the clients that had been treated at the Center had improved. Not only that, but these people were able to cite specific behaviors which had changed for the better. They were enthusiastic over the treatment they had received and the results that had been obtained in their lives. That is why we feel confident in recommending that you not only read this book, but that you also put into practice the procedures it offers you for bringing about real change in your life. You will be learning skills which you will want to keep forever.

---

1. Psalm 1:1, 2, The Amplified Bible.
2. Matthew 5:3, The Amplified Bible.

CHAPTER ONE

What Is Misbelief?

"Why do I feel the way I do?" cries the troubled person. Typically, he or she wants to put the blame on something or someone else. "It's my wife. *She's* the one who makes me feel this way." Or, "It's all my *husband's* fault." "My *job* isn't satisfying me," or "My *friends* are disappointing," or "My *children* are a disappointment." Some people blame their problems on their church. They find fault with their pastor, complain that the people aren't friendly enough or that everybody *else* in the world is a hypocrite.

There's something in all of our lives we'd like to change. Nobody's life circumstances are perfect. But what are we *telling* ourselves about these circumstances?

A few years ago a man we'll call Jerry was a wreck of a man. He was a Christian and had believed in God most of his life. Now, however, after 15 years of marriage, he was forced to live alone, separated from his family and facing a divorce he didn't want. He thought it was the end of the world. He was really miserable. He spent many evenings trying to anesthetize his painful feelings with liquor. He was so unhappy he wanted to die because he just couldn't see any other way out of such sad circumstances.

Finally, he decided to see a Christian psychotherapist for help. Once in therapy, he gradually began to see that his life didn't have to be over. He stopped thinking about taking his own life, and his faith in God began to stretch. He started thinking of

God as a giver of *good*. He came to know Him in a new dimension, and little by little, his life changed.

He explained it this way. "One day while I sat groveling in my sorrows, I listened to the words I had been telling myself, things like, 'Oh, what's the use? I'm all alone. Nobody loves me or cares about me. Nobody wants to be with me. I'm rejected and useless . . . ' Suddenly I was shocked. I thought, 'What am I telling myself anyhow?' "

Jerry questioned his self-talk. He recognized something radically wrong with what he had been telling himself and realized his depression was not due to his impending divorce, but what he was *telling himself about it*.

As a result he began to change the sentences he said to himself. This took some hard work and determination on his part. It wasn't easy at first, but because he refused to be a "chump" to a pack of self-destroying lies, he taught himself to confess the truth.

INSTEAD OF:	HE SAID:
I'm a failure and no good.	The marriage failed, but I am deeply loved by God. Therefore I am important.
I'm so lonely and miserable.	I'm alone, but I am not lonely.
I'm separated from my family and there's no joy anymore for me.	I'm separated from my family and that hurts. I can function even though I hurt.

He also stopped drinking completely. He argued with the destructive sentences he had been telling himself. "Just because I'm alone doesn't mean I have to be lonely!" he said. He told himself the *truth* and used his situation as an opportunity to celebrate, enjoy and revel in the presence of the Lord Jesus Christ in his life.

His circumstances hadn't changed, but what he *told himself* about the circumstances changed! He discovered that he had been telling himself a lot of lies, straight from the devil.

14

Three steps to becoming the happy person you were meant to be are:

1. *Locate your misbeliefs.* (Jerry realized that he was telling himself lies.)

2. *Remove them.* (He argued against them. "I am *not* lonely!")

3. *Replace misbeliefs with the truth.* ("It's nonsense to say I'm unlovable and useless. I'm loved with an everlasting love by the God of the universe. In Him, I have countless talents and uses and I am infinitely valuable to Him.)

Jerry learned that being alone could actually be an exciting experience with the Lord. If he had hung on to his ridiculous misbeliefs, he might have gone to his grave in gloom and misery long ago. Happily, he recovered completely and now leads a wonderfully fulfilled life. He will never again suffer the self-destructive anguish he was duped by once. When he learned to see the *truth* about himself, he also learned to argue and get rid of the lies that would have destroyed him.

TRUTH: WHAT IS IT?

Many philosophers and thinkers through the ages have been fascinated by the idea of *truth*, what it is and what it means in our lives.

One of these people was a man named Rene Descartes. He was a devout Roman Catholic who lived at the beginning of the seventeenth century. He made a name for himself by trying to discover clear and indubitable truth.

Descartes was fed up with the never-ending arguments among philosophers and decided to put an end to their disagreements forever.

In order to find some truth which would be so unquestionable that no one could doubt it, Descartes decided to start at the point of his own doubt of things. He systematically doubted all that he could possibly doubt. In doubting everything imaginable, he told himself he was *thinking.* Then he reasoned, since he was thinking, he had to *be.*

Thus emerged his famous words, *"I think, therefore I am."*

Descartes had finally discovered what he considered an indubitable truth: He believed the most important thing about truth was to arrive at it. The trouble with his proposition is that it doesn't tell us much about how to *live* or be *happy* with that truth.

Marcus Aurelius was another thinking man. He was emperor of Rome about 150 years after Christ, and he too was concerned with the *truth*. Marcus Aurelius was a stoic ruler and noted as one of the most high-minded and conscientious of all the Roman emperors. He had many failings, one of them his dislike for Christians; but in spite of this sorrowful indiscretion, he pursued a quest for *truth*. In his book *Meditations*, he shares an earth-shaking discovery, one that can make a difference in the way we live today.

Marcus Aurelius saw that human emotion is not just a product of chance circumstances, but is determined by the way people *think*.

Where Descartes said, "I think, therefore I am," Marcus Aurelius might have said, "I think in order to *determine* the way I am."

Precisely.

In the book of Proverbs in the Bible, it reads, *As a man thinketh in his heart, so is he.*[1] In exploring this and other scriptural references pertaining to the importance of right thinking, we discover the Bible solidly teaches that man's feelings, passions and behavior are subject to and conditioned by the way he thinks.

Marcus Aurelius had unearthed a truth whose fullness he could not wholly appreciate because he did not know the Lord Jesus Christ who said, *"I am the Truth."*[2]

As human beings we are not doomed to a cold, emotionless, machine-like existence. We are creatures throbbing with mental, emotional and physical energy. Once we yank out the irrationalities and lies from our thoughts and replace them with the *truth*, we can lead satisfying, rich and fulfilling emotional lives.

These irrationalities are not always easy to label. Most of what we tell ourselves is not in word form. Our thoughts are often images or attitudes without words attached to them. You may feel uncomfortable and isolated in crowded places but never actually put these feelings into words. You may be fearful of a thing

16

and avoid it without really knowing what's going on in your belief system at all.

But how do we change? How do we make contact with what's really going on within us?

"Doctor," a patient will weep, "I think the root of my problem goes back to my childhood!" How often we hear this statement!

Our culture, intinctured with Freudian philosophy, has nearly made it mandatory to believe that no one can be healed psychologically without exploring the past in detail and in depth.

It is not, however, events either past or present which make us feel the way we feel, but our *interpretation of those events.*

Our feelings are not caused by the circumstances of our long-lost childhood *or* the circumstances of the present. *Our feelings are caused by what we tell ourselves about our circumstances,* whether in words or in attitudes.

What we tell ourselves can be either (1) truth or (2) lie.

If you tell yourself untruths or lies, you will *believe* untruths and lies. If you tell yourself you're a dumb jerk who can't do anything right, you'll believe it. If you *believe* something, you'll *act* as though you believe it.

That's why your *beliefs and misbeliefs* are the most important factors of your mental and emotional life.

MISBELIEFS

What are misbeliefs?

The word *misbelief* is an important word. In fact, it's the most appropriate label we can think of for some of the ridiculous things we tell ourselves. The amount of suffering we experience due to sustained bouts of negative thinking and battered emotions is outrageous.

Misbeliefs are the direct cause of emotional turmoil, maladaptive behavior and most so-called "mental illness." Misbeliefs are the cause of the destructive behavior people persist in engaging in even when they are fully aware that it is harmful to them (such as overeating, smoking, lying, drunkenness, stealing or adultery).

Misbeliefs generally appear as truth to the person repeating them to himself. They might even seem to be true to an untrained counselor. That is partly because they often do contain some shred of truth, and partly because the sufferer has never examined or questioned these erroneous assumptions. But, please understand, the misbeliefs we tell ourselves are directly from the pit of hell. They are hand engraved and delivered by the devil himself. He is very clever in dishing out misbeliefs. He doesn't want to risk being discovered so he always appears as if the lie he is telling us is true.

Words like, "Oh, I can't do anything right. I'm always making mistakes" are good examples. You'll believe these lies when you've just made a mistake.

"Oh, I can't do anything right" is a *misbelief statement*. If you believe words like that, you are believing a lie.

Martin Luther, teaching the meaning of the sixth petition of the Lord's Prayer ("Lead us not into temptation") wrote: "We pray in this petition that God would guard and keep us lest the devil, the world, and our flesh lead us into misbelief, despair and other great shame and vice." The consequences of misbelief do lead to despair and other "great shame and vice."

Think for a moment about the things you tell yourself. If you tell yourself your mother-in-law hates you or the guy next door is a rotten neighbor and a no-good so-and-so, what will you be influenced by? *You'll believe what you tell yourself.* Therefore, you'll treat your mother-in-law as a personal enemy and you'll treat your neighbor exactly like a no-good so-and-so.

More than likely your mother-in-law and neighbor gave you some reason to tell yourself those things about them, so you can feel justified with your self-talk. But you're a victim of misbelief.

Why?

The Apostle James shows us where destructive self-talk comes from. "This [superficial] wisdom is not such as comes down from above, but is earthly, unspiritual [animal], even devilish." [3] Negative and distorted statements which a person repeats to himself come from the devil. Your flesh accepts them without question and then, like spoiled, rotting food, these words of mental poison create painful emotional aches and pains.

This diet of deadly toxins will kill you, according to Saint

18

Paul. He says to set "the mind on the flesh . . . is death."[4] If you continue to tell yourself distorted statements, you're going to have negative feelings and you're going to engage in negative behavior.

Persistent painful feelings are contrary to God's will.

God does not want His children to suffer depression, worry and intractable anger.

Did you know God wants us to be able to control our feelings and actions?

We can do it when we get rid of our misbeliefs and start paying attention to our self-talk.

A client named Bob sits in the therapist's office for his sixth therapy session. He fidgets with his hands as he talks. "It's getting so I feel tense and knotted up most of the time," he tells the therapist. "I've prayed about it, and I know the Bible says we aren't supposed to be nervous about things, but I can't seem to help myself. It's getting worse."

"You feel tense *all* the time?" asks the therapist.

Bob frowns. "All the time. Sometimes it's worse than at other times. I go to church but that doesn't help. Last Sunday morning in church I could hardly stand it. I wanted to run out."

"Why didn't you get up and leave?"

Bob is surprised at the question. "I couldn't do that! Everybody would stare."

"And suppose they did stare? Can stares hurt you?"

"They'd think I was crazy or backslidden. Oh, I could never just walk out of church."

"But you said you could hardly stand it. Do you mean that because you were with people, you felt you *had* to stay there?"

"Well, of course. I mean, they'd think something was wrong with me if I just got up and walked out."

"Would that be so bad?"

"Well, what if they knew what was going on inside me? What if they found out how tense and upset I am most of the time? I'm always afraid people will find out how uptight I am."

"What if they did know some of your inner feelings?"

"They'd think I was a kook, maybe. Or maybe I'm not a good Christian. After all, Christians are supposed to be happy and calm."

19

"Let me ask you something, Bob. If you had a friend who was having tense and nervous feelings, would you call him a kook or a terrible Christian?"

Bob shifts his weight, glances at the floor. "Of course not."

"You seem to think that what others think of you is more important than your own feelings."

Bob is quiet for a moment and then says, "I do want everyone to think well of me. I want to be liked, do what people admire—"

"Let's examine what you've told me so far and see where the misbeliefs are."

Bob shakes his head up and down. "I can see one for sure."

"What is it?"

"The misbelief that everybody should like and appreciate me. If they don't, it would be just awful."

Bob made a huge discovery that day. He discovered how important the words are that he tells himself. These words, or our *self-talk*, are what we listen to in order to hear our misbeliefs.

One of Bob's misbeliefs was that in order for him to be happy, he had to know he was acceptable to people and liked by them.

Misbelief: "I must please people. My actions must not cause others to disapprove of me in any way. If someone disapproved of me, it would be intolerable."

This string of related misbeliefs causes anxiety and an endless source of pain.

Truth: The Christian doesn't have to strive for the approval of everyone around him.

Bob needed to understand that the people he was worried about pleasing actually had no power to hurt him, even if they weren't pleased with him. He learned that very rarely do people get as upset with us as we imagine them to be. He was able to make dramatic changes in his thinking when he at last realized that the actual consequences of disapproval could never cause as much despair and anguish as his misbelief caused him. He also realized that it was God's approval that was most important.

Bob was one of the fortunate ones. He didn't land in a hospital or become dependent upon various drugs. He was able to take control himself.

You are the controller of your happiness and your unhappiness.

You'll be on the road to freedom when you take the first step and identify your misbeliefs for what they are. Learn how to recognize them and put them in their place as lies of the devil.

"You will know the truth, and the truth will set you free" [5] is a promise of Jesus. Let the truth expose your misbeliefs for what they are!

You can be free from such ugly feelings as bitterness, oppression, depression, anxiety, resentment, anger, over-suspiciousness and hypersensitivity. You can learn self-control and have fun while you're doing it.

In emotional and mental health, what you believe is *all important*. It makes a difference what you believe. Other people, circumstances, events and material things are *not* what make you happy. What you *believe* about these things is what makes you happy or unhappy.

If you believe it would be horrible if nobody talks to you at a dinner party, your mental and emotional self will react accordingly. Getting ready for the party you feel tense; on the way to the party you're feeling anxious. Once there you're sweating and uncomfortable. Your every impulse is to find someone to talk to, to be a part of things, to be liked. You wonder *why* you're so nervous. You may excuse your feelings by telling yourself, "Oh, those parties aren't for me. I'm basically a shy person."

Do you see how misbeliefs cause us to deny ourselves pleasure as well as the good blessings of life in Christ?

The misbeliefs in the above are:
1. It will be horrible if nobody talks to me at social gatherings (or if I don't know the people).
2. It's terrible to feel self-conscious and nervous.
The truth is:
1. I can enjoy myself wherever I go, and I do not need to have someone to talk to in order to have a good time.
2. Feelings of self-consciousness won't kill me.

It's all right to experience these feelings.

Discomfort never killed anyone, but our misbeliefs tell us that discomfort is terrible, awful, wretched, horrible, when in fact, although not a lot of fun, it can be endurable.

What you think and believe determines how you feel and what you do. It is our endeavor to change the fundamental negative misbeliefs in you to the point where you will energetically and actively set about to get rid of them—permanently.

If you are a counselor, you can help people by helping them discover their misbeliefs. You can watch lives change and blossom before your eyes as people shunt their misbeliefs and actively inject the *truth* into their lives.

The question now is, do we really want to be happy?

---

1. Proverbs 23:7.
2. "I am the Way and the Truth and the Life; no one comes to the Father except by (through) Me" (John 14:6).
3. James 3:15.
4. Romans 8:6.
5. John 8:32.

CHAPTER TWO

Do We Really Want To Be Happy?

A very nice thing about changing your misbeliefs in order to be a happier person is that it will work for you *now*. You don't have to wait for months and years for a grand breakthrough. You can begin to change negative and unwanted persistent feelings immediately.

You have an advantage in working with a book like this. A misbelief that is frequently encountered in psychotherapy is that it is the *therapist's* job to make the client a well-adjusted and happy person.

Sometimes we expect a psychotherapist to treat us the same way a medical doctor does. You go to his office, present your body and your symptoms and he diagnoses your condition and prescribes proper treatment. Maybe you require medication or surgery. He puts you in the hospital. He operates. You take your medication, rest properly and soon you're much better.

Learning to be a happy, adjusted, productive and attractive person cannot be done for you in this way. Your therapist can't do it for you. He or she can't push a button and presto, you're no longer depressed or anxious.

It takes work on your part to be happy.

With misbelief therapy the client is informed immediately that the plan of action involves his hard work at changing the lies and misbeliefs which have victimized him.

Reading this book won't make you a different person, but *do-*

ing something about what you read here will. We hope you have decided that you *can* change your emotions, you *can* be an adjusted and happy human being, no matter what you have experienced in your life and no matter what your circumstances are.

BUT I CAN'T CHANGE THE WAY I BELIEVE!

Some patients have no trouble accepting the truth that what they tell themselves makes them feel and act the way they do. But they may argue, "That's fine for you, a therapist, to say, but I can't change the way I am!"

The misbelief is, *others* can be happy, *others* can have an experience with God, *others* can correct and change their misbeliefs, *others* can be free from anxiety, depression and anger, but I can't!

Perhaps they have learned to believe these lies through critical and fault-finding parents, or maybe they have formed habits of comparing themselves to others and believing they come out on the short end. There may be many causes for such misbeliefs.

The chemical dependent believes he can't quit using drugs. The obese patient believes he cannot lose weight. The depressive neurotic says, "I can't help myself."

"I can't even if other people can" are crippling words. Changing your misbeliefs will change your feelings and actions. You *can* do it.

There may be some things in life you actually cannot do. Perhaps you cannot run a four-minute mile, hit a home run over the ball park fence, or kick a football sixty yards. But you *can* change your misbeliefs.

You may say to yourself, "Misbelief Therapy may work for others, but it won't work for me. I've tried everything and I can't make anything work in my life." Are you saying something like that? Let's change that misbelief right now.

As long as you're convinced that you can't change, you won't try. There have been many people who have believed they could never change. And yet, these same people have dug in and changed their misbeliefs in spite of themselves, and the result has been transformed lives.

24

Misbelief Therapy *will* work for you. It will work for you even if nothing else has because its effectiveness depends upon very explicit psychological laws which are as universal as the law of gravity. The law of gravity is evident when you drop something, causing it to fall straight toward the center of the earth. So it is with the laws governing the relationship between belief and behavior. What you believe affects how you behave.

OUR EARLY YEARS

We talked earlier about the misbelief that all our problems stem from our childhood. This belief is widespread largely because of the influence of Freudian psychoanalytic theory, a magnificent but frequently erroneous personality theory which, a few decades ago, was generally accepted as the definitive word about human behavior. Now, however, psychoanalysis is not nearly as universally accepted among psychologists, and is losing ground among psychiatrists. Many excellent scientific investigations have demonstrated that it is entirely unnecessary to uncover the childhood antecedents of current behaviors in order to change them. Freudian psychoanalysis may actually provide an exercise to avoid working on changing behavior.

This is not to say that a problem is not better understood by looking into its history. Most therapists engage in exploration of the patient's past because it's important to a certain degree. We began thinking the way we now think at some time or another in our lives and often our thoughts and beliefs originate in childhood. Some of the primitive beliefs and behaviors that cause our unpleasant feelings and maladaptive behavior as adults were acquired in our early years. They may have been conveyed to us through the behavior and words of a significant person in our childhood. The impressions we learned in early years are important to us in order that we may change the misbeliefs we incurred then as well as the current misbeliefs we may have about our childhood.

Examining your early years may be important for the following reasons:

1. To discover your misbeliefs learned in childhood.

2. To discover your misbeliefs about events in your child-hood.
3. To examine your self-talk:
   What did you tell yourself *then*?
   What do you tell yourself *now*?

When you were a child you may have thought it was terrible if you lost something or if someone was cruel to you, mistreated you or treated you unjustly. Examining your early self-talk may reveal some of your current misbeliefs.

Once these are discovered, you can go to work changing your present thoughts and attitudes. By working on the lies you tell yourself *now*, you can successfully learn how to be a happy person in spite of anything that has happened to you in your life.

WHAT CAUSES US TO FEEL THE WAY WE FEEL?

The state of your biochemistry can affect the way you feel. There are ways to change your biochemistry; one of the ways is through drugs. Another way to change is to begin maintaining an adequate nutritional base and a properly-functioning body. Your thoughts, too, can change your biochemistry. That's right; what you are thinking right now can actually change the chemical composition of your brain cells and the rest of your central nervous system.

Would you believe that the sentences in your self-talk can actually alter your glandular, muscular and neural behavior? It's true. That's what we mean when we talk about emotions.

Some psychologists are uncovering the fact that the way you *think* influences the way you *feel*. They speak of it as a brand new discovery, a modern-day revelation. Actually, this truth has been around for thousands of years. The book of Proverbs says, *"As he thinketh in his own heart, so is he,"* and "The *thoughts* of the righteous are right . . . " [1] and the book of Psalms gives us many words regarding man's thoughts and the material he puts into his mind: "I thought on my ways, and turned my feet unto thy testimonies." [2]

Our thoughts determine our behavior. When we speak of behavior, we mean not only our actions but also our emotions.

26

Jesus kept telling people to believe, believe. Have faith, trust, believe. "According to your faith be it unto you,"[3] He said.

"Faith" is a noun that refers to the act of *believing*. Jesus' statement clearly teaches that we can expect certain things in our lives to take place as a direct result of how we believe.

What if you believe your life is hopeless and that you're nothing but a failure? "According to your faith, so be it done to you" is what Jesus said.

What if you believe that in spite of the ups and downs of life, you are not a failure, you'll never be a failure; it's impossible for you to be a failure! What if you believe that life is challenging and good and with Christ as the strength of your life, you're a winner through thick and thin?

"According to your faith be it unto you."

Don't let anybody tell you that what you think or tell yourself isn't important. It was the main core of Jesus' teachings.

During the 1970s many experiments in psychology were done to demonstrate that changing misbeliefs resulted in changing feelings like fear and depression. Psychologists have spoken of "cognitive restructuring" or rational emotive psychotherapy or alteration of personal constructs. No matter which term the psychologists prefer, they are all excited about one major discovery, a fact which has long been known to wise men, including the authors of the Scriptures: *Change a man's beliefs and you will change his feelings and behavior.*

In order to accomplish our goals in this book and in life, we must systematically discover, analyze, argue against and replace with truth the misbeliefs in our lives.

Before starting, however, you will have to answer the question, do *you* really want to be happy?

If the answer is yes, then move on to the next chapter of this book, and the next chapter of your life!

---

1. Proverbs 23:7, Proverbs 12:5.
2. Psalm 119:59.
3. Matthew 9:29.

CHAPTER THREE

Misbelief in Self-Talk

Yes! We want to be happy. The business of making yourself a happier and more fulfilled person can be a lot of fun if you let it be. Sometimes it may be a bit painful, as you become more and more aware of yourself and what you have accepted as you; but foremost, it promises to be an exciting time of discovery and renewal for you. Listen carefully, follow the scriptural course outlined, and trust the Lord to bring you through with flying colors.

Please get a notebook and pen now as we are learning new life skills and getting rid of the old destructive ways. You will be able to watch your own progress and learn much from the entries you make in your notebook. This chapter begins with an investigation of self-talk.

THE WORDS WE SAY TO OURSELVES

Self-talk means the words we tell ourselves in our thoughts. It means the words we tell ourselves about people, self, experiences, life in general, God, the future, the past, the present; it is specifically, *all of the words you say to yourself all of the time.*

What are the lies and half-truths you repeat to yourself? Which misbeliefs keep you unhappy and upset? First you must learn how to identify the misbeliefs in your life.

Where do the lies and misbeliefs start?

The answer to that is in your *self-talk.*

28

Angie is a 31-year-old housewife who has been repeating negative things about herself most of her life. As an adult her negative self-talk has increased. "They're harmless words," she says: words like "Oh, dumb me. There I go again, being my old stupid self. That's just like me. What a dumb thing to do." "Boy, if I didn't have my head screwed on, I'd lose it for sure." "I can't do anything right," and "I have no interests." Finally, she says, "I'm really a nothing person. I don't see how anyone can stand me."

After many years' experience with such self-talk, she finds herself with a marriage of eight years hanging in shreds, her children disturbed and maladjusted, her friends few and her family helpless to assist. No amount of love and attention from anyone can convince Angie that she is a worthwhile and lovable person, although she says her biggest pursuit in life is happiness.

The words we tell ourselves are more important than we realize. If you tell yourself something enough times and in the right circumstances, you will believe those words whether true or not. Angie's jokes about herself were not really jokes at all. "Dumb me" said often enough is not funny.

"I can't do anything right" said enough times will find you *not* doing anything right, at least in your own eyes. Then, with a few negative remarks from those around you, such as, "You did wrong *again*," your belief in self-failure is reinforced.

If you tell yourself, like Angie, "I have no interests," you will find yourself behaving as if you had no interests. (That's impossible, by the way. Everyone is interested in something, no matter how trivial or unimportant it may seem.)

Psychiatrist Willard Gaylin said, "A denigrated self-image is a tar baby. The more we play with it, embrace it, the more bound we are to it." With each self-destructive sentence uttered, we ply another wad of tar on a developing tar baby which could eventually hold us desperately bound.

Listen to the words you tell yourself. Are you building a tar baby?

Angie believed she was basically an inept person with no skills or assets of any kind. She didn't see herself as personally attractive or interesting and believed she was not worthy of being loved or wanted by anyone.

Angie, by the way, is a Christian.

Rarely, if ever, did she tell herself that she was loved and cherished by the Lord of love. Rarely, if ever, did she count personal blessings. Rarely, if ever, did she thank God for her own special gifts and talents because she had been telling herself she had none for so many years she believed it. She had never told herself the truth, that she was unique and beautiful in the eyes of the Lord.

WHAT SENTENCES ARE YOU TELLING YOURSELF?

In the following, check the words you tell yourself in the appropriate column. Be honest.

___ I am dumb.	OR: ___ Thank you, Lord, for giving me intelligence.
___ I am unattractive.	___ Thank you, Lord, for making me attractive.
___ People don't like me.	___ Thank you, Lord, for making me likable.
___ I have no talent.	___ Thank you, Lord, for the talents you've given me.
___ I'm miserable.	___ I'm content.
___ I'm lonely.	___ Thank you, Lord, for my friends.
___ I'm poor.	___ Thank you, Lord, for prospering me.
___ I'm nervous.	___ Thank you, Lord, for peace.
___ I'm uninteresting.	___ Thank you, Lord, for making me unique.

_____ I'm no good.	_____ Thank you, Lord, for your righteous- ness in me.
_____ I'm sick.	_____ Thank you, Lord, for perfect health and healing.

If you checked more sentences on the left than on the right, you need to change the sentences you are saying to yourself. Ask what you are measuring yourself against. Are you comparing yourself and your life with someone else who seems better in some way, or are you looking at yourself in the light of God's Word? D. L. Moody once said that the best way to show that a stick is crooked is not to argue about it or to spend time denouncing it, but to lay a straight stick alongside it.

The straight stick in the lives of Christians is the lovely and indestructible love of *Christ*! When our eyes lose sight of this dazzling truth, there remains only shadows to stare at. Shadows such as envy, jealousy, or comparing ourselves with others. Unhappiness or a state of discontent often is the result of longing to be different or to be in different circumstances, especially someone *else's*.

Not long ago, a poll was taken of 5,000 middle-class single and married men and women of average and above-average intelligence. The poll revealed that the single people were no more or less happy than the married people and the married people no more or less happy than the single. Common, however, was the finding that single people envied married people. Married people, on the other hand, reported envying single people. Many married people revealed they were happy because they were "supposed to be happy," not because they actually had feelings of happiness in their lives.

A single woman said, "I envy my friend, Jane. She's really happy. She has a husband, kids and a home. She has everything."

A married woman said, "I envy Connie. She has it made. She's free to come and go when and where she wants. Her time is her own; her money is her own. She's out in the world doing things. She's single and she's the really happy one."

31

What do you recognize in the words these two people are saying? Envy isn't usually realistic—it doesn't have all the facts. The words "I'm miserable and someone else is the happy one" are basically untrue. Everyone has some unhappiness in his life somewhere and sometime. Everyone has difficulties to face and problems to solve. Both Connie and Jane may have good lives, but they also have trials to overcome.

Picture a little boy jumping with delight as he tightly clutches a nickel in his fist. His mother gave him the nickel and told him to go outside and play. The little boy feels light and happy. But then he meets a playmate who has a quarter. His nickel suddenly loses its luster. He's not feeling so light anymore. He goes home and asks his mother for a quarter, and his mother gives him one. Now the little boy jumps happily once again until he meets another playmate, and this time the playmate has fifty cents in his hand. The little boy is crestfallen. His quarter looks pitiful next to two quarters. So back home he goes to get fifty cents from his mother. When he does, he runs into a playmate with a dollar bill . . . and on it goes.

If we do not find worth in what we are and what we have now, we will tell ourselves we are less important than others or we have less than others. When we tell ourselves these things, we create unrest within ourselves and in striving to be or have what we think others have, we are always seeking after an invisible unattainable state of happiness which is always out of our grasp. Somebody somewhere will always be or have more than we.

Carol is a soft-spoken grandmother who lives in a modest home which is usually in need of repair. Her sons are successful businessmen and own homes twice the value of hers. Their wives are smartly dressed and have every convenience at their disposal. Carol cannot afford expensive clothes. She drives a second-hand car and takes her laundry to the laundromat. She is happy, outgoing and content with her life. "Grandma is my bestest person!" her small grandchildren exclaim. Carol is not only adored by her family, but by her friends, neighbors and acquaintances. There is a peaceful, loving and unselfish quality about her which draws people to her. Her son marvels at how his mother avoids complaining. Carol knows the value of the words of the Apostle

Paul, "I have learned, in whatsoever state I am, therewith to be content," [1] and she lives them. Envy has no place in her life.

A young man who lost a limb in Viet Nam is able to praise God for blessings in his life and to lead a vital and productive life in spite of his loss. He tells himself, "I can do it. I have much to offer."

A middle-aged woman who lost her husband and three small children in a private plane crash finds courage and strength in Christ to go on and live a full life helping others and being a blessing to those in need. She tells herself, "I shall always miss my family, but I do not want to prolong grief and sorrow beyond the limits of God's will. It is His will that I be happy and useful—and I am!"

A soothing tongue is a tree of life, but perversion in it crushes the spirit. [2]

Choose to say truthful things about yourself to yourself. When you hear yourself saying something false about yourself, *stop.* You can do it. Just say aloud, *"No. I don't want to say that. It is not true."*

Lorraine, a single woman of twenty-six, told us about the following event in her life: "I had moved back home to my father's house after quitting college. I had been gone from home for a couple of years and I didn't know anybody in the neighborhood anymore. It was all very strange. My father was nagging me to get a job, but I wasn't sure what I wanted to do. In the back of my mind I thought it would be great to get married and get away from it all, but I wasn't even dating anyone seriously. Anyhow, one night I was in my room and I wasn't doing much of anything when I heard this little thought-voice coming from the back of my head somewhere. It said in a real high whiney voice, 'I'm sooo lonely.' I sat down on my bed and in a few minutes I heard myself sighing in a high, whiney voice, 'I'm sooo lonely'—just like I had heard in my head. It really scared me. I jumped up and shouted, 'I am *not* lonely. That's ridiculous. I am *not* lonely. I didn't mean that!' "

Lorraine was wise enough to recognize false thinking. She probably could have found enough evidence to support the thought of being lonely, but she chose to gather evidence to prove she was *not* lonely instead. She told herself out loud, "I am *not* lonely," resisting the temptation to verbalize the lying thought. She didn't start forming the tar baby which could have given her a lot of unnecessary sadness later on.

We can all tell ourselves we are lonely, inept or incapable at some time or another in our lives. A glamorous Hollywood actress, the envy of many women, was found dead in her bed with a suicide note beside her, "I am without hope." A magnificent poetess of considerable literary success believed she was a failure in spite of the awards her work had won and the acclaim she had achieved. At the height of her career, in utter despair, she committed suicide.

These illustrations prove the need for something more in life, some meaning and fulfillment beyond the external layers. They show a need for a spiritual relationship with the God who created us and His Son, Jesus Christ, who redeemed us. Release from self-denigration and hopelessness is available through faith in Him. The Christian finds within his grasp the dynamic results in such practices as:

> . . . *whatsoever things are true, whatsoever things are honest, whatsoever things are just, whatsoever things are pure, whatsoever things are lovely, whatsoever things are of good report; if there be any virtue, and if there be any praise, think on these things.* [3]

as well as:

> *Casting down imaginations, and every high thing that exalteth itself against the knowledge of God, and bringing into captivity every thought to the obedience of Christ.* [4]

It is not pleasing to the Lord when we speak evil of anyone, or for that matter, when we speak evil *period*. To speak of yourself in a belittling or destructive way is, in His sight, evil.

> *Keep thy tongue from evil, and thy lips from speaking guile*[5] (against *yourself* as well as against anyone else!). *Depart from evil* (saying evil words and believing evil

34

thoughts about *yourself* as well as about anyone else!),
and do good; seek peace, and pursue it.[6]

Pursuing peace means to choose it. You will never have peace
if you are putting yourself down. The peaceful person is the one
who is at peace with himself. Dag Hammerskjold said, "A man
who is at war with himself will be at war with others." When you
like yourself, you will be free to like and appreciate others. When
you are hard on yourself, you will be hard on others.

Write in your notebook the things you tell yourself about
yourself every day. Listen to your thoughts and your words. Remember, any thoughts that reflect hopelessness, desperation,
hate, fear, bitterness, jealousy or envy are the words and
thoughts generated by demonic falsehood. These are the words
and thoughts you will be changing and eliminating from your
life.

Now, are you ready to go to work? Let's begin by examining
some familiar maladies and the misbeliefs associated with them.
See how many you can recognize.

---

1. Philippians 4:11.
2. Proverbs 15:4 (NAS).
3. Philippians 4:8.
4. 2 Corinthians 10:5.
5. Psalm 34:13.
6. Psalm 34:14.

CHAPTER FOUR

Misbelief in Depression

One of the most familiar causes of psychological suffering is depression. Patients seeing psychologists and psychiatrists all across the world have such diagnoses as "depressive neurosis," "psychotic depression," "involutional psychosis," "manic-depressive," "psychotic: depressed," or "depressed," as well as other diagnoses with depressive symptoms. Worse, however, are the millions of people who, for various reasons, do not have the advantage of psychological or pastoral help, struggling through long miserable days in depression and believing there is no end in sight.

The Bible speaks of depression as the "soul cast down," and in Psalm 42 we can sense the agony in the words, "My soul is cast down within me" and "Why art thou cast down, O my soul?" Then triumphantly in 2 Corinthians 7:6 are the wonderful words, "God comforts those who are cast down."

The ancient church fathers had another word for depression. They called it "sloth." It was considered one of the seven deadly sins, on the same list with greed, anger and lust. Sloth was described as sadness of heart and reluctance to engage in any activity requiring effort.

Today we don't define depression in quite the same way. What exactly is depression? It can be described from various perspectives. If you looked at your biochemistry when you're depressed, your metabolism, the behavior of your smooth muscles

36

and glands, you would see that it is not only your verbal and motor behavior that has depressive symptoms.

Depression usually occurs with some provocation. Most depression-causing misbeliefs enter the stream of self-talk after some loss has occurred.

Many times a patient will be unable to explain why he is depressed. "I don't know why I feel this way," he may say. "I just don't feel I can do anything at all. I just don't want to do anything. I cry a lot. I don't sleep well, and I don't have any energy or interest in anything . . . I don't know why . . ." His voice may trail off inaudibly or he may sigh, slump in the chair or just stare at the floor.

In spite of the inability of the depressed person to explain how he got that way, it is extremely rare for depression to occur without some special provocation. The misbeliefs that cause depression can become activated by a single event. This event represents a loss of some kind. Someone special or dear leaves or dies. Or it could be financial reverses and a loss of money. It could be physical illness, aging, an accident, stroke or loss of physical strength. Separation and divorce are frequent occasions of loss in depression, and situations where rejection, fear, and low self-esteem are triggered.

Any of these events can be an opportunity for the devil to slip a few suggestions into a person's self-talk. A college student may tell himself, "Boy, you sure are dumb. You failed your math exam. What are you doing in college anyhow? Look at all the money you're wasting. You'll never make it!"

The above example shows the three misbeliefs known as the depressive triad. Here they are:

Activating events followed by negative self-talk founded on *misbelief:*

1. *Person devalues self:*	"Boy, you sure are dumb."
2. *Person devalues situation:*	"Lately life has been a drag; nothing is worth doing; I don't know why I get out of bed!"
3. *Person devalues his prospects for future:*	"You'll never make it!" And you'll never be anything! Life is hopeless!"

37

If you repeat these things to yourself enough times, you will find yourself behaving accordingly. When time rolls around for another math exam, the student may panic, sinking to new depths of depression and worthless feelings. He may even quit school before the quarter is up because of his *misbeliefs*—not because of anything real or true at all.

A 37-year-old woman named Jennifer makes an appointment with a Christian counselor because she is suffering severe depression. Two months earlier her fiance called off their wedding and broke up with her. She can hardly go on, she says. Nothing seems worth living for.

At the first interview she appears attractive, intelligent and charming, although she insists her life is over and it's futile to go on.

She tells how she's lost interest in her job, how she has lost her appetite and doesn't want to do much of anything except sleep. "Life is a pain," she says listlessly.

Her friends had tried to console her with words such as, "You ought to be thankful you found out your boyfriend's true colors before it was too late and you were married to him. Then you'd be in a fine mess!" Or, "If that's the kind of person he is, you're better off without him!" and "You're better off staying single than married to a guy who is fickle and unfaithful." All of these words made sense to Jennifer, but they didn't help her.

Her belief system was already so jam-packed with misbeliefs she couldn't respond favorably to her friends' homespun common-sense advice. For several years she had been afraid of becoming an old maid. She had believed maybe there was something wrong with her, harbored fears and worries that maybe she wasn't attractive and desirable to men; otherwise, why was she getting older by the minute and still a single person? This engagement was the most wonderful thing that had ever happened to her, she told herself. This was really her last opportunity for happiness and wedded bliss.

Her self-talk had included, "If I blow it this time, I'll end up an old maid. That would be terrible. Awful! That would be so dreadful, I could never stand it." She worked hard at pleasing her fiance and doing everything "right." She was determined to be the greatest thing that ever happened to him, to be his "Miss Perfection," his Dream Bride.

Because she worked so hard at being what she hoped he wanted her to be, it made her feel all the more miserable when he rejected her. She told herself, "Even my very best stinks. I couldn't go through this again. It's all over for me. Nobody will ever love me. Even when I do everything I can to make a man love me, he leaves me. I'm the worst. The lowest."

You can see the familiar triad here:

1. *Devalues self:*   "Even my very best stinks. Even when I do everything I can to make a man love me, he leaves me. I'm the worst. The lowest."

2. *Devalues situation:*   "It's all over for me." (Meaning that since she is such a dud and since no one can love her, life is utterly unrewarding and negative—a pain.)

3. *Devalues prospects for future:*   "I'll never be happy. I have no hope. It's all over for me. Nobody will ever love me.

Jennifer's misbeliefs are: she is a failure or worthless; she is guilty and inadequate; her situation is intolerable and lacking in everything containing hope; her future is hopeless and she might as well roll over and drop dead.

She has convinced herself through years of self-talk that to be unmarried is awful and to be rejected is the worst thing on earth, especially if it is by someone she worked so hard to please. ("How could he do that to me? And after I tried so hard? My best isn't good enough for anybody!")

Jennifer's awful fears and dreads have now come true. She tells herself she is the rejected castaway, useless, unlovable, ugly and hopeless. "To be me is the most awful thing I can think of."

Actually the only awful thing in Jennifer's life is the crock of lies in her belief system, her *misbeliefs.* They are awful, not Jennifer.

Her attributes are many, including an ability to teach handicapped children. She has many friends and is highly respected at the school where she has taught seventh grade for several years. But Jennifer is a Christian and Christians don't have to base their worth on achievements or attributes. Even without any achievements and without any special merit or attractiveness, the Christian can know for certain he/she is important and loved. Our lives have been bought and paid for with the blood of Jesus Christ and that means we're free from the pressure to *be* something, *do* something, *own* something, *achieve* something or *prove* something in order to be important and loved. We can do all these things or not do them and still be loved and important.

Jesus loved Jennifer so much that He was willing to die on the cross so she could have eternal life with Him one day, as well as a fulfilled life here and now. If Jennifer is as worthless as she says she is, then none of the things God says of His love for people can be true.

But His words *are* true and Jennifer needs to come to grips with them. According to God, Jennifer has worth and value and so does every other human being. The worth of a person is not based on success or accomplishment. It is not based on performance, achievement or even on how many people love and respect us. Our worth is based totally and solely on the declaration of God: "For God so loved the world." *God loves people.* No circumstance, no matter how bad it looks, can change this fact. The treachery and suffering of man is not from the hand of God, but from his own hand.

It is a misbelief to tell yourself that you are a failure. It is rare indeed that a person cannot do anything at all. Jennifer told herself that she was a failure because she had failed to hold on to her fiance. But that does not mean she is a failure in everything in life. She over-generalized.

The depressed person says that his/her situation is hopeless. "He left me and so I am nothing," Jennifer says. "My life has no meaning or value." Once the enemy, the devil, has a person deeply convinced of the lie that something or someone other than Jesus Christ is the foundation of life, he is open prey for the crippling pain of misbelief.

Our lives hold meaning because God loves us and because we are His. Our lives do not depend upon someone else loving us, staying with us, respecting us, noticing us or pledging their eternal devotion to us. It's nice to have friends and loved ones, but having them is not what makes us important. If you believe you cannot live without a certain person or that your entire existence depends on somebody else, you are setting yourself up to be hurt by that *misbelief.* If that person leaves you or because of circumstances you find yourself without them, you will tell yourself things like, "My life has no value or meaning." "Since I lost X, my world has no significance. I'm nothing now that X is gone."

That's not true at all. You are not reacting to X's leaving; you are reacting to your *misbelief.* We hear the popular songs with lyrics to the effect, You're-my-very-existence, without-you-I-wouldn't-know-how-to-take-air-in-and-out, I'd-be-an-empty-shell-and-a-worm-if-it-weren't-for-you. The romances on our screens and printed page teach us that love means to tell ourselves that all happiness and breath depend on someone else, on their reciprocal affection and acceptance.

SELF-CENTERED RETALIATION

One way some people have of combating depression is to tell themselves: "I'm *me,* I'm *somebody.* Nobody's gonna get in the way with what *I* want and need. After all, I'm a *human being. I'm me.* I'm running the great show of my life. Yessir, *I'm* the star of this number. I'm *me—Numero Uno,* kiddo. You live only once and I'm gonna get all I can because I only pass this way but once and if I don't look out for *myself,* who will? If you love me, fine."

This philosophy is costly because there is no way to love others as long as the star of the great show is you—only you and you to the tenth power.

Jesus Christ is the foundation of our lives, not ourselves alone and not another person or persons. When we become God's children the great *I* dies and there's a change, sweet as morning, that takes place and we trade banners: the old used *I* for a shiny impenetrable *His.* Self-talk that degrades others degrades ourselves. We cannot undermine other people's importance and

41

overestimate our own importance without trouble.

BURNED AND STAYING THAT WAY!

Many times when a person has been hurt by another person resulting from misbeliefs such as, "People should be nice to me and love me," he or she will react in still another way. Instead of admitting to anger or hurt, he or she will tell himself, "I'll never be so dumb as to let somebody do this to me again!"

You may be saying things to yourself you are not even aware of until you start consciously listening to yourself. The person who has been rejected by another person may believe that rejection is the worst thing in the world. To be rejected certainly is unpleasant, but it's *not* the worst thing in the world.

Listen to your self-talk and then engage in some honest and daring truth-telling.

Truth-telling such as, "This feels bad. I don't like it. It isn't what I wanted and it certainly isn't something that gives me pleasure." Notice we aren't lying about the situation—not saying, "Oh, this doesn't hurt a bit. Who cares if he/she rejects me?"

We're speaking the truth, not making stupid remarks about not having the emotions we were born with. When you cut your finger you say, "Ouch," right? When your heart hurts, it's truthful to say, "I hurt."

But you don't end the self-talk at that. Here's where so many counselors lock up shop. They advise, "Admit the hurt," then wave good-bye. But what do you do next?

You *continue* the truth-telling about the hurt. Here is some more truth to replace the lies that create anguish and leave it raw:

- It's true I'm feeling bad. It's only *unpleasant*, however; it's not doomsville.
- It's not doomsville because I'm not letting it be. I will allow some good healthy pain, but I *won't* allow anguish, misery, woe and disaster.
- I'm in control here. God has created me as an emotional being and so I can expect to have emotions. But God has also given me the fruit of the Spirit: self-control. So I will control my feelings and they can't control me.

42

- I am angry. I can, however, handle anger in the biblical, healthy manner. I do not lie to myself about this emotion and I do not try to squelch it or hold it in. I am also not a person of temper tantrums. I choose self-control.

When we lose someone or something important to us, we will feel hurt, yes; but if the hurt deepens to despondency and depression and remains that way for weeks or months, the cause is not the loss but misbelief. Two misbeliefs undergird this kind of despair:

1. God is not the source of life. Man is.

When we are despondent over loss, we are telling ourselves that the person or thing we lost is crucial to our lives and happiness.

The untruth lies in the fact that nothing and nobody but God is crucial to anyone. This truth is revealed in the first commandment: Thou shalt love the Lord thy God and thou shalt have no other gods before Him.

To ascribe the all-sufficiency of God to any person is idolatry, and the basis for idolatry is deception and misbelief. James, the apostle, wrote, "Do not be deceived . . . every good and perfect gift comes from the Father of lights" (James 1:16, 17); those truly good and perfect gifts do not come from someone or something other than God. God is the giver of all good and all love. *He* gives us our relationships and our blessings. Now the second misbelief:

2. Since I lost X, my world has nothing of any significance in it.

Experience bears out the deception here. Many of us have told ourselves we "cannot live without" some person, object, scheme or notion. Then this adored "whatever" is removed from our lives and wonder of wonders, we recover. Some people without the skills we are learning in this book prolong their sufferings. They go on muttering destructive, irreligious, "without X I'm nothing" self-talk.

But many who have suffered loss in their lives recover and find satisfying and exciting alternatives. "I used to consider my health indispensable," an ex-football star says. "When I lost what I considered absolutely essential to living, I thought there was nothing for me to do but die." The handsome ex-athlete was in a car accident and lost both legs. He went on, however, to discover he had many interests in other areas. He graduated from college with honors and became a skilled musician. He is now married and working as a biologist. Although he encounters many problems as a handicapped person, these problems don't render him hopeless or helpless.

A famous artist was thrown into a Nazi prison during World War II. When it was discovered he was an artist, his torturers had his right hand chopped off. It could have been the end of his world, but he taught himself to use and draw with his left hand. He went on to a prolific career as a productive and skilled artist.

A person can lose his/her health, reputation, vision, hearing, legs, hands, even family members, money, homes, physical attractiveness, life goals and plans—and yet recover and go on living a wonderfully rewarding and meaningful life.

When you suffer a loss of any kind in your life, you are going to feel the sting of that loss; but the key to recovery is not to repeat that someone or something is of such importance that you cannot go on after losing it. You *can* go on. You *are* important. Martin Luther's great hymn counters this misbelief with the truth which stands the test of experience.

> Take they our life,
> Goods, fame, child and wife—
> Let these all be gone.
> They yet have nothing won,
> *The Kingdom ours remaineth.*

Part of the self-talk of nearly all depressives includes the statement, "The future is hopeless." Having lost her fiance, Jennifer was telling herself that she would doubtless have to live and die without marriage and family, that there would never be anyone that could replace him, and that even if she should meet other good men, she was such a loser she'd never be able to hold their interest.

The depressed person believes he or she can never be happy without the thing they now do not possess. Jennifer tells herself that she will never know true happiness if she doesn't get married. Many single people suffer with this misbelief. "Only through marriage can I experience life fully." If that sentence fol-

44

lows with, "I'll never get married. Nobody will ever love me," there's trouble. "All I can expect from life is frustration and unfulfillment" will be the words in the person's self-talk.

Examine those words and you will expose the misbeliefs. To begin with, no one can predict the future with certainty, least of all a person whose prediction is determined by the pain and hurt of depression. We cannot predict that all of the events in our lives are going to be happy and enriching, nor can we predict that all ahead is gloom and despair.

Life at any given moment offers a mixture of pleasant and unpleasant, desirables and undesirables, fulfillment and disappointment. Some experiences are more gratifying than expected, but then some are worse than expected. Anyone predicting that life will be horrendous forever is as wrong as if he were predicting a nickel thrown through the air one hundred times will turn up tails one hundred times.

In actual fact, while nearly all depressed people tell themselves they will always feel devastated and down, *virtually all recover*. It is helpful to predict recovery if you are suffering from depression or if you are counseling a depressed person. That is because recovery from depression is in fact the most likely outcome! Speak the truth and say, "Even though I feel I have no hope, my recovery is assured. Thank God, these feelings of depression won't last."

Pray this prayer with us:

Dear Lord, thank you for giving me emotions. I'm thankful I can feel pain as well as joy. Thank you for setting me free from being a victim of my own emotions.

Thank you for caring deeply about me even though I'm sometimes unaware of it.

I choose now, in the mighty name of Jesus, to speak the truth to myself instead of misbeliefs. I am yours and so are my emotions.

In Jesus' name, Amen.

CHAPTER FIVE

Misbelief in Anger

Marilyn had resented her husband, Jack, for years. At least once a day she told herself words like, "I can't stand this any longer," and, "I'm wasting my life with him."

Her husband was a minister who issued admonitions from the pulpit to abide in brotherly love, live in humility and honor your neighbor higher than yourself. At home he complained, found fault, made cutting remarks and compared his wife with younger and more attractive women. She felt insignificant and inadequate, and quite angry.

Marilyn didn't say anything to anyone about her feelings, although there were many clues which demonstrated how angry and hurt she really was.

She sat in her pew listening to Jack's sermons week after week as her insides twisted and her muscles tightened. She developed headaches which sent her to bed, sobbing with pain. Jack considered the headaches just a ploy to get attention. He preached about love and forgiveness from the pulpit and gave hours of loving advice in the counseling room, but at home he was impatient, critical and often cruel. His church face and personality was quite different from his home face and personality.

Years passed and Marilyn and her husband continued to appear in public as a happy couple, when actually they were worse off than the couples who came to them for help.

Many Christians try to deal with anger as a single moral

problem. "Anger is bad," a sweet little Christian lady will tell her Sunday school class. "Anger is a sin, children, and you mustn't get angry!"

"We need to banish anger from our lives!" shouts the moralist. "Get rid of the anger in your life and you'll be a happy person."

The problem of anger cannot be dealt with so simply. Like taxes, anger doesn't just go away, even if you decide it ought to. And like your nose or your hair color, your angry feelings are part of you and your human nature.

There is a difference between being angry and expressing anger toward someone else. There is a difference between being assertive and aggressive. There is a difference between being capable of honest expression and being punitive.

Marilyn believed she had every right to be bitterly angry with her husband, Jack. She believed she had the right to *remain* angry as long as he refused to change his habits. She was ruining her emotional and physical health.

Both Marilyn and Jack had certain expectations of each other. They believed they had every right to demand the fulfillment of their expectations.

Specifically, Marilyn told herself the following:
1. It was shocking and intolerable to be treated unfairly by her preacher-husband.
2. She was right in *demanding* her husband treat her and their children with love, tenderness, consideration and kindness.
3. Since Jack was her husband, he *owed* her love. He should behave the way the Bible prescribes for husbands; namely, he should love his wife as Christ loved the church.
4. Her husband was terrible to criticize her and compare her unfavorably to other women. This behavior was dreadful and outrageous and absolutely intolerable.

The headaches were the cause of her visit to the Center for Christian Psychological Services.

"Marilyn, it sounds as though you're telling yourself you have a right to demand Jack be a good husband," Dr. Backus told her after hearing some of her symptoms.

47

Marilyn looked surprised. "Of course, Doctor. Don't you think I do?"

"Marilyn, when you were married you expected to have a husband who would be kind, considerate and thoughtful, but that isn't the same as having a guarantee from God that your husband would act that way."

"But why not? I'm considerate to *him*. I consider *his* feelings. I never compare him to other men. I build up his ego. I'm kind to him. Why can't he treat me the same way?"

"I don't know why Jack behaves as he does. I do know that you apparently haven't succeeded in changing him."

"But I can't take any more!"

Marilyn was now near tears and pressing her fingers to her forehead, indicating she was getting another headache.

"Marilyn, people rarely do what they *ought to* just because we want them to. Seldom is there a wife or husband who suddenly becomes habitually kind and loving just because their mate would like them to be that way."

"But he ought to practice what he preaches! What about all his talk about charity beginning at home? What about all that stuff he tells his congregation about humility and love? Sometimes I want to laugh out loud when I listen to him preach."

Tears now streamed down her face. She knotted her hands in frustration.

Whereas we don't want to make excuses for her husband's behavior, Marilyn needed to differentiate between what *ought* to be and what actually *is*. It is easy to look around us and locate disparity between what *should* happen and what actually *does* happen. We live in a sinful world. The fact is, as the Bible teaches clearly, "there is not a just man upon earth that doeth good and sinneth not." We can't find an environment on earth that is sanitized and sin-free.

Yet many people go through life giving themselves headaches, ulcers and high blood pressure over the fact that other people are not perfect. They confuse what *ought to be* with what *is*. Every time another person treats them unfairly, they tell themselves they have a right to get furious and stay that way.

"Marilyn, what sense does it make to tell yourself what Jack

48

should be like?" Marilyn listened unhappily. "Since years of upsetting yourself over his faults haven't changed anything and
have only made you miserable, wouldn't it be wise to start telling
yourself the truth?"

Her eyes narrowed. "Which is?"

"Which is that it doesn't matter what Jack *ought* to be like or
how you feel he *ought* to treat you. The fact is, he *does* treat you
and the children in a way you consider unfair and inexcusable.
Rather than constantly telling yourself how dreadful and intolerable your life is, you can decide right now to stop upsetting yourself over his behavior."

"But he treats everybody else better than he treats me, including the organist, the choir director, the Sunday school
teachers, and the wives of the elders. What do you mean, upsetting *myself*?"

It wasn't her husband's behavior that upset Marilyn; it was
her own self-talk.

"Suppose you were to stop telling yourself how terrible it is
that your husband doesn't treat you the way you want to be
treated. Suppose you tell yourself that while he may not do the
things you'd like him to do and while it's an unpleasant situation, it's senseless for you to upset yourself over what you haven't
been able to change."

She was quiet. "People have lived quite well with some very
undesirable situations in their lives. Almost no one has everything just the way he or she wishes it to be."

"Yes, I know of many marriages having a lot of big problems."

"Nearly half of American marriages end in divorce. A good
share of the other half are troubled."

*If you're telling yourself you must have a perfect marriage in
order not to be miserable and upset, you are telling yourself a
misbelief.*

Marilyn was taught how to get rid of her anger and headaches
by learning how to change her self-talk. She learned the difference between the truth and misbelief. Here's a page from her
notebook:

MISBELIEF	TRUTH
1. It's terrible to have a husband like Jack.	1. Jack is my God-given husband, and, although I would prefer him to act differently, I can live with him without making continued demands that only go unmet anyhow.
2. It's impossible to be happy with Jack as he is.	2. It would be nice if he would change, but it is not essential for my personal happiness.
3. I can't stand it any longer.	3. I can live a satisfactory and happy life even if Jack doesn't treat me as I want him to. My life can be fulfilling and enjoyable even if he never changes.
4. I'm wasting my life.	4. I'm not wasting my life. I'm believing in God to work in Jack's heart and make him the person He wants him to be. I am also believing God is working in my own heart, making me the person He wants me to be.

Marilyn did face reality. She discovered her husband's behavior was *not* terrible, although it was undesirable. She learned to discern when her expectations of others weren't realistic. It is not the end of the world if others are not thoughtful, kind or considerate. It's merely unpleasant.

If her husband's behavior toward her was not a source of happiness, she could find other rewarding activities and involvements in life to bring her satisfaction. She did not depend on her husband to make her happy by his acting the way she wished he would act. She could face up to him as he actually was.

It wasn't easy at first. Marilyn had lived with guilt over her anger for a long time; but little by little, as she felt better about herself, not only the anger but guilt feelings as well were diminishing. She began looking for the better qualities in her husband and appreciating things in him she had hardly noticed before. As a result of Marilyn's new behavior, Jack began to enjoy Marilyn's company. He had felt her disapproval of him for years and reacted by defending himself with attacks of criticism. When Marilyn stopped behaving in punishing ways toward him, he spontaneously reduced his critical and inconsiderate actions.

Often, but not always, relationships change dramatically when one person drops the misbeliefs that generate and perpetuate bitterness and anger.

Always the person who works to change misbeliefs will benefit even if the other person does not change.

The constant repeating of misbeliefs is what sustains and perpetuates angry resentment. Constant repeating of the truth generates peace and health.

Common Misbeliefs Connected with Anger:

1. Anger is bad and if I'm a good Christian, I will never get angry.
2. Anger always means to yell and throw things or do whatever else it takes to "drain off" the emotion.
3. If I do get angry, it's always better for me to swallow the anger than to express it.
4. I have every right to be angry when another person does not live up to my expectations. I have no choice but to stay angry as long as things don't change.
5. It is outrageous and insufferable when others do things I don't like, or if they fail to treat me as well as I ought to be treated.

You may have one or more of these misbeliefs. They are lies and distortions. They have, in each instance, the peculiar power to cause considerable suffering. Now here is the *truth*.

51

The Truth About Anger:

1. *Anger is not always bad.*

On the contrary, anger can be normal and has adaptive significance in appropriate situations. Remember, Jesus experienced anger. The simple emotion of anger is not always harmful or unloving. It is what you *do* when you are angry that has moral significance. Paul wrote, "Be angry, and yet do not sin; do not let the sun go down on your anger." [1] The Amplified version of this verse reads, "When angry, do not sin," which surely indicates we may sometimes feel anger. Paul is telling us that anger in itself is not wicked; that *what we do when angry can be sinful*; and that we should not allow ourselves to remain angry by continuing our destructive, resentful self-talk. He is telling us to deal with the issue *promptly.*

2. *Sometimes it's better to express your anger.*

There will be times when the Lord will want you to express this emotion, just as Jesus did on several occasions. He was genuinely angry at the buying and selling going on by the opportunists in the temple, for example. He saw ungodly people making ungodly gains in a holy place and this misuse of God's house angered Him.

As we can see from Jesus' example, it may sometimes be loving to reveal to another person that what he has done against you has made you angry. Matthew 18:15-17 really instructs in how to deal promptly with situations causing anger: "If your brother sins against you, go and tell him"—not "scream at him" or "prosecute him," not "kick things and slam doors so he'll figure it out." "Tell him his fault." It is a simple procedure. You can say, "What you did hurts me and I'm angry about it. I'd like to get you to stop."

3. *Anger does not mean yelling and throwing things or other intemperate behavior.*

Research on aggression[2] has demonstrated that if such behavior is rewarded and encouraged, the aggression increases; it does not decrease. The "steamboiler theory" held by some psychotherapists concerning the emotions asserts that emotions are like steam in a pressure tank and must be released vigorously or they will cause a terrible explosion.

This assertion is not substantiated by the experimental evidence. Our emotions are not a kind of gas or fluid which must be expelled in order to prevent our popping all over the place in a million pieces.

Anger is behavior. Anger is responses of your body and mind to a stimulus. When the stimulus is withdrawn, the anger responses will cease—that is, *if* you do not continue to tell yourself how unfair and unjust your treatment has been and how miserable you are because of it.

If it were essential for our mental health to express all anger by shouting, screaming or punching something, then the Word of God would be mistaken in urging us to develop self-control. This does not mean we swallow anger and pretend everything is fine when it isn't. Sometimes it is healthier, wiser and more loving to say words like, "I am feeling anger right now. I'd like to talk about it because I feel it concerns us both."

4. *I do not have every right to be angry when another person does not live up to my expectations. I do have a choice whether or not I remain angry.*

So many Christians keep asking God to free them from anger and they go through motions of asking for and receiving forgiveness. It doesn't occur to them that between their prayers they are telling themselves terrible things. "Naturally I'm angry," a person will say, "as long as so-and-so continues to treat me so badly."

There is no necessary connection between the behavior of another person and your anger. It doesn't matter how unfairly, unjustly or thoughtlessly someone has behaved toward you, you are angry because of your own self-talk. One psychologist tells his patients that the truthful statement to make when you're angry is, "I make *myself* angry." Other people cannot force you to remain in a stew over their behavior. This is something *you* do yourself. To take it one step further, you make yourself angry by what you *tell* yourself.

You tell yourself in words, images, and attitudes the very things that cause you to feel anger. "Isn't it terrible how Jim always keeps me waiting?" "It's disgusting and rotten that I'm the one who gets stuck with the job of mowing the lawn and raking the leaves while she sits inside drinking coffee!" "It makes me

53

sick the way their dog eats better than a lot of people in this world."

When you are counseling a person who is angry or when you are dealing with your own chronic anger, it is vital to ask, "Why do I insist that someone else is making me upset when I am the only one who can make myself angry and keep myself angry?" If I'm angry I'm telling myself that something the other person is doing or saying is terrible; it shouldn't be that way; things aren't as I think they should be; and the resulting assumption is that it's awful, terrible, horrible, disgraceful, shameful and/or just plain horrendous. You can use only irrational notions to support such assumptions which are, in themselves, already irrational.

The truth is, such things are not horrendous at all. It is unpleasant when things don't go as you'd like them to or when someone says unkind words to you, but it's not awful or terrible.

5. *It is not dreadful or even especially unusual if others do things I don't like or fail to treat me as well as I treat them.*

We waste a lot of time, energy, and thought when we brood over the offenses of others. All of us have sinned, according to the Word of God. Those who keep telling themselves how others ought to treat them confuse what *ought* to be with what actually *is*.

It would be nice if everybody was loving, considerate, thoughtful, kind and fair. The Bible warns us to expect sinful behavior in people since all men and women have chosen their own way. To those who are born into His family, God says, "Be ye perfect as I am perfect," *not*, "Try to make all those around you be perfect." God's perfection includes His perfect forgiveness and forbearance. It was His great compassion and love that took Him to the cross so that while we were yet sinners, He died for us.[3] So part of the perfection He desires in us is the same quality of forgiveness and forbearance.

The better you get to know another person, the more deeply aware of his or her shortcoming you will likely become. If you dwell on the negative characteristics, you can continually find plenty to criticize and be unhappy about. Your parents, siblings, spouse, children, and friends all have something about them you don't like. More than likely there is something about everyone you know that you would like changed.

The people in your life will not always be kind, just, loving, and thoughtful to you. You yourself do not always behave perfectly and fairly in every instance. But your heavenly Father loves you in spite of yourself. You can change your self-talk and love and accept the people around you. He accepts them and so can you. (God does not accept sin. It's sinners He loves.) He loves the sinners thoroughly and sent Jesus to die on the cross for them so they could know God and be saved from the penalties of their sins.

WHEN ANGER IS NORMAL

The simple *brief* emotion of anger is normal. The anger which explodes into rage or stews in bitterness is maladaptive and sinful. Scripture gives two views of anger. *"Be angry, and yet do not sin"* it reads in Ephesians 4:26. Then James writes, "Be slow to anger, for the anger of man does not achieve the righteousness of God." [5]

Anger in itself is not always sinful. We have already mentioned how Jesus on occasion became angry. "And after looking around at them *with anger*, grieved at their hardness of heart, He said to the man, 'Stretch out your hand.' And he stretched it out, and his hand was restored." [6] None of us can go through life without ever having had the emotion of anger.

WHEN ANGER IS A PROBLEM

Anger becomes a problem when it is made worse or perpetuated by misbeliefs—misbeliefs such as, "I must never get angry." This misbelief leads to the self-deceptive words, "I'm *not* angry," when one is quite plainly saying and doing hostile, angry things and even hurting others. The internal conflict and destructive behavior then becomes hard to interpret, identify and control. More self-deception develops and neurotic behavior follows. "I'm *not* angry. I'm a forgiving, nice person," says the bitter person between clenched teeth. He or she smiles, laughs and says friendly words while furious inside, refusing to confront the truth.

Christians are often prime targets for such deception. Many Christians think they must be nice fellows—always-smiling, above-it-all, super-people who are perpetually happy no matter what. When they are hurt and react with genuine anger, they hide it and cover it up with various shrouds, such as religious-sounding words, smiles, grins, shrugs, silence.

Jack and Marilyn, the couple at the beginning of this chapter, are examples. Jack resented Marilyn's obvious disapproval of him. He felt she was judging his every word and action, which made him feel uncomfortable and angry. He did not discuss his feelings with his wife, but his behavior showed how angry, hurt, and bitter he was. He felt her disapproval so strongly that he took every chance to show her she had bad traits of her own. Misunderstanding was compounded and walls were built between them. Neither one of them could discuss their hurt or anger, but their hostile behavior toward each other was vicious and cruel.

Both Jack and Marilyn refused to admit to angry feelings because they thought anger meant to yell, throw things, or act in a violent way. They were able to deceive themselves by thinking their angry behavior and bitter, resentful words were not caused by anger. Jack admitted, "I never hit Marilyn, nor threw anything or yelled, so I thought I was a person with the fruit of self-control. What I did do, however, was probably worse than yelling or throwing things. I belittled her with my sharp tongue or else I wouldn't talk at all. I'd stew in silence and not say one word."

Besides acting violently, silence is one maladaptive way to say, "I'm angry." Expressing anger by yelling, breaking things, stamping feet, or punching something is as dangerous as not admitting you're angry at all. Whoever said, "Never bottle up anger, let it out!" was missing the mark. There is a proper way to express anger, but erupting in riot is not the way. The notion to "let it all hang out" will never work the "righteousness of God." Untempered anger earned its position as number five on the ancient "Seven Deadly Sins" list because it *is* deadly.

Another unhealthy response to angry feelings is the "Fight! Fight! Fight!" attitude, not unlike the football fan cheering the team at a game. "Let 'em have it! Push 'em back, push 'em back, harder! Harder!" is the idea. The misbelief behind this notion is that the harder you fight the person or thing causing you to feel angry, the quicker the hurt will go away. But it doesn't go away. It gets worse, and so does the anger. One day you may find yourself screaming at the wind, hating and mistrusting even the dearest people closest to you for no good cause.

There is a healthy way to express anger. It is not through violence, nor is it by holding it in while pretending it isn't there.

THE HEALTHY WAY TO EXPRESS ANGER

Perhaps you've known someone who is chronically angry, always seeming to be nursing a grudge and ready to ignite any minute. Most of these people have one common trait. They are markedly uncommunicative and withdrawn. They are reluctant and shy about expressing their desires truthfully and openly. They are fearful of simply telling someone else what hurts them or how they have been offended.

Jesus teaches us appropriate and effective ways to have healthy relationships with others. When He tells us how to deal with anger and its causes, He says, "Go to the other person." Speak up honestly and openly, without accusing or manipulating the person. Tell him, "I am feeling anger right now. The reason for my angry feelings is that I heard you say such-and-such or you did such-and-such. These things have hurt and offended me and I feel angry."

Effective behavior such as this prevents you from becoming bitter and resentful, both sins in the life of a Christian, and will very likely get the attention of the other person. It will preserve rather than destroy your relationships. Prayerful assertive behavior that uses no harsh or hurtful words or action will bring a dramatic change in your life.

Each time you find yourself in a situation where someone aggravates you or hurts you, pay attention to what's going on in your mind. What are you telling yourself? If the words you are telling yourself are misbelief-centered, correct yourself immediately with the truth.

DON'T LET MISBELIEFS HAVE ANY ROOM IN YOUR MIND WITHOUT IMMEDIATELY COMING AGAINST THEM WITH THE TRUTH.

Arnold is angry at Ben because Ben just bought a new car and came over to show it off to Arnold who cannot afford a new car. Arnold thinks Ben is rubbing in the fact that he can't afford a new car. He tells himself Ben is purposely trying to show him up and make him feel bad.

Arnold has a couple of misbeliefs going, as you can see. One is that it is intolerable that Ben can afford a new car while he can't. (The truth is it isn't intolerable. It may not be desirable, but it's obviously not intolerable.) Second, it's terrible for Ben to rub it in by showing off his new car when poor Arnold can't have one, too. (It is not terrible. It may be a minor irritation, but it is not terrible.) Third, Arnold says self-depreciating words to himself and feels that he is a loser. If he doesn't check his misbeliefs soon, he'll really be miserable. (The truth is there is nothing at all wrong with not being able to afford a new car. True value does not depend upon what you can or can't buy; it depends on what you as a person are before God.)

In dealing with his misbeliefs, Arnold has to face them and replace them with the truth. But there's one point he isn't sure of and that is whether Ben is purposely trying to get his goat by showing off his new car. He decides to talk to Ben about it, which demonstrates some constructive behavior.

"Ben," he says with a serious expression on his face, "I'd like to talk to you for a minute about something that is bothering me." (Please note when you are about to talk to someone about your angry feelings to use an appropriate expression—not a face twisted with rage and blazing red with fury, and not a face smiling pleasantly and benignly as though you merely ate too much.) Face the person, use a normal tone of voice and look them square in the eye.

"Sure, Arnold, what is it?" Arnold's friend responds.

Arnold takes a breath. "I value our friendship and it's important to me that I be honest with you."

"Oh?"

"I want you to know I'm feeling angry right now."

"Angry? Yeah? How come?"

"I feel angry when you boast about your new car. You know

58

I'd like to buy one, too, but I can't afford to. I get the feeling that you are kind of rubbing it in. Is this what you want me to feel?"

Arnold has opened the channels for positive and honest communication with his friend. He has avoided carrying around senseless bitter resentment and adding deeper feelings of low self-worth.

Anger should be expressed honestly, not hidden hypocritically. There is a difference between revealing the fact of your anger to someone and forcing him to taste the sting of your rage.

We can learn to admit to ourselves when we are angry and, furthermore, we can be free to express to the person who has hurt us how we feel, if we desire. It takes self-control and honesty. Raw emotions blustering loudly or seething silently won't do a thing but cause more emotional distress, not to mention accompanying physical complications such as headaches, backaches, high blood pressure, stomach disorders, and heart disease; and, most grievous of all, our Savior is hurt by our sin.

The Scriptures teach us to deal with our anger and the cause of it and to prevent the emotion of anger from running away with us. This constructive behavior is described in Ephesians 4:26, "Be angry, and yet do not sin; do not let the sun go down on your anger." Anger that is harbored and nurtured offers great potential for our acting in ways that are sinful and unhealthy. That is why it is important to identify angry feelings immediately and to be free to talk about these feelings.

The one person you should talk to at all times when you are feeling angry is the Lord. Confess any sinful anger to Him. Ask Him to show you your misbeliefs and allow the Holy Spirit to guide you into the truth. A promise we can count on is found in John 16:13: "He will guide you into all truth."

At times there will be no need to talk about your angry feelings to the person you're angry with because you will have taken care of it by talking it over with the Lord alone. With your cooperation, He often can remove anger from you in the privacy of your prayer closet.

Tackle your misbeliefs; replace them with the truth. Allow God to penetrate into your emotions and thoughts with His Holy

Spirit of truth and you will find your self-talk, your thoughts, and your emotions with the presence of heaven in them. You're thinking, talking, and behaving to the glory of God.

WHEN SOMEONE ELSE IS ANGRY AT YOU

No matter how effectively you learn to deal with your anger and its causes, you have to live in a world where other people sometimes become angry, and there are times when someone will be angry with you.

Here are some of the ways to deal with the anger of others:

1. Don't be upset every time someone becomes angry with you. It isn't a disaster. You *can* cope with it effectively.
2. Don't shape your behavior just to prevent others' getting upset with you; they will anyway and when they do, it's their problem, not yours.
3. Be careful not to reward the angry outbursts of others. Ignore them when they yell at you, but be very attentive when they speak reasonably.
4. Don't be intimidated. Speak up and say, "Please talk to me reasonably."
5. Be kind and loving. Just because someone is angry at you doesn't mean you have to be angry back. Say words such as, "I am sorry you are feeling bad. Can I do anything to help you feel less upset?"
6. When there is truth in an accusation directed at you, admit it. Don't lie and defend yourself. You don't have to be right all of the time. Say words like, "It's true. I wasn't using my head at all when I came over here boasting about my new car. I can see where I was just showing off and I'm ashamed of myself. Please forgive me."
7. Give others the right to be angry with you sometimes and don't be shocked and offended when it happens. If you insist everyone see and respect you as the Perfect Human Being With No Faults, you will be deeply disappointed, not to mention the victim of a gross misbelief.

Sometimes the anger vented at you by someone will have nothing to do with you. You may be merely the target of some-

60

one's frustrations and unhappiness. Learn to identify such things, refusing to take personally every word spewed at you. Always remember, the angry person's problem is *theirs*; don't make it yours.

The victims of child abuse and wife beating are increasing in number every year. Don't allow yourself to become one of these statistics by allowing the situation to go unchanged. If you are the victim or the perpetrator, there *is* help for you. You can be free from the horrors of uncontrolled rage.

ANGER AND PRAYER

You're learning to listen to your own self-talk, and it becomes necessary to listen to your prayers as well. If you hear yourself complaining, pleading, begging, and reiterating grievances, it is time to take a new direction. Instead of praying the problem, pray the answer.

The words you say can move mountains. You need faith only the size of a mustard seed to do it. Jesus said nothing shall be impossible to you! Instead of, "O Lord, I just can't take it anymore. I've had it with this job. Nobody is nice to me; they're all so mean and nasty—the boss takes advantage of me, the workers are so stuck up and unfriendly. O Lord, it's just terrible," try this instead:

"Lord, I know nothing is impossible to me, so since I have to be at this job, I'm going to be there in your name. You tell me in your Word in Matthew 17:20 that my faith, even if it's small, can move mountains. I believe that, Lord, and I believe you can change me as well as my boss and the people I work with until we work in harmony. I know that you can lift this job from the level of drudgery, making it more than tolerable. Holy Spirit, move in my place of work and leave no heart untouched by your presence."

After praying like that, you wouldn't want to return to complaining; after all, you just gave the whole situation to Him. When you pray the answers instead of the complaints, you, too, will move mountains. Some mountains take a while to move, maybe even years, but you can manage that. It's a misbelief that

God absolutely must answer immediately or else it's terrible and dreadful. Misbeliefs like that are anger-related and might start a string of other blatant misbeliefs, finally getting to the point where you're impatient and angry enough to accuse God of not caring about you or not existing at all.

When you pray God's Word and the truth, which you have substituted for your misbeliefs, you will begin to sense great changes in your personality and life. In Christ nothing is impossible to *you*. You can bring about great changes by believing those words and praying answers instead of problems.

SUMMARY: HOW TO HANDLE ANGER

1. Confess your sinful anger to God, and receive His forgiveness.
2. *Locate and identify your misbeliefs.* What are you telling yourself that is not true?
3. *Replace the misbeliefs with the truth.* Eliminate the lies you've been telling yourself and start repeating the truth to yourself.
4. *Behave according to the truth.* Your old behavior resulting from misbelief has to come to an end. The old destructive ways of expressing or repressing anger, for instance, are gone now. In their stead is a person reacting according to the Word and will of God. You're honest, direct and sensitive to other people as well as yourself.
5. *Pray answers instead of problems.* You must believe that in Christ nothing is impossible to you, including the elimination of bitterness and anger from your life.

---

1. Ephesians 4:26 (NAS).
2. Bandura, Bandura & Walters.
3. Romans 5:8.
4. Romans 3:23.
5. James 1:19-20 (NAS).
6. Mark 3:5 (NAS).

CHAPTER SIX

Misbelief in Anxiety

Suzie is stacking dishes in the dishwasher for her mother when she accidentally drops a glass and breaks it. Her heart pounds. She knows this means punishment. When she broke things in the past, her mother usually did three things: yell, call Suzie names, and spank. Suzie shudders in fear, thinking of what is to come. Then Mother enters the kitchen. When she sees the broken glass, she seizes Suzie by the arm, raves about the glass being fine crystal, calls her clumsy, careless and useless, and then wallops her.

The next day Mother again tells Suzie to stack dishes in the dishwasher. Suzie isn't very eager to do it. She tries to come up with an excuse to get out of the task. She says she has to go to the toilet or she has a stomachache and has to go to bed. Suzie feels anxious because she has been *conditioned* to feel that way. If she stacks the dishes, there's the danger of breaking something; and if she breaks something, she will surely get yelled at, called names and spanked, and that would be painful. In time, if Suzie has enough of these painful experiences—that is, breaks enough glasses and receives enough insults and spankings—she will develop anxiety that spreads into her very feelings of self-worth.

Pair these events with Suzie's social contacts. She goes roller skating and has trouble staying upright on the skates. The other children ridicule and tease her. In school and at home her brother calls her names in front of other people. Her father often calls her lazy and her mother yells when she doesn't perform according to her expectations.

Suzie teaches herself how to be anxious. When her playmates ridicule her, she feels pain; therefore, she feels anxious when she sees them playing on the ice skating rink or playground, as well as when she *thinks* about them. Her family's demands, which she cannot always meet, present additional anxious feelings.

So Suzie does something typical of anxiety neurotics. She begins to avoid the things that make her feel anxious. She begins to avoid contacts with her playmates. She avoids her family, stays by herself. She teaches herself that when she withdraws from situations that make her feel anxious, the anxiety level drops. This is reinforcing to her.

Carol is a 22-year-old person. She has spent several years of her life piling up anxiety responses, just as Suzie is doing now. She is riddled with fears and can't force herself to go out and get a job. She says she wants to get a job but she just can't get one. She has her own apartment near her parents' home which she rarely leaves. "If you could get out and get a job, you'd pull yourself out of the dumps you're in," her mother tells her over the telephone.

"I can't get a job," she protests. "I've tried and I just can't." In desperation, her parents insist she see a psychologist.

"I hate job interviews," she tells her therapist. "They scare me."

"Why is that?"

"Well, they're awful, that's why. The job market is tight and there are so few openings."

By her eighth session she is able to identify her thoughts and beliefs. She identifies her feared objects as other people. Her inability to land a job is not due to the job market but due to the anxiety she suffers at the *thought* of going out and being with people. She fears what the people could do to her.

"Carol, you said you hated being in crowds."

"That's right. I really hate it."

"What could a crowd do to you?"

"Well, they might make fun of me or laugh at me."

"Would that be terrible?"

"Yes, it would be terrible. It would be horrible. I'd hate that."

"Would it really be the end of the world for you if someone laughed or made fun of you?"

"Well—I'd hate it, but—I guess it actually wouldn't be the end of the world."

Carol didn't realize it, but she had just made a big and important step of progress.

1. She listened to herself and heard what was really going on in her mind.
2. By listening she realized she had been telling herself that to be laughed at and made fun of would be terrible, horrible. (Misbelief.)
3. She then argued that misbelief with the truth by telling herself that although she wouldn't like the situation, it would *not* be the end of the world.

People who suffer from anxiety tell themselves, "If the thing I worry about actually happened, it would wipe me out. It would be awful, horrible." Dr. Albert Ellis, director of the Institute for Advanced Study in Rational Psychotherapy, calls this "awfulizing." Anxious people do a lot of it.

Little Suzie does it when she avoids her playmates. "It would be awful if they were mean to me." Carol does it by avoiding job interviews. "It would be awful if I didn't do well."

Carol will realize that the idea of being in a crowd makes her anxious not because of the number of people or discomfort brought by the press of a lot of people, but because she fears they might make fun of her or laugh at her. She will overcome this lie as she de-"awfulizes" the thought in her mind and replaces it with the truth.

Some common lies are:

- He/she/they might not like me. That would be terrible.
- I might not meet people's expectations of me. That would be terrible.
- I might be rejected. That would be terrible.
- I might fail. That would be terrible.
- I might say or do something dumb. That would be terrible.
- Once I've gained happiness, I might lose it. That would be terrible.

65

- Once I've gained love, I might lose it. That would be terrible.
- I might not look as good as other people. That would be terrible.
- He/she/they might not approve of me. That would be terrible.
- He/she/they might discover what a nothing I really am. That would be terrible.
- Nobody will ever love me. That would be terrible.
- I might be a terrible lover. That would be terrible.
- I might get hurt. That would be terrible.
- I might be asked to do something I don't know how to do. That would be terrible.
- I might lose everything I've got. That would be terrible.
- I could die. That would be terrible.

There are many more. How many of them can you recognize?

WHAT OTHER PEOPLE THINK OF ME

The central theme running through the misbeliefs in anxiety is that *what other people think about me is of such crucial importance that I must anticipate it in advance of all my actions. I must do all I can in order to prevent others from thinking badly of me. If they think badly of me, it will be a mortal blow to me. It would be terrible.*

Nearly all anxious people believe and tell themselves that they are in danger of other people's reactions to them. These words, like all misbeliefs, are lies from the enemy. While we are certainly glad if others think well of us and love us, we can still live very well if we don't have the affection and approval of other people. The Scriptures teach us to consider others in verses such as "Love your neighbor as yourself" and "Beloved, let us love one another," but that does not mean we are to strive and aim for the approval of everybody and drop dead if we don't receive it.

It's great to be liked. It is, in fact, more desirable to be liked than disliked. There is nothing wrong with learning how to be liked and appreciated by others. There are skills of personal communication which are beneficial to learn. But it is silly and destructive to believe that you *must* succeed in making everyone endorse you and everything about you. There is no reason why you cannot learn techniques for pleasing, influencing, persuading and changing the behavior of other people. But this is different from dwelling on such misbeliefs as, "I *must* be important to someone." It's nice to be important to someone, but it's healthy to leave out the "must."

The philosophy that says you should be liked and appreciated by one and all is not only silly, it's non-biblical. If you are learning techniques to please, influence, persuade, and manipulate people, what are your motives? Are you saying to yourself, "I *must* be important to someone—I *must* be liked—I *must* be accepted—I *must* be . . ."?

Let's assume your "musts" aren't fulfilled after all. Suppose people still don't particularly like you after you work diligently to gain their approval? Suppose someone actually hates the sight of you—outwardly rejects you? Suppose someone you respect and desire the approval of tells you to go fly a kite or jump in the lake or some similar brush-off? What do you tell yourself then? Because placed as paramount in your gallery of "musts" is the notion that everybody should approve of and like you, you'll probably respond to rejection with such miseries as, "I'm really a loser," or, "What a failure I am," or, "I'm a real nothing," or, "I'll get them for this. I'll show the world!" "I don't need *anybody*!"

The Bible does not teach us to please everybody on earth. It does not tell us to work overtime trying to get people to love us. Jesus never told us to go out and take a course in how to get people to like us. He told us to love *Him*, trust *Him*, have faith in *Him*, glorify *Him*, and to genuinely care about others.

The price an anxious person pays to please people is too great. Jesus, above all others, demonstrated that if a person is really serious about pleasing God, there will be times when his behavior will be just the opposite of what others expect of him. Jesus himself wasn't loved by everyone and still isn't. Jesus wasn't accepted by everyone when He lived, and He still isn't. Many have found fault with Him. When He was alive on earth He made the leaders and molders of public opinion quite upset with His social behavior. He befriended prostitutes and thieves and sought the company of traitorous tax gatherers. This did not make Him Mr. Popular with the religious folk. In fact, many of the things He did didn't win him friends. People found fault with the way He talked and worshipped; they didn't like what He said, didn't like His friends, didn't like what He did—they even criticized the way He *ate*. But He wasn't devastated by what others thought of Him because He kept His eye on the Father and doing His will.

In fact, He had joy through it all and says to us, "*My* joy I give to you." Jesus didn't live to please people. He lived to please His Father in heaven.

Nobody other than you has the power to make you miserable. That power is yours alone.

You make yourself miserable by the things you tell yourself. Sometimes, however, an anxious person cannot define what it is that is making him anxious. The term anxiety covers a large number of behaviors, including cognitive activity (such as worrying, fretting, obsessing) as well as physiological events appropriate under stress (dry mouth, perspiring, rapid heartbeat and respiration, dizziness, light-headedness, tremors, butterflies in the stomach, tense muscles). Anxiety is ordinarily defined as fear in the absence of actual danger. The event a person fears is highly unlikely to do to him what he fears.

Anxiety is:

1. Fear in the absence of real danger.
2. Overestimation of the probability of danger and exaggeration of its degree of terribleness.
3. Imagined negative results.

The acrophobic person has a fear of heights and is afraid he will fall from the highest floor of a tall building to his death even though he is indoors with the windows closed or standing on a heavily screened observation platform. He *grossly overestimates* the likelihood of falling. Granted, it certainly wouldn't be a pleasant event if a person were to trip off the edge of a high building and plunge twenty floors to the pavement below, but the likelihood of its actually happening is extremely remote. In spite of that, the acrophobic person is horrified that such a thing might happen to him. His life can be made miserable because of his fear of heights. Driving along a mountain road may be a living night-mare to him. He may get hysterical if he has to climb a ladder or scale a catwalk. Just the thought of a high plane can bring a cold sweat to his brow. He is trapped by this fear in spite of the fact that he is actually in no danger at all.

The zoophobic is another person with exaggerated fear. His anxiety, due to imagery, is related to animals and he is deathly afraid of them. He may turn pale and tremble in the presence of a tiny kitten. What he is doing is *exaggerating* the degree of evil he would suffer if the kitten were to jump on him and bite or scratch. He may imagine being clawed to death, disembowelled, or being suffocated by it. In reality, he is in very little danger at all. The zoophobic realizes that most domestic pets are not dangerous, but he is tormented by images of danger.

The claustrophobic person is afraid of small places. Elevators, small rooms without windows, crowded narrow hallways and other enclosed areas will be an agonizing torture for this person. He is afraid that if the building were to catch fire or if some disaster were to occur, he couldn't get out fast enough. He overstresses the likelihood of these improbable events happening. He is tormented by this fear.

Another person who experiences agonizing anxiety is the agoraphobic person who is fearful of open places. He is afraid that if he goes to these places, he will have an anxiety attack at being there and be unable to escape. He tells himself he will become so anxious in such places that his heart will race, his breath will come in gulps, his limbs will tremble, his head will swirl, he'll black out and lay squirming on the ground making a public spectacle of himself. Maybe he'll die or maybe he'll get carted away to some hospital where he'll be pronounced hopelessly insane.

How probable is such an event?

Little Suzie at the beginning of this chapter has become an agoraphobic. She sits in the big leather chair of the consulting room, her eyes darting back and forth at the furnishings and out the window.

"Suzie, is it true you haven't been to school for several days?"

"I guess so. I'm never going back."

69

"Never?"

"Never. I hate it. It's too big. My other school wasn't so big."

"Did you like your other school better?"

"No. I hated that school, too. I don't want to be around so many people. They make me nervous."

"What happens when you become nervous?"

"I don't know. I just get sick, I guess. I feel sick."

"Where do you feel sick?"

"Everywhere. I just feel sick. I feel like I'm going to faint or lose control. Like I'll lose control."

"What do you mean by that, Suzie?"

"I'll just lose control, you know, like start screaming or crying or maybe I'll fall down or something and lose control."

Little Suzie, whose parents can't understand how they could possibly have such a "disturbed child" wonder if she is brain damaged. There is nothing wrong with Suzie's brain, however. She is a bright child who suffers anxiety at phobic proportions. At first she doesn't want to receive psychological help, but after a few sessions she begins to respond and she likes her therapist.

"Suzie, what would happen if you actually did lose control, as you say, in the middle of a crowd?"

Her eyes widen and the pulse beat at her temples quickens. "Oh, I uh—I would lose control. I'd—I'd—I don't know, maybe go crazy."

"Do you *really* think you would go crazy?"

"Do you think I would?"

"No, I don't."

She is quiet for a moment. She is fumbling with her hands. "I uh—I don't know. I'd lose control in front of all those people. In front of the other kids. It would be the worst. The worst."

"Would it really? What would be so bad about that?" She wants to laugh, but she just groans. "Oh, that would be so terrible."

Several sessions later, she is able to honestly say to her therapist, "I suppose it wouldn't be the end of the world if I lost control."

"And do you *really* believe you will lose control?"

"Well, I don't know. After all, we did go to school twice last

70

week and I didn't lose control. I went this morning—"

"Is it unpleasant to be around all those kids?"

"Yes, it's unpleasant."

"It's endurable, though, isn't it? I mean, a thing can be unpleasant and still endurable, can't it, Suzie?"

Suzie smiles her brightest smile since she has been coming for therapy. She shrugs then and says, "I s'pose. I just never thought that something could be unpleasant and that I could still get through it."

"Are you willing to go to school again tomorrow?"

"I think so."

The "terrible" consequences Suzie imagined were based on nothing but anxiety. Some people's lives are organized around the effort to avoid anxiety. The fear of fear consumes their waking hours and anxiety about anxiety brings such tension and stress that it becomes self-fulfilling. The agoraphobic cries like Job, "The thing which I greatly feared is come upon me." [1] The misbelief is exaggeration of the badness of the anxiety attack. For even though it may be truly uncomfortable, it is not likely to do a person any harm.

We don't want to make the answers to Suzie's problem sound simplistic, and we don't want you to get the idea that phobias are cured miraculously after a few little talks with a Christian psychotherapist. Suzie has come a long way, though, and is on her way to true recovery. She is beginning to understand and *act* on the truth. She is learning how to argue against her misbeliefs. Her parents' unrealistic expectations of her, rejection from her brother and friends, as well as failure at sports and schoolwork all contribute to her anxiety responses. The wonderful fact is, however, she will not have to wait until she is an adult to learn the skills that make for a healed and normal life. She is learning them now with God's help.

The love of God reaches into Suzie's fears. This love surrounds, engulfs and pierces into her soul where her emotions and thoughts live. She imagines the Lord accompanying her to school; she sees Him standing beside her in the school gym softly whispering, "I'm with you always, Suzie"; she chooses to replace some of the self-condemning lies she has believed with such

71

truths as: The same spirit that raised Christ from the dead dwells in me.[2] Gradually and slowly, Suzie will take part in the youth group at church and she will be a sparkling star for the Lord whom she is finding to be very real.

Perhaps Suzie has suffered more than most little girls in the sixth grade, but she has learned something many adults are still groping to discover. *Even though things may be unpleasant, I can live through it without falling apart* and *things are only as unpleasant as I tell myself they are.*

Let's look at the major misbeliefs in anxiety.

1. If the thing I worry about were to happen, it would be *terrible.*
2. Even though the likelihood of the *terrible* happening to me is utterly remote, I believe it's actually inevitable.

Most of our anxieties do not reach phobic proportions. You may feel tense and anxious when you have to get up and give a speech or when you are in a new and unfamiliar situation that demands your best; but more than likely, your reactions won't reach phobic proportions. You may think your legs are turning to putty and your stomach is popping with flying objects, but you do eventually recover.

An actor tells himself on opening night of his play that he will surely have a heart attack before the curtain goes up. He perspires, his hands are cold, his feet feel numb. He has difficulty breathing. "I'll never live through it," he tells the floor. "I don't remember a word of the script. I'm sick all over."

Two and a half hours later, when the curtain rings down, he feels great. Why? He got through it. He shows us one of the best cures for situational anxiety. Avoid it and you'll increase the anxiety. Face it and go through the anxiety and you'll remove it.

It may be unpleasant, but who ever told us all of life was supposed to be pleasant? The actor somehow pushed one foot in front of the other and got himself out on stage at his cue. From then on, he was okay. He got through it, and on top of it—got through it well. Whether or not the play was a critical success is not important. What is important here is that he plunged through his anxiety and didn't turn back.

When you are feeling anxiety, stop and ask yourself:

1. What am I telling myself is terrible?
   (The actor tells himself he'll forget his lines, he'll do a bad job in the play. He thinks that's terrible.)
2. Will the results really be as terrible as I tell myself they'll be?
   (The actor says *terrible* things will happen if he forgets his lines or does a bad job.)
   Now argue the case—like this:
1. It's not terrible. It may be unpleasant, but that's a long way from *terrible*.
   ("Some of the things that I believe to be absolutely terrible really are only annoying.")
2. Even if what I fear were to happen, it wouldn't be *terrible*. It might be unpleasant, but it surely wouldn't be the end of the world or me.
   ("If the worst happened, the consequences wouldn't really be as bad as I've been telling myself.")

AVOIDANCE BEHAVIOR

The actor could have refused to go on stage the night his play opened. He could have chosen to run away from the unpleasant feelings he was experiencing. But he didn't. He forged ahead, plowed through his anxieties—and afterward? He felt good.

Many situations in your life may be less than pleasant. In fact, oftentimes you'll be faced with problems that seem to be insurmountable. Avoiding the problem or situation usually makes it more intense. Avoiding anxiety is not the way to get rid of it. Tell yourself:

1. Even though I'd like to avoid the circumstance or situation, I will *not*. Avoidance behavior will only increase my anxiety. I will go ahead, experience the unpleasant feelings, and I'll get through it.
2. I do not have to be afraid of unpleasant feelings. They are a part of life and they won't kill me. It's acceptable to have unpleasant feelings at times.

Margaret is a beautiful woman of forty with the energies of a teen-ager. She busies herself caring for the needs of her family as well as working a full-time job outside the home. She has several hobbies and is active in her church as a prayer group leader and Sunday school teacher. She is well loved by those closest to her and has many friends and acquaintances. She has one problem: she is deathly afraid to drive a car and refuses to learn how.

This problem was magnified when her husband decided it was time to move to a larger home in the suburbs. Margaret would no longer have the convenience of the city buses to help hide her fear of driving. She would no longer have the familiar busy routine with which she felt safe and secure. She was faced with the threat she dreaded most: sitting behind the driver's wheel and driving a car on dangerous streets and highways. The thought was horrible. It nearly cost her her marriage.

"I won't move," she told her husband flatly.

"But we'll move into a bigger and better home," he tried to reason. "We'll have everything you could want."

"I'm not going."

"But why not? What's wrong?"

"I hate the suburbs."

Her husband could not understand her attitude. He attempted a rational discussion. "But you've always said how much nicer it would be to live in the suburbs. The children would have more outdoor freedom, we'd have a more modern home with more space, it would be more quiet than the city . . ."

"I don't want to talk about it. If you want to move, go ahead. You move without me, though."

"I don't *want* to move without you. That's a foolish thing to say."

"If you really loved me, you wouldn't do this to me."

"Do *what* to you?"

Her husband was unaware of the proportions to which Margaret's anxieties had grown. She had been able to develop her fears without revealing how painful they were. Her lies were, "If I drive a car, I'll have an accident and that would be terrible. I could kill someone. Or I could be killed."

Margaret and her husband sought professional marriage counseling and the truth emerged. Margaret's fear of driving was deeper than they realized.

Very gradually and over a long period of time, Margaret was able to overcome this fear. Eventually she was able to take driving lessons and even own her own car. She was able to *get through* her unpleasant feelings; she *could* do the thing she dreaded.

But how does Margaret or anyone else experiencing intense anxiety get to the point where their fears pass? The answer is to *listen* to the words you tell yourself, *argue* against those words, and *replace* the misbelief with the truth.

In a very short time Margaret was able to see her misbeliefs clearly. They were: "Driving cars is the most dangerous thing a person can do. I might do something stupid or make a mistake, costing a life. That would be the most terrible thing I can think of." She then taught herself to challenge such nonsense: "Driving cars is *not* the most dangerous thing a person can do. Living without Jesus is more dangerous. Furthermore, if I make a mistake, I will handle the consequences."

She learned to speak the truth to herself, "Even though it is anxiety-arousing for me to get behind the wheel of a car, I *can* do it." Gradually she progressed from sitting behind the wheel to starting the engine. ("I *can* do it. In Christ nothing is impossible!")

Then, with someone sitting beside her in the front seat, she would put the car into drive, step gently on the gas and drive only to the end of the driveway; then she would brake, put the car in park, and turn off the engine. ("I *did* it! I drove the car! I got through it! Thank you, Lord.")

The next day she repeated driving to the end of the driveway. She did this for three days. We asked her how she felt driving to the end of the driveway for the fourth time.

"I felt fine."

"No anxiety?"

"No, not really. I felt fine about it."

"Why do you think you felt fine about it?"

"Well, I knew I could do it. I had done it three times before and it didn't do me in. I guess I just felt confident it wasn't going to be that terrible."

We were delighted and congratulated her. Then we asked,

"Are you ready to drive to the corner?"

Margaret made the drive to the corner. She did it several times with someone with her and then she soloed. "I did it!" she exclaimed. "I never dreamed it would be possible."

Most anxieties are related to four things:

1. Dread of making public mistakes.
2. Fear of making someone else angry or upset.
3. Losing love.
4. Physical pain and death.

These fears are exaggerated and often needless. In reality, *you* create anxiety, not situations or events. Anxiety is brought about by your telling yourself something is *terrible.*

What does "terrible" mean? Usually it means something far worse than you think you can endure. You tell yourself the "terrible" is beyond human endurance, worse than anything on earth. Truly, nothing of this sort exists.

"Terrible" is something that you firmly believe ought not to be. *It's terrible; therefore it must not exist.* This, too, is a misbelief.

Inconvenient, annoying, unfortunate, unpleasant stimuli will always exist. *You,* however, control your own feelings. *Thinking creates feelings.* You'll never get rid of every unpleasantry around you, but you can gain the skills to handle them effectively. The mistaken belief that life should be sweetsey, nicey, and without problems will make you quite miserable. With these ideas in your mind, you will seek to avoid or run from trouble rather than overcome it.

Jesus tells us quite clearly that we will encounter negatives in this world and that there will be problems, trials, and temptations of all sorts. He said, "In the world you shall have tribulation." He warned us of a devil, the enemy of God who seeks to destroy man; but then He said triumphantly, "But be of good cheer; I have overcome the world."[3] We can be free of crippling anxiety when we rest in this beautiful fact: In Christ, we are safe, loved, protected, watched over, and one day bound for eternal glory.

Getting rid of your anxiety means to (1) minimize the danger you tell yourself you're in (remember, your fears are exaggerated); (2) realize *you* create your anxiety (you create your own misbeliefs); (3) dispute these misbeliefs, challenge them ("is this really as terrible as I'm telling myself?"); (4) replace the misbeliefs with the *truth*. Don't worry about how weak you think you are. Jesus said, "My strength is made perfect in weakness." [4]

Here are some words of truth with which to argue those lies:

> *For our light affliction, which is but for a moment, worketh for us a far more exceeding and eternal weight of glory (2 Cor. 4:17).*

> *Behold, I give unto you power to tread on serpents and scorpions, and over all the power of the enemy: and nothing shall by any means hurt you (Luke 10:19).*

> *And I say unto you, Ask, and it shall be given you; seek, and ye shall find; knock, and it shall be opened unto you (Luke 11:9).*

> *Submit yourselves therefore to God. Resist the devil, and he will flee from you (James 4:7).*

> *Greater is He that is in you than he that is in the world (1 John 4:4).*

> *But they that wait upon the Lord shall renew their strength; they shall mount up with wings as eagles; they shall run, and not be weary; and they shall walk, and not faint (Isa. 40:31).*

Let's pray together, "Create in me a clean heart, O God; and renew a right spirit within me." And now let's expect great things as He answers our prayer. Anxiety will no longer have controlling power over you.

---

1. Job 3:25.
2. Romans 8:11.
3. John 16:33.
4. 2 Corinthians 12:9.

77

CHAPTER SEVEN

Misbelief in Lack of Self-Control

Ann's eyes are downcast, her voice low and quivering. "It just all seems so hopeless . . . sort of, well, like I'll always be in this awful rut . . . like there's no way out . . . I just can't seem to get going on anything . . . I mean, God knows I pray and pray, but nothing ever seems to happen. My prayers are just never answered. It's just so . . . hopeless."

Tears slide down her pale cheeks. "I expected Jesus to change me when I gave my life to Him five years ago, and He certainly has—that is, so many things in my life are really changed for the better and He has blessed me in so many ways—but there's one thing I just can't seem to get anywhere with and that's self-control. You know what I mean?"

She continues miserably. "See, I need to get a job, but I just don't go out and look for one. I always make some excuse for not going out, although I do read the want ads and sometimes I find certain jobs that look good, but I need to lose weight, as you can see, at least 30 pounds; I want to get down to 125 pounds, but I just *can't do it.* I've prayed and prayed about this, and then I just can't seem to get going. . . . "

For the next 40 minutes Ann delivers a barrage of "can't do's," each one prefaced by the sentences, "It's all so hopeless" or "I can't," "I lack," and finally, the crunch: "God doesn't care about me. If He did, He'd change me."

David is a handsome 35-year-old used-car salesman. His

twinkling eyes and bright smile fade as he explains, "It's like I'm a victim or something. You should see the paper work I've got to do—a ton of it—and I just can't get to it. My discipline stinks. And that's not all. I'm late everywhere I go. I oversleep, I do lots of things I really shouldn't do. I've always got a good excuse, but this last month being late cost me about $3,300. The month before my being late cost me plenty, too. I can't keep on like this!"

Shirley dabs her cigarette out in the already overflowing ashtray of butts. "I'd love to quit smoking, but I don't have the self-control. I'll probably croak of lung cancer and my dying words will be, 'Got a light?' I've tried quitting and once I lasted three months without taking a single drag on a cigarette, but here I am, smoking two packs a day. Some people have the self-control, and others, like me, don't."

For most of us there is no easy way out of life's difficulties and responsibilities. It's a lot easier to blame Jesus for our not going out and getting a job than it is to do something about the problem. It's a lot easier to oversleep and avoid the monumental task of long-overdue paper work than it would be to sit down and begin work on it. It's a lot easier to keep on smoking than it is to quit. It's a lot easier to sit in a comfortable chair with a bag of potato chips watching TV than it is to engage in a series of physical exercises or to diet.

Elaine, a distraught mother of two children, cries, "I feel like I'm a rubber ball, just bouncing along where I'm thrown. I make all sorts of new resolutions—like, how I'm going to get into reading the Bible more; or, how I'm going to start exercising to get rid of this flab on my body; or, how I'm going to get the house clean by noon and then do this or that. But then I'll sit on the phone all morning, or watch soap operas instead of reading my Bible, or I'll eat a dish of ice cream wishing I were thin. Where is self-control in my life? Aren't I supposed to have self-control? Isn't that one of the fruits of the Holy Spirit?"

Many people try drugs, hypnosis, and even surgery in their desperate flight from facing responsibility and difficult tasks, but seldom do these methods bring lasting results or the happiness so passionately sought.

We asked Ann to face the reasons why she couldn't go out and get herself a job. "Well, I don't know. I just can't."

"Are you afraid to apply for a job?"

"Yes, I suppose so. I'll probably be turned down."

"But you said you were qualified enough to get any number of jobs."

"Yes, that's true. But that doesn't mean anything. I guess I'm just afraid of rejection."

"But why are you afraid of rejection? What's so bad about being rejected?"

"Are you kidding? What's so *bad* about rejection? That's the worst thing in the world. A person likes to feel accepted and wanted."

"You said you're qualified enough to land a good job. You said you've had two years of business school and that your skills are good. What makes you think you'll be rejected when you apply for a job?"

"Well, they want pretty girls . . . "

"Now wait a minute. Are you telling yourself you're not *attractive* enough to get a good job?"

"Isn't that obvious? Look at me, I'm at least 30 pounds overweight."

Notice the self-talk here. Ann tells herself she can't get a job, but then reason tells her she probably could because she does possess the skills to get the kind of job she'd like. So then she tries another lie: she's not attractive enough. (If this were true, we'd have a world with no overweight or unattractive people working.)

"I used to have a body of a model. I was what they called a real knock-out. Now I'm really disgusted with myself."

"And is it important for you to be a knock-out in order to feel good about yourself? Suppose what you consider attractive isn't attractive at all? Suppose it was considered gauche for a woman your height and build to weigh less than 200 pounds?"

"I weigh 140 now."

"Well? What would you do?"

"I'd probably gain weight."

"And if you did gain the weight, putting yourself 75 pounds heavier than the 'knock-out' weight you speak of? Would you consider the weight-gain to be the result of a lack of self-control?"

"Probably not. I would have gained it because I set my mind to it."

"Suppose you 'set your mind' to losing weight?"

"I'd lose it."

The easy way out for Ann is to avoid her problems and do nothing. She puts up high goals for herself, worries she won't attain them, shrinks in dismay at imagined rejection, frets and feels angry and guilty and never gets around to "setting her mind" to doing the things she desperately wants to do.

Ann and others like her who suffer from lack of self-control tell themselves enough lies until the point is reached where they shout accusations at heaven, "Jesus doesn't answer my prayers! He won't change me! He doesn't love me!"

Lies.

It is not surprising when a Christian lacks self-control that his accompanying complaints are discontent, guilt, deep dissatisfaction with life, lack of self-confidence, and anger at God.

We learn many of our misbeliefs through the media.

The misbeliefs associated with poor self-control are encouraged by the media. Watch enough commercials on television and you'll begin to believe that you should have everything you want. We easily grasp the invitation to "own" something appealing or to "be" someone who has the approval of everyone around. These misbeliefs tell us to *get* what we want and get it right away (while we're still young or while the sale lasts or while it's there to get).

Misbeliefs related to lack of self-control are:

1. If you want something you should have it—no matter what considerations are involved.
2. It's terrible and unjust if you have to wait to get something you want, especially if you want it very much.
3. To be uncomfortable or frustrated is terrible, intolerable. (Avoid distress at all costs.)
4. You cannot control your strong desires. They are "needs" and you can't stand it when they are not satisfied. Any time you have to spend being frustrated or ungratified is unendurable.

5. You can't stand pain or discomfort.
6. You can't stand not sleeping very well.
7. You can't stand it if others don't treat you as your doting parents did.
8. You can't stand it if circumstances aren't the way you want them to be. You may "endure" things as they are, but they are terrible and you'll let that be known.
9. You can't stand exerting yourself or having to make an effort.
10. You can't stand failure of any kind.
11. You can't fight your desires—they're much too strong for you to expect yourself to handle them.
12. You can't quit because you're too weak and besides, even though X is bad for you, it meets your need for gratification. (X stands for whatever habit happens to be the problem.)
13. You're entitled to inflict your demands upon others.

Several generations of parents have been reared on these notions and have passed them on to their children. Psychologists' and pastors' offices swell with men, women and children who are the extensions of these misbeliefs. So-called "progressive" educational methods often foster the belief that we ought to get and have what we want and like, discarding all else.

A young couple is having Sunday dinner in a restaurant with their two-year-old son. He sits on a toddler's seat placed on a chair and begins kicking the table with his foot.

"What's the matter, Sweetie?"

"He wants some bread."

Mother hands the child a chunk of bread. Two-year-old son throws it on the floor and emits a shrill scream.

"He didn't want the bread. What's the matter with him?"

"He wants your pie."

"He didn't eat his own pie. Something's upsetting him."

Father wiggles his fingers at Screaming Child. "What's the matter, Son? What is it? Here, play with your spoon."

Son hurls the spoon across the table at Father.

"*You* take care of him. Maybe he has to go potty."

Mother wiggles fingers at Screaming Child. "Want to go potty, Sweetie?"

Child screams and writhes on the seat.

"Milk. Give him some milk!"

"Here, Sweetie. Here's your milk. Come on, Sweetie, open the mouth. Attaboy, here comes the choo-choo headed for the tunnel. Choo! Cho—oh, oh, all over my dress." Mother turns helplessly to Father. "Why don't *you* do something?"

"Maybe his stomach hurts," he offers.

The interaction here is getting obvious. The child is quite capable of communicating his needs, but he has been systematically trained to believe that his parents exist primarily to spare him the trouble of coping and even of making his wants clear. Although the child could feed himself, he doesn't have to. Although he could handle some of his own problems or else ask for help, he doesn't have to. He was reinforced for yelling by the constant attention he received. Not only that, when his desires were gratified (milk, pie, spoon, potty), he learned that he could have everything he wanted and should not have to wait for it. He also learned he should never have to endure the slightest distress or discomfort.

Later in life, Screaming Child has many of these misbeliefs reinforced and strengthened as his parents continue to give him everything he expresses the least longing for. He has things done for him which he could do for himself and is never made to wait. He is also taught that to be uncomfortable is *terrible* and that above all he should *never* suffer distress.

Now what happens to Child? He grows up and discovers his friends don't comply with his demands and wants. ("Everybody hates me.") His teachers don't dote on him or make excuses for his lack of obedience. ("Nobody understands me or cares about me.") He finds that other people don't want to do for him what he can do for himself. ("The whole world is rotten!") He faces a society that requires him to comply with a certain moral code. He can't imagine denying himself something he wants, so when his peers offer him drugs, he has no reason to say no. He grows fat and sloppy in his appearance because he doesn't want to be inconvenienced or put upon. Living a chaste life is something he is not sure of; after all, one ought to get what one wants when one wants it. He believes all his fancies are vital *needs* which must always be gratified. These mistaken "needs" must be fulfilled or

he's miserable. ("Life stinks. I might as well kill myself.")
Self-control? What's that?

If your teen-ager sounds like Screaming Child in advanced stages, don't be in a hurry to condemn yourself as a parental failure. You aren't. You have the right to make mistakes, the same as everybody else. *Behavior is learned.* Your child can learn to develop self-control in his or her life as well as learn to avoid it. It's never too late. Most of the happy, productive people we know today are that way because they worked at it. They *overcame.* Perhaps they weren't always sterling examples of self-control and dedication, but today they have attained personal gains far exceeding anything they've known before.

The devil has managed to convince millions of people that self-control is something other people have. "I just can't control myself," someone says matter-of-factly. As long as a person continues to believe this lie, it will cause itself to come true! You will find that you actually *can't* quit whatever it is you wish you didn't do; you *can't* do the thing you want so dearly to do; you *can't* resist whatever it is you know you should resist.

The can't is a lie. You *can.* Recognize the lie immediately. Look at these statements for a moment:

1. I *can't* lose weight.
2. I *can't* control my physical passions.

Remember what we said earlier: you control your feelings by your thinking. If you *think* and *tell yourself* you can't control yourself, you probably won't be able to. Can you change those sentences?

TRUTH

1. It's ridiculous and dumb to think I can't lose weight. Of course I can lose weight! I can say no to myself and my appetites. I can stop eating fattening foods, I can count calories, I can join Overeaters Victorious,[1] I *can* lose weight! I can do all things through Christ who strengthens me!

2. I certainly *can* control my physical passions. Jesus died on the cross to deliver me from every shred of unrighteousness, and I certainly will *not* sink to fleshly indulgence, not I. It's a lie that I have no self-control.

84

ONCE-FAIL-ALWAYS-FAIL MISBELIEF

There are many lies regarding self-control or lack of it. Some people actually *train* themselves to believe they are weak, worthless, and inadequate. These people tell themselves, "I can't do X because I'm so helpless. I'm a failure at absolutely *every*thing."

Marsha failed to finish her two-year course of study at a church-affiliated Bible school. She didn't keep her job, either, and had to move in with her sister and her husband. She began going to singles bars where she met a young man and began a relationship with him that included sex. He vanished from her life when he learned he had gotten her pregnant. Without a job, without money, without a home except the couch in her sister's living room and pregnant, Marsha's outlook on life was grim.

Marsha taught herself to believe she was a weak person; she believed she was worthless, inadequate, and helpless. She told herself that she had piled up so many failures in her life, what else was there left for her but more failure? "Failure, failure, nothing but failure. What's the use? Why go on?"

Once-fail-always-fail is a misbelief and a lie! If you look at history, you can see what a gross lie it is! The old adage "If at first you don't succeed, try, try again" is not unsound advice. Marsha, with help, needed to learn to appreciate herself, to value herself, to see that she was indeed an important human being whom God was deeply concerned about.

From there she could learn to practice those behaviors which reinforce that truth—things that were good for her and not harmful. Eventually she realized she could return to school and finish her education. She found an apartment for herself and the baby in the same building as her sister, and developed many intimate friendships with other Christians who loved and cared for her. Marsha found her real self in Christ Jesus who never ever said, "Once-fail-always-fail."

Shirley is a woman of 36, pretty and hard-working, but distraught over her cigarette smoking. She feels trapped in a vise with no way out.

"It's no use. I've tried quitting and I can't. I always start again."

"Do you believe that when a person tries and fails at something it then becomes impossible?"

Shirley thinks for a moment. "I guess not. I applied to several schools for my teaching job. I was turned down eight times before I finally landed the job I have now."

"So that destroys your original hypothesis: 'I failed before so I always have to fail.' "

"My brother quit smoking a few years ago and he says he doesn't even think about smoking anymore. Says he doesn't even miss it."

"Had he ever tried quitting before?"

"Sure. He tried lots of times. He managed to quit for a few weeks once and then he quit for a couple of months another time. But then one day he just gave them up and hasn't lit another one since."

"Shirley, do you see the point? Your brother tried to quit several times, the same as you have. Then one day he finally *did* quit for good. It's absolutely untrue to tell yourself that past failures prove you must continue to fail."

Shirley clung to her misbelief like a child clings to a teddy bear. If she could convince herself that her habit wasn't her own fault, that she was somehow an innocent victim, she could go on smoking and not have to experience the unpleasantness of saying no to herself. The lie "I can't do something because I haven't been able to do it before" is untrue and defeating.

Jesus sets us free to be the people we were meant to be— whole, beautiful, and capable of taking His strength as ours.

Fear thou not; for I am with thee: be not dismayed; for I am thy God: I will strengthen thee; yea, I will help thee; yea, I will uphold thee with the right hand of my righteousness. [2]

To gain self-control it is important to identify the misbeliefs in what you tell yourself. Very likely you will find that your self-control problems are related to the following list of lies. Never let yourself get away with mouthing one of these lies once you identify them.

MISBELIEF SELF-TALK

• Nobody cares about me anyhow, so why should I even try to

86

be (slim, sober, even-tempered, a non-smoker, or what-ever)?

- I've had such a terrible time of life (or I've been so mis-treated) I owe myself a little indulgence. So I'll go ahead and (smoke, drink, eat, steal, or whatever).
- I'm such a worthless wretch, it doesn't really matter one bit if I (destroy myself, hurt myself, get addicted to something harmful, or whatever).
- I've worked so hard and done so well, I ought to just (steal something, drink, smoke, gorge on food, or whatever).
- I *need* _____ .
  (fill in blank)
- I can't go on without _____ .
  (fill in blank)

Use determination and energy in arguing against each of these misbeliefs with the *truth.* The Lord is upholding you with His right hand!

The Apostle Paul says, "Blessed is the man that endureth temptation: for when he is tried, he shall receive the crown of life, which the Lord hath promised to them that love Him." [3] He tells the Corinthian Christians, "Be ye steadfast, unmovable, always abounding in the work of the Lord," [4] and his prayer for the Christians at Ephesus was that the Lord would "grant you, ac-cording to the riches of his glory, to be strengthened with might by his Spirit in the inner man." [5]

Where are we strong? In the inner man, the inner *person*, in our souls where our thoughts toss and tumble waiting to create our feelings and our actions. When Paul says, "I can do all things through Christ which strengtheneth me," [6] he gives us a dynamic lie-shredding principle to stake our very lives on. This verse is true of the entire domain of self-control behavior. Paul was writ-ing of his own experiences as he voluntarily went without, suf-fered and was deprived for the sake of Christ. "I *can do* all things!" he triumphantly declared for the ages to hear.

In order to have self-control, you must actively counter your misbeliefs with the sword of the Spirit, the *truth.*

How much of our behavior is helpless? Connie, who is 65 pounds overweight, says she can't lose weight, she's *helplessly* fat. Her weakness is ice cream. We asked her to imagine she was sitting in an ice cream parlour with an enormous ice cream concoction sitting in front of her. Picking up her spoon she is about to dive into the thing when suddenly from behind her she hears someone speak.

"Drop that spoon!" he says menacingly.

She's stunned for a moment. "I said *drop* it, lady!" the voice repeats. She then feels something cold and hard against her temple. The voice is fierce. "This is a gun, lady, and if you take one bite of that ugly mess, I'll blow your head off."

Connie's reaction is immediate. "I wouldn't eat the ice cream!" she gasps.

"You mean, you wouldn't touch it?"

"I wouldn't touch it!"

So much for helplessness.

Shirley, who insists she absolutely *can't* quit smoking has a sudden change of mind when we ask her to imagine a thousand dollar bill placed between her and a package of cigarettes. "Imagine someone saying to you, 'If you refuse to touch another cigarette for the rest of the day, this thousand dollar bill is yours.'"

Shirley's face brightens. "I wouldn't go near a cigarette," she laughs. We continue the story. "And then suppose at the end of the day when you've received your thousand dollar bill, another one is placed before you and a voice says, 'Shirley, if you stay away from cigarettes for 24 more hours, you may have another thousand dollar bill.'"

Shirley is delighted. "At this rate, I'll be rich! I wouldn't even *want* a cigarette."

"Suppose then, at the end of the 24-hour period, when you've earned yourself another thousand dollars, there's held before you a ticket for a round-trip four-week vacation to Hawaii. You're told, 'This Hawaiian vacation is yours if you refuse to smoke for three days in a row.'"

"Great!" Shirley says.

And then as a bonus, your benefactor tells you, "For every week that you do not smoke or take one puff of a cigarette, you will receive a certified check for one thousand dollars."

Shirley laughs loudly. "I see what you mean! With that kind

of an offer I'd quit smoking in a huge hurry. I'd even go on an anti-smoking campaign!"

You are *not* helpless. You *do* have control over your life. You *can* do what you think may be impossible.

"I CAN'T DENY MYSELF" MISBELIEF

Is it so painful, really, to deny yourself something? Is it, in your mind, somehow in the same category as death and dismemberment? When you feel hungry, thirsty, sleepy, frustrated, nervous or dissatisfied, do you think you're in the pits of hell? When you are forced to endure discomfort, interruption or thwarted plans, do you tell yourself the world is coming to an end?

Sometimes it is not easy to deny yourself. It's not easy to go without something you desperately want, not easy to give up something you dearly prize, not easy to lose something you cherish. BUT sometimes for the sake of a higher, more noble life, it's necessary. Most of the time, in fact, you'll find that gaining something valuable in your life will depend on being willing to tolerate distress, anxiety, discomfort and discontent. Your greatest achievements are often won because you are willing to put up with situations which are often downright unpleasant.

You *can* deny yourself. You *can* say no to yourself. It is *not* the end of all things if you have to suffer pain. You can stand it. You really can.

Max, a brilliant graduate student in psychology, thought he was a person who would go to pieces if he had to deny himself something that was really precious to him. Then one day his wife left him and took the children with her. Max took it hard. He managed to stay in school in spite of his suffering, but his life was a wreck. He started drinking to ease the pain, which only increased his feelings of guilt and self-worthlessness.

It took a lot of effort on Max's part to finally say to himself, "Okay, so my family is gone. I'm alone, but I don't have to be lonely. I don't have to drink to ease the pain either. I *can* stand pain. It won't kill me."

Max did three dramatically life-changing things.

1. He realized he was self-destructing with his misbelief that

his life and happiness depended upon another person. Happiness depends upon our relationship with Jesus. No other person should be the controlling force in our lives. "Thou shalt worship the Lord thy God, and him only shalt thou serve." [7]

2. He argued against his misbeliefs. He spoke truth to himself. ("I loved my wife and still do, but Jesus is the Lord of my life.")

3. He denied himself the temptation to wallow in self-pity and loneliness by refusing to continue drinking to ease his pain. ("I *can* stand pain!")

You *can* deny yourself.

You *can* wait for the thing you want. "In your patience possess ye your souls!" [8] Your soul is your intellect, emotions and will. How large a part patience plays in the security of your soul!

Speak the truth to yourself. Tell your soul that all is well. You *can* successfully live through inconvenience, discomfort, distress, and other negative feelings.

THE "I NEED" MISBELIEF

We get two things confused: "I need" and "I want." The word *need* implies that you cannot exist without the thing so described. An automobile *needs* oil in the crankcase, plant life *needs* water, human beings *need* oxygen; but when you tell yourself you *need* a glass of wine or a pair of blue shoes, you're not talking about need; you're talking about *want*.

All of us at one time or another have told ourselves we passionately or desperately *need* something that perhaps we really only want very much. "I *need* my favorite pillow to sleep soundly and peacefully." "I *need* my tranquilizers. If I don't take them, my nerves would fall right out of my body." "I *need* acceptance from other people in order to accept myself." "I *need* a man (or woman) to love me in order to lead a satisfying and fulfilling life."

These sentences, of course, are not true.

If you tell yourself you *need* something, or you *can't stand* something, or you *must have* something, try to stop yourself and step back for a bit of observation. Listen to those words you're telling yourself.

"I *can't stand* living in this house another moment," or, "I absolutely *must have* people around me who care about me," "I *can't stand* loneliness" are examples of fictionalized sentences. You can, in fact, carry on very well in spite of these annoyances and trials. You have withstood many hassles in your life and if you had to, you could survive more arduous tests than these.

By telling yourself you *can't stand* something, you increase the likelihood of avoiding or evading suffering through it. By avoiding and evading everything unpleasant in your life, you rob yourself of the rewards of endurance, patience, hope, courage and even faith. This is *not* to say that you should accept without question everything disagreeable and burdensome or ask God for trials and troubles. There are certain things that always ought to be gotten rid of, cast out, removed and avoided. You don't want to willingly hurt yourself or perform destructive acts that are against the will of God. You don't want to "accept" negativity or some woeful situation as your lot in life if the Lord clearly states in His Word that you are set free from it through the shed blood of Calvary.

The Bible says to "resist the devil, and he will flee from you," [9] and that means we are not to blindly accept or wallow in negativity, sickness, and disaster. Jesus died on the cross to redeem our lives from sin, sickness, and destruction. "In righteousness shalt thou be established: thou shalt be far from oppression," Isaiah 54:14 tells us. That's a dear and encouraging promise.

And yet, there you are, looking for a way out of getting a job. You'd rather stay home. You don't want to face the work-a-day world, the people, the demands; you just want to stay home where you tell yourself it's cozy and safe.

But then you tell yourself there's no way out except to become and remain sick and you're too smart for that, so you fight the defeating urges and form a plan for job hunting. "People have to work in order to eat," you rightly tell yourself. "I'm no different from anyone else." When you land a job and report for work, you continue to tell yourself the truth and refuse to recite complaints and words of fear or worry. You say, "I'd rather stay home, but I'm now a working person. I'll work for the glory of God. I'll face this new experience and not run from it. Even though it's difficult for me, I can do it!"

You'll discover new and exciting experiences in life as well as pleasing things about yourself when *need* and *want* take their rightful place in your thinking. You'll find that you can do very nicely without everything you want, although the wants often look like needs. You can live very happily, even be a better person for enduring without some of those wants, even though the wants may seem quite respectable and reasonable to you.

Saint Paul was free from the confusion between need and want. He was able to rise above the cloying, complaining anguish of unfulfilled wants and needs. "I know both how to be abased, and I know how to abound: everywhere and in all things I am instructed both to be full and to be hungry, both to abound and suffer need. I can do all things through Christ which strengtheneth me." [10] It didn't seem to drive him to despair when things went wrong, when his plans were ruined or changed or when he suffered persecution. He then tells us confidently, "*My God shall supply all your need according to his riches in glory by Christ Jesus.*" [11]

Learn the difference between need and want in your life. Write a list of your wants in a notebook. Alongside this list write down your needs. How many of your wants have you considered to be needs?

CHOICE—THE DOORWAY TO JOY

When you tell yourself you can't do without something or that it's terrible you have to suffer discomfort or you just can't help yourself, you're engaging in an activity called *choosing.*

Instead of saying, "I *need* _____," say the truth,
(fill in blank)

which is, "I *choose* to have _____."
(fill in blank)

We are responsible for our choices.

92

Connie is a young college student in her Junior year. She tells herself she is "weak and easily intimidated." She talks of a domineering mother and explains that she is in college for her mother's sake.

The truth is, Connie *chooses* to let her mother be domineering. She *chooses* to go to college to please her mother. She *chooses* weak and intimidated behavior.

Too often we avoid admitting we are responsible for our own lives. We'd like to pin accountability on other people, circumstances, events, but not on ourselves and our own *choices.* How often we hear words like the following:

"If my husband would act more like the man of the house, I wouldn't be so frustrated."

(Not true. The truth is, "I *choose* to be frustrated because I *tell myself* my husband doesn't act like the man of the house.")

"If I weren't so upset and lonely, I could stop overeating."

(Not true. The truth is, "I *tell myself* I am upset and lonely and I *choose* to overeat.")

"If only I could find the right church, I'd attend every Sunday."

(Not true. The truth is, "I *tell myself* I can't find the right church and I *choose* not to attend.")

"My kids behave so terribly I've developed a temper I just can't control."

(Not true. The truth is, "I have *taught myself* to respond to my children's poor behavior with outbursts of temper. I *choose* this behavior.")

When you catch yourself in the act of telling yourself lies, be quick to label them "not true" and to replace them with the truth.

I AM ACCOUNTABLE FOR MY CHOICES

- Admit *you* make your choices.
- Remind yourself that *you* are responsible for what you are doing.
- Prepare to accept the consequences of your behavior even if unpleasant.

An unmarried pregnant girl says, "I couldn't help myself. We were just drawn together like magnets and I couldn't say no."

The president of a respected local ministry is asked to resign because he has been stealing from the donations. "But I needed the money. I worked harder than anyone else. What else could I do?"

Both of these people are saying that someone or something else is responsible for their behavior. Both are deceived.

SELF-CONTROL IS A CHOICE

When you admit you are responsible for your behavior and that it's *you* who makes the choices in your life, you will be taking the first and most important step to becoming a person of self-control.

"But I didn't want to move to this town," a pretty 42-year-old woman named Dee Dee argued. "How can I tell myself that I am responsible for my actions? I didn't choose to move here. My husband made this choice, not I."

"What are your feelings about living here now?"

"I hate it. I don't want to live here. It's not my choice, that's my point. You're saying that *I* make the choices in my life. But my husband makes the choices, not I."

"Does he choose your emotions?"

"He causes them!"

"He causes them? How does he do it? Does he stand over you with a sledge hammer and shout, 'Feel this-or-that or I'll clobber you'?"

"No, he doesn't. He tells me what to *do*, though."

"And you do what he tells you to do?"

"Yes. If I didn't, he might leave me, or stop loving me or who knows what. He's a very demanding man. I've always done everything he asks, including moving here, which I didn't want to do."

"But you did it."

"Yes, I had to."

"Not quite. You *chose* to."

"*He* chose to, not I."

94

"But *you* chose to let him."

"But I had to."

"No, you didn't. You weighed the circumstances and then you *chose* to let your husband move you here to this city. You told yourself you had to do what he wanted to do or lose him. That's choosing."

"It's been that way our whole life together. Whatever he wants, that's what we do. I have very little say in anything."

"You choose it that way."

"No! It's just the way it is, that's all. It's *not* my choice. I'm not stupid or insignificant. I ought to have a say in things, too."

Dee Dee began at point one and studied our three checks. They are:

1. Admit you make your choices.
2. Remind yourself that you are responsible for what you are doing.
3. Prepare to accept the consequences of your behavior even if unpleasant.

We helped Dee Dee analyze what she had been telling herself. She didn't like uncovering the truth. "I came here because I wanted to work on my temper—I wanted to gain some self-control. In fact, I had hoped you'd prescribe some sort of medication."

She worked hard at facing herself and her behavior. Her gains were greater than she expected. She learned to develop skills that far surpassed the temporary effects of a pill. After several counseling sessions, she explained the three Choice Checks.

"First, I must admit I make my choices. I always thought everyone else made my choices. If I felt sad, I thought it was because of something or someone else. I never thought I was actually choosing to feel that way. My temper, the worst part, I always blamed on something else. Then the second thing, I need to remind myself I am responsible for what I am doing. Boy, that's hard. It's hard to admit I'm responsible for most of my own unhappiness. I realize that I have chosen to allow my husband to act aggressively and hurtfully to me. I also realize that I am responsible for choosing to have a bad temper."

Dee Dee is on the right track.

"Then the third Choice Check," she continued, "I remind myself of the consequences of my behavior. I am responsible; therefore I am going to have to accept it, even if unpleasant. I blamed my husband for making me move to this city. I was wrong. The truth is I *chose* to let him make this decision. And I'm choosing to feel miserable about it. The consequences for choosing to be a doormat are pretty great."

"Can you name some of these consequences?"

"Sure—my bad temper! I have been frustrated and angry at my husband, but I've chosen to avoid discussing these things with him. I have chosen to help him treat me as a doormat."

Dee Dee's communication with her husband increased and, to her surprise, he liked her honesty with him. He also liked the changes in her attitude toward herself. With the Lord's help, their marriage relationship was strengthened and enriched. "I'll never teach my husband to treat me like a doormat again," Dee Dee told us recently. "And I'll never treat him like a tyrant again, either. I found out he's really a nice guy who I never allowed to be the terrific husband he could be."

LEARN TO REWARD YOURSELF

Many times the hard work it takes to develop self-control isn't worth it because there aren't enough rewards in sight.

Take Fred who wants to lose 60 pounds. It may take him six months to do it. He begins a weight-loss program and at the end of two weeks he's lost seven pounds. Instead of celebrating his victory, he's ready to throw in the towel. The thought of the 53 pounds that are left to lose is menacing; furthermore, the smell of pizza is pure ambrosia. It doesn't seem rewarding at all to painfully stick to a regimented weight-loss program, especially since gobbling up half a pizza is an extremely rewarding thought.

Where was the reward for losing seven pounds? DO reward yourself wisely and appropriately. (For the person on a weight-loss program, food can no longer serve as a reward.)

WHEN SHOULD YOU REWARD YOURSELF?

• DO reward yourself for small successes.

- DO reward yourself when you've accomplished what you set out to accomplish.
- DO reward yourself often.
- DO reward yourself when you've exhibited self-control.
- DO reward yourself even if nobody else does.
- DO reward yourself when you've worked hard at something.
- DO not wait to reward yourself.

For some Christians the idea of rewarding themselves is nothing short of shocking. "Who *me*, reward myself? (nervous laughter). I wouldn't know *how*!"

We respond with, "Do you ever put yourself *down*?" The unhesitantly spoken answer is usually, "Yes! All the time!"

Which is more godly? Is it more Christlike to put someone down, grinding them into the dust for every fault and error committed, or is it better to bless with gentle, loving words, often and regularly?

Billy is a seven-year-old boy who bites his fingernails. His mother punishes him for this behavior, using a variety of punishers. She slaps, takes away his allowance, paints his finger with a salt solution, calls him names, raises her voice in disgust, sits him in corners, threatens until she's weary—and nothing works. One day she tries rewarding him for *not* biting his fingernails. It proves far more effective than the barrage of punishers she had been using.

She begins rewarding Billy *often* and regularly for not biting his fingernails. For every hour he keeps his hands out of his mouth, she tells him sincerely and in a pleasant manner, "You lasted an hour without biting your nails. I'm proud of you. Very good. You did it." We advised her to reward him every hour at the beginning of the program and then taper off as it progressed.

When you are working on changing behavior and developing self-control, reward often for exercising the self-control you desire. Then, as the behavior improves and changes, ease off a bit, but always continue to reward.

What are rewards? First and very importantly, the *words* you say are rewards. Billy was told often and regularly how terrific it was that he didn't bite his fingernails. He won other rewards as a point system was initiated between him and his parents.

At the beginning of the week it was mutually agreed upon

97

between Billy and his parents that he would receive a reward for earning so many points. The first week they decided together that if he earned five points, he would be allowed to stay up a half hour later than his bedtime. He chose other rewards, including having a friend over to stay all night and going to a baseball game with his dad. He responded to the reward system favorably and in a manner of a few weeks, the nail-biting problem was licked.

Billy learned that it feels good to exercise self-control. It is not punishing to have self-control. So often we shrink from self-control because we think it's so difficult to attain such a pain-inducing thing. Billy learned it isn't painful to have self-control. He felt good by the rewards he received and good about himself. The punishers only served to help him hate himself and chew his nails more.

You don't control your behavior by putting yourself down or finding fault with yourself. If you lose ten pounds and gain three back, do you punish yourself for the three you gained or do you congratulate yourself for the seven you lost? More than likely you'll punish yourself first.

God doesn't spend all His time punishing. In fact, He loved us so much He sent us His Son, Jesus Christ, to take the punishment for our sins from us! Forgiveness is one of our most precious gifts. To refuse forgiveness is an insult to the work done on the cross. God is love!

Picture the Lord saying to you, "Well done, thou good and faithful servant" when you exercise self-control or when you have conquered a misbelief. Say "Well done!" out loud to yourself. Smile at yourself! You deserve it!

Stop dwelling on negatives, stop making lists of your failures. Stop saying hurtful words to yourself, stop calling yourself names, stop putting yourself down for being such a lousy Christian. Stop telling yourself you don't deserve any blessings from God. Stop piling on the guilt and condemnation.

Jesus died on the cross for you to take the guilt and condemnation from you. If you have sincerely repented from the sins in your life, go on from there. Stop dwelling on them. Pick yourself up and carry on.

Naturally, don't reward yourself for failure or pretend you're something greater than you are, but at the same time don't go on punishing yourself for every mishap in your life. Much better results will be achieved by rewarding yourself for doing well than punishing yourself for every nonsuccess.

There is therefore now no condemnation to them which are in Christ Jesus, who walk not after the flesh, but after the Spirit. [12]

WHO DID IT? JESUS OR I?

One misbelief that prevents some Christians from rewarding themselves for real accomplishment is the notion that they didn't do it—it was the Lord who did it. This is a misbelief because it teaches an impossible and unscriptural psychology.

It *is* true that out of our old sinful selves no good thing can flow. It *is* true that without the Holy Spirit we can do nothing (good). But it is *also* true that with the Holy Spirit at work within, *we* do the good.

You cannot have faith without the gift of faith, but the faith you have is yours. *You* do the believing. It is not the Holy Spirit's faith, but *your* faith which saved you. When you gain a small victory over a bad habit, you might want to say you had nothing to do with it. But you had plenty to do with it. Through Him, *you* did it.

It's true that you cannot accomplish anything or gain victory over sin and self without Him ("Without me ye can do nothing," [13] He tells us)—but we must realize we live our lives *through*, *in*, and *with* Him. When you were born again into Christ, you didn't move out of your body. You are still there, only now you are a new person with a new godly nature. ("Old things are passed away; behold, all things are become new." [14])

Saint Paul said, "I am crucified with Christ: nevertheless I live; yet not I, but Christ liveth in me: and the life which I now live in the flesh I live by the faith of the Son of God, who loved me, and gave himself for me." [15] By this Paul is saying he has been crucified (by choice) and the self who ruled his life pre-

99

viously has been put to death. When Jesus went to the cross on our behalf He gave us that great possibility of being *saved from ourselves* by allowing His life to enter and transform ours.

We as Christians have the opportunity of making a commitment so all-inclusive and permanent that temptation to selfishness and sin will not have the binding hold on us as in the former days. Christ, living within us by His Holy Spirit, will have the chief position in our lives! This thundering truth is the very purpose for writing this book. We are showing you in a practical and tangible way how you can cooperate with the provision Christ has made for you, enabling you to crucify the "flesh with its affections and lusts" which previously enslaved you, and release the new, born-again Christian, Spirit-indwelled *victorious* you!

Praise God for your victories! Because of Christ, you can gain the victory! Reward yourself with kind and soothing words for your obedience to Him.

HOW TO REWARD YOURSELF

- DO reward yourself by telling yourself "Well done!" or "Good job!" or other words of honest appreciation.
- DO reward yourself with activities you enjoy. Examples: "When I finish cleaning the oven and scouring the appliances, I am going to reward myself with words of appreciation and then I am going to take a long, luxurious bubble bath." Or, "Now that I've lost two and a half pounds, I am going to reward myself by setting aside an evening to relax in my favorite chair and read without any interruptions."
- DO reward yourself, as you can, with token awards. Examples: "I've done such a good job of building these shelves, I'm going to buy myself a new set of screwdrivers." "I have improved nearly 100% getting places on time and I'm pleased with myself. I'm going to reward myself by getting my watch fixed."
- DO reward yourself by helping others learn what you've learned.
- DO reward yourself for spiritual victories by enjoying the feelings of joy and confidence which come through the Holy Spirit.

DISCONNECT THE TRIGGERS THAT
SET OFF THE BOMB

List your trigger situations. What triggers the behavior you don't want? Then begin cutting the triggers one at a time, gradually reducing the number of situations in which you allow the behavior to occur. For example, if you're trying to quit smoking, eliminate some of the triggers that make you think of having cigarettes. They might be:

1. Sitting at the table after a meal with a cup of coffee.
2. Sitting in the smoking section of restaurants.
3. Taking a soft-drink break.

After gradually eliminating the triggers, then imagine yourself in these situations doing these same activities *without* cigarettes. Prepare yourself for not smoking.

Finally, after you have disconnected all the triggers but one, you can either remove the behavior from your life entirely, or you can keep practicing the behavior, linking it only to that little trigger.

You can do yourself a big favor by getting rid of all the triggers that set off the bomb. Don't allow yourself to be in places of temptation with your girlfriend or boyfriend if you're trying to maintain mastery over the sin of lust. Don't keep candy in your cupboards if you're trying to lose weight. Don't carry your credit cards when you go shopping if you're a compulsive buyer.

If you disconnect the linkage between the trigger and the firing pin of a gun, the weapon won't fire. Most behaviors have triggers or situations which cause the behaviors to occur. Recognize yours.

YOU CAN BE A SELF-CONTROLLED PERSON!

He feedeth on ashes: a deceived heart hath turned him aside, that he cannot deliver his soul, nor say, Is there not a lie in my right hand? [16]

The most important thing you can do to increase your self-control is to identify the misbeliefs in the words you tell yourself. Then argue against those misbeliefs. Never let yourself get away

101

with misbelief talk. Use determination and energy in arguing and refusing each misbelief with the truth.

You can be self-controlled in every area of your life. People who exercise self-control have discovered a major key to living fulfilled lives.

Laziness, apathy and lethargy, avoiding responsibility, are not inroads to happiness and the fulfilled life. It is not surprising that when a person complains of lack of self-control the accompanying complaints are discontent, guilt, deep dissatisfaction with life, and a lack of self-confidence.

Self-control, a fruit of the Spirit, will become a part of your life as you diligently cultivate it, as you reject discouragement, and as you teach yourself to reward yourself for your successes. "Let us not be weary in well doing: for in due season we shall reap, if we faint not," Paul tells us in Galatians 6:9. Allow the Holy Spirit to help you. With God, nothing is impossible. Sometimes things may seem difficult, but with the Lord as your helper, strength and guide, it's not impossible.

You can shout to the whole world, " 'Greater is he [the Holy Spirit] that is in me than he [the devil who tempts me to sin] that is in the world.'[17] Therefore, I can be and am a self-controlled person!"

---

1. Christian weight-loss organization with chapters all over the U.S.
2. Isaiah 41:10.
3. James 1:12.
4. 1 Corinthians 15:58.
5. Ephesians 3:16.
6. Philippians 4:13.
7. Matthew 4:10.
8. Luke 21:19.
9. James 4:7.
10. Philippians 4:12.
11. Philippians 4:19.
12. Romans 8:1.
13. John 15:5.
14. 2 Corinthians 5:17.
15. Galatians 2:20.
16. Isaiah 44:20.
17. 1 John 4:4.

CHAPTER EIGHT

The Misbelief in Self-Hate

Arnie is 29 years old. He suffers with intense anxiety attacks. He is nervous, tense and often feels depressed for seemingly "no reason at all." At home he frequently has outbursts of temper where he flies into a rage over small things. Outside the home he is usually as gentle as a lamb; on the job he has been called Mr. Nice Guy, and in his church he has been known as the person who will do anything for anyone, Good Old Arnie.

Arnie has been people-pleasing for years. He has done what he has felt people expected of him. The major decisions in his life such as education, marriage, and a career choice were made largely through the influence of others. When he had the approval of others, he felt he was doing right. He felt worthwhile when he was approved of and pleasing others.

When he was a teen-ager, it was very important to him that he be accepted as one of the crowd. He worked hard at being popular, cool and "with it." He was well liked by the other teen-agers and had many friends. He was also popular with the girls.

There wasn't anything unusual about his behavior because being liked and fitting in with the group is important to all teen-agers. It's at this stage of life that fear of social rejection is greater than the child's fear of being hurt or dying. Arnie was an average teen, then, you might say, because he pursued being liked and approved of by others.

But then Arnie graduated from high school. Most of his

103

friends went to the State University, so Arnie went to the State University. Drugs and booze were now the big thing. Arnie followed the crowd. His friends got high, so Arnie got high; his friends had loose morals, so Arnie had loose morals. His parents worried about him because he was missing school. Everybody's pal, Arnie, began to flunk out after two semesters.

He managed to stay in school on probation, but many of his friends were dropping out. Some of them were getting married. Arnie began to date a girl who didn't smoke or drink, which pleased his parents, and they encouraged the relationship. Arnie wasn't sure he wanted to be serious with her and about the time he was making a decision to break up, she disclosed the news that she was pregnant.

Arnie married the girl, as was expected of him. He dropped out of school entirely, abandoning the idea of evening classes, and took a job in his father-in-law's company, where he works to this day.

Three years ago Arnie and his wife had a conversion experience and they gave their hearts to Jesus Christ. Their two children are Christians and love the Lord, too, and they are an active family in their church. But Arnie is unhappy.

He can't understand what's wrong. When he became a Christian he gave his testimony many times telling what the Lord had saved him from. He told about his past life in drugs and loose living and how glad he was to be a new person in Christ, washed in the blood of Jesus. The Christians in his church were thrilled to see what the power of God could do in a person. So how come he was so miserable?

"What's wrong with me?" Arnie asked. "I'm supposed to be filled with joy. I'm a Christian!" He feels he has to control his negative feelings because that's what other people expect him to do. He feels that if he allows his true feelings to emerge, he will be judged and condemned for them. He has given testimony to how much better his life is now that he is a Christian, and he doesn't want to look like a hypocrite by exposing his unhappy and depressed feelings.

Arnie has taught himself over the years that he has to meet the expectations of the people around him. At church he does and says exactly what he thinks other people expect. He dresses, talks, walks and does as he thinks the congregation and pastor would expect of a fine upstanding Christian man.

At the job he does exactly as expected of him, also. He gets along with his father-in-law because he has his approval. The truth of it is, he doesn't really like the work he does, but it's more important to him to be accepted and liked than it is to be doing something he wants to do and likes to do. In fact, he gets the two confused. He associates being approved of with being happy.

At home he thinks his wife has certain expectations of him and so he fulfills those. The house, the car, the furniture, the appliances, even the vacations—he provides acceptably and agreeably. Everybody's satisfied, everything is fine and dandy. What's wrong?

For most of his life Arnie has not allowed himself to think of himself and his own needs as very important. He brought these beliefs into his Christian life, and because they're not always easy to detect, he was able to carry on as his usual Terrific Guy self without being found out, least of all to himself. After all, isn't the Christian supposed to honor his neighbor higher than himself?

You can't honor your neighbor as he ought to be if you don't give any honor to yourself. At best your feelings are neurotic and self-debasing. God does not want us debased. He wants us healthy and sound of mind.

The self-debaser flatters others to get their approval. If others don't approve of him, he feels worthless. His own good opinions of himself don't mean a thing. Other people's opinions are what count.

Arnie doesn't consider his own needs and feelings as important. As long as he is pleasing others, he feels his life is going along okay. As long as others like him and approve of him, he feels things are fine. But now he is finding out things aren't okay or fine at all.

Almost 30 years old, he is still living the anxieties of an adolescent. Because of it he can't really love others.

Some of Arnie's misbeliefs are:

1. The way to be liked by others is to be what others want me

to be and to do what is most pleasing to them.

2. It is more Christian to please other people than to please myself.
3. Other people have every right to judge my actions.
4. It is wrong and un-Christian to think of my own needs, or to consider my own needs important, compared to the wants of others.
5. It is wrong not to be willing to forget my own wants to please friends and family when they want me to.
6. Pleasing others is an insurance policy which guarantees that people will be nice to me in return. When I am in great need they will forget their own needs to help me.
7. When others are displeased with me, I cannot enjoy one moment's peace or happiness.
8. Approval from everyone else is essential to my feeling of well-being and peace of mind, since God doesn't want me to be happy unless everyone else is approving of me.
9. Being what other people want me to be is the only way to be liked.
10. Pleasing others and doing what they expect of me is the only way to win friends.

If you believe any of the above, you're believing lies.

In 1 Samuel 18:1, we read that the soul of Jonathan was knit with the soul of David and that Jonathan loved David "as his own soul." When the true knitting of souls in sincere friendship occurs, it is not lopsided or out of kilter; it is not living to please and gain approval of another. It is a *joint* relationship, a knitting of souls. Jesus taught that we are to love others *as* ourselves.[1]

"Thou shalt love thy neighbor as thyself" means to consider the needs of others as *equally* important with your own, to value others' opinions equally with your own, to respect the rights of others as much as your own rights. It means that other people are not less important than you and they are also not more important than you. This thinking takes effort. Sometimes it is easier and more comfortable to degrade yourself and believe that others' opinions of you are more important than your own. Arnie was a person who relied on other people for his own feelings of self-worth. If someone didn't like or approve of him, he thought it

106

meant something was wrong with him.

The Scriptures teach us two important truths about our self-worth.

1. Our life, including our opinions, feelings, wants and needs, is not less valuable or important than anyone else's and
2. Our life, including our opinions, feelings, wants and needs, is not more valuable or important than anyone else's.

When you gaze out the tour bus window at the hungry illiterate peasants of an underprivileged country, remember your needs are not more important than theirs. And at the same time, the needs of others are not more important than yours.

When Jesus said, "Greater love hath no man than this, that a man lay down his life for his friends,"[2] He prepared the way for us to be able to love ourselves in the purest sense. Condemnation, guilt, despair, self-degradation, shame and self-hate have all been nailed to the cross in His body. By His taking our sin on the cross with Him, we are set free to live healthy and abundant lives with wholesome, pure, swept-clean attitudes. When our lives are really beautiful in the eyes of God, they are pure and clean in the holiest sense. When do we please Him but when we are right before Him, living as He has shown us to live? If we lay down our lives out of guilt and self-hate, we are not fulfilling the very meaning of the above verse, "Greater *love* hath no man . . . "

> *Hereby perceive we the love of God* [notice: *the love* of God], *because he laid down his life for us: and we ought to lay down our lives for the brethren.*[3]

What good does it do God or anybody else if you lay down your life because you can't stand yourself? Jesus died on the cross for you, and to despise yourself is to insult Him. We despise *sin*, not people.

We ought not to forget that our lives are made up of such things as honesty, courage, sense of humor and most precious of all possessions, *wisdom.* These we can give to one another as loving, unselfish gifts.

Elaine is a woman who is a lot like Arnie, but whereas Arnie reacts to his misbeliefs with depressed and woebegone feelings,

Elaine reacts with rage. She is a woman of 35 who looks more like 45. Haggard, worn, droopy, she rarely laughs or relaxes. She has believed for years that she has to sublimate her own wishes for everyone else's and she's tired of it. She says she has been a doormat for her family and friends; even strangers have pushed her around. "The Bible says to give and so I give," she says angrily. She's upset because she feels guilty about feeling angry. Her words snap with bitterness and resentment.

"Nobody ever does anything for *me*," she says; "and no matter what I do, they don't have any respect for me. I'm just a *thing* for people to *use*, that's all. I shouldn't be angry, I know. I suppose it's just selfishness on my part. I just don't know what to do about it. I'm probably a lousy Christian, but I can't help it."

The Word of God tells us to fellowship with one another, to love one another, to give and share and forgive; to be kind, generous and tender-hearted. Indeed, the Lord tells us to bear our lives toward one another; but not in a downgrading way and not for self-denunciating motives; not to become slaves to other people's whims, and not for *people-pleasing* motives. All of these are self-hate indicators. Elaine's "doormat" really *was* selfishness in different attire.

"What makes you think you're a lousy Christian?" we asked Elaine.

"A Christian shouldn't get so mad. I'm supposed to be above it all. I'm supposed to just give-give-give and not ask for anything in return; I know all that self-denying stuff."

She slaps the chair with the palm of her hand. "I bend over backwards for my friends, for my kids, for my husband. And not only that, I've got a very demanding mother. She still has me driving her all over town because she doesn't drive. I've got six kids and I'm in the middle of eating dinner and she calls and expects me to drop everything and come running for her."

"And you do?"

"Of course! She'd probably have heart failure if I didn't. She expects it of me. That's how everybody treats me. I'm just a *thing* to be *used*."

"You've said that before. What does that mean—a thing to be used?"

"I'm a nothing. N-o-t-h-i-n-g!"

"Says who?"

"Says everybody! Look how they treat me!"

"Does everybody else decide your importance?"

"What do you mean by that?"

"Well, why is it you think everybody else decides whether or not you are an important and worthwhile person? What happened to your own opinion of yourself?"

"My opinion of myself stinks."

"If your opinion of yourself stinks, how do you expect other people to treat you with consideration and respect?"

"I don't know and I don't care. All I know is that the whole world can go take a flying jump."

You can hear the bitterness in Elaine's words. She has worked all her life for approval and love and now sees it hasn't paid off. For all her years of sacrifice she sees nothing but dust and emptiness. She has made herself a victim of other people's whims in order to please them and earn their approval and love. If someone else would tell her she was a giving and dear person, she might feel worthwhile for a moment or two, although she would disagree. When no words of acceptance and approval are forthcoming, she feels desperate and hopeless. She really believes she is nothing but a *thing* to be *used.*

The people Elaine gave the most to, such as her mother who thought it not presumptuous to call her at any hour of the day to be driven somewhere, gave her the least returns in acceptance and love. Elaine believed she had to *earn* her worth and *earn* the right to be loved and so the harder she worked, the worse she felt.

You have more than likely already labeled many of Elaine's misbeliefs.

- If I don't give, give, give, I'm not a good Christian. (Elaine wasn't really *giving*; she was *doing* things to *get* something for herself.)
- I'm supposed to be appreciated for all I give. (True giving doesn't even need acknowledgment.)
- My self-worth depends on the opinions of other people.
- Love is something you *earn* and *work* for.
- Respect is something you *earn* and *work* for.

109

- If I don't do what other people want and expect me to do, they won't like me.
- If I don't do what other people want me to do, I don't *deserve* their approval or friendship.
- Other people have the right to ask anything they want of me in order that I won't offend anyone.
- If others do not tell me I am a good person, then I must not be.
- If someone does not like me, there is something wrong with me.
- If someone is angry with me, it must be my fault.
- It's my duty to make everybody happy and comfortable.
- It's my duty to work my fingers to the bone for my family. If I don't, they might reject me.

Elaine thought her problem was not being able to give *enough*. Some of the additional lies she told herself were:

- Rejection and not being liked are terrible.
- In spite of how hard I work to earn approval, some people still don't like me and reject me; therefore I am terrible.
- It's terrible to be angry,
- I am angry; therefore I am terrible.
- It's terrible to be a *thing* other people *use.*
- I am a thing other people use; therefore I am terrible.
- It's terrible not to be able to conquer my bad feelings.
- I can't conquer my bad feelings. Therefore I am terrible.

Elaine had to learn, first, that she was important and valuable because *God* says so, and secondly, because she agrees with God. People do not respond favorably to someone who hates himself/herself. Elaine wanted respect from her friends and family, but she had no respect for herself, realizing her own underlying selfish motives. She depended upon others to prove whether she was worth anything or not. Other people did not show her the respect she tried so feverishly to earn.

There is a difference between self-respect and selfishness. The person who truly respects himself is genuinely interested in others, giving of himself without fear. He may even find on occasion that the most loving thing he can do for another person is to say no to him. A selfish person, however, is greedy, fearful, and manipulative. Elaine had many of these behavior patterns and she was forced to face them. Usually the tendencies toward greed

110

and selfishness in an individual motivate him to live for the approval of others, always striving to satisfy an insatiable need within himself.

Both Elaine and Arnie had to learn that a Christian is an important person, special, and loved, *period*. Their self-worth, as well as yours and ours, does not depend upon others' opinions, but upon God's declaration. We are God's temples on earth—real, honest living temples where the King of Power lives and makes His home. "Know ye not that ye are the temple of God, and that the Spirit of God dwelleth in you?" [4] A most godly thing for you to do is to have respect and love for yourself.

"Godly?" asked Elaine. "How can it be godly to love myself? I thought that was vanity." In order to love yourself, you must be a lovely person; and that happens when a person allows himself to be crucified to sin (selfishness) and come alive to God through the power of the Holy Spirit.

Vanity is not accompanied by contentment and peace. You can recognize your own godly motives by the contentment and peace that surround them. You won't be living in strife if your motives are godly.

GODLINESS AND CONTENTMENT

"Godliness with contentment is great gain" [5] is a verse for the self-hater. When you are doing what the Lord is showing you to do, you can experience real contentment even through hard times and in hard tasks. A sign of a people-pleaser is a lack of contentment. When the going gets rough, the people-pleaser starts to find fault and complain. Eventually, if things continue to go wrong, he becomes enraged.

Elaine cried in exasperation, "The whole *world* can go take a flying jump!" Arnie threw temper tantrums at home and yelled at the children for the slightest mistake.

Loving yourself is to be content with yourself whether or not other people approve of you. With God's approval, you no longer are compelled to *earn* love and acceptance. You're free to be you—for better or worse.

Loving yourself is not selfish. You don't become an aggressive

111

bully who demands his/her own way from all those around. Far from it!

Loving yourself is seen in your self-respect, your wisdom, and in your integrity. You see the nobleness of humility. You love and respect yourself because you belong to the Lord Jesus. Your life is His and the Holy Spirit lives in the temple of your being. The Lord has wonderfully created and designed you, as He has those around you. You love yourself; therefore you can love others.

Arnie's moment of truth came when we asked him to seriously answer the question, "How important is it to you that you always please and gain the approval of others?"

He was stunned to discover how much of his life was lived solely to please and impress other people. As of this writing, he has made many changes in his life and learned to respect himself for who he is. Elaine, also, has made changes in her life. By changing her attitudes and the misbeliefs we listed, she has found that she can have the respect of others just by being herself.

When you stop striving to get the approval of others, you'll gain it without trying. When you like yourself, others will like you, too. When you accept yourself, others will accept you, too. And if they do not approve, accept or like you? What happens?

You discover you can live with it. It's not *terrible* not to be liked!

Tell yourself these words of truth instead of the misbeliefs you may be harboring in your own belief system. *It's all right if everybody doesn't like me!*

TRUTH

- It is *not* necessary to be liked by everyone.
- I do not have to earn anyone's approval or acceptance.
- I am a child of God. I am deeply loved by Him, I have been forgiven by Him; therefore I am acceptable. I accept myself.
- My needs and wants are as important as other people's.
- Rejection is *not* terrible. It may be a bit unpleasant, but it's not terrible.
- Not being approved of or accepted is *not* terrible. It may not be desirable, but it's not terrible.

112

- If somebody doesn't like me, I can live with it. I don't have to work feverishly to get him/her to like me.
- I can conquer my bad feelings by distinguishing the truth from misbelief.
- It is a misbelief that I must please others and be approved of by them.
- Jesus died on the cross for me so that I can be free from the misbelief that other people decide my value.

Meditate on the following:

1. Pleasing others is a principle which may be directly opposed to the basic rule of the Christian's life: to *please God*. God's will for you may be at variance with others' claims, demands and whims. God's will for Jesus, for example, was contrary to the demands of the multitude who wanted to make Him king after He fed 5,000 people with the little boy's meager lunch (John 6). The disciples objected strenuously to the will of God for Jesus when He foretold His coming crucifixion and death, also. Peter was upset at the news. "May it never be!" he said. Jesus answered, "Get thee behind me, Satan."

2. Frequently, God's will for you will require that you consider your own needs first and set aside the wishes of others. There were times when Jesus put His own needs for rest and food ahead of ministering to others. If you try to neglect yourself and your own needs (unless you are under direct instructions from the Lord), you will court spiritual and psychological troubles. Being cruel to yourself is not necessarily holy. Jesus did your penance for you on the cross. You're free now to live in love, receiving as well as giving.

3. In making judgments about what you should do, it is too simplistic to base priority on the rule: Whatever pleases others must be right. True, the critical needs of another human being will very likely often be given precedence over your own plans and less critical needs, and at times even over your own crucial needs. If you encounter a dying man at your doorstep when you are on the way to a prayer meeting, you would probably give up the prayer meeting to help the man. But notice, the question to answer is not: Is someone else expecting it of me? but rather, *Is God directing me to do it?*

4. If you live to please others, any negative feedback, criti-

cism or displeasure will tend to ruin you. It will disturb you terribly to think that others are not perfectly happy with you. You must learn to take criticism and handle it as a "very small thing," to quote Saint Paul who knew it was the Lord who was the true judge.[6]

5. Even if everyone disliked you and disapproved of you, you could still survive. Jesus did. Many others have managed to live through large amounts of disapproval by others. If you are willing to take God at His Word, "I will not leave you nor forsake you!" [7]—there is no reason to believe that you will collapse or disintegrate when others disapprove of you. Of course, the displeasure of others is often unpleasant for us to tolerate, and it may be very difficult to endure, especially when those who are important to us do not approve of us. Nevertheless, if we have to, we can stand it. And most of the time disapproval by others is short-lived and restricted. It is very unlikely that we will encounter a circumstance where absolutely *everyone* will dislike us and disapprove of us.

Much of our social custom teaches us to manipulate for acceptance and approval. If you invite the Joneses to dinner, they'll invite you in return. If you help the Joneses paint their house, they may help paint yours; if you take the Joneses to lunch they may take you to lunch; it's the "if you scratch my back, I'll scratch yours" philosophy.

Godly motives are higher. They say, "I care about you and I want you to care about me. I will not demand or insist you care about me, however, and I will not strive to earn your approval, affection or friendship. I care about you and I also care about me because Jesus died for each of us."

Godly motives say, "You are important and so am I. Jesus loves us—and He loves us equally."

You can be released forever from the grip of self-hate when you freely and fully know the approval of God is far more precious than the approval of people.

---

1. Matthew 19:19.
2. John 15:13.
3. 1 John 3:16.
4. 1 Corinthians 3:16.
5. 1 Timothy 6:6.
6. 1 Corinthians 4:3, 4.
7. Hebrews 13:5.

CHAPTER NINE

Misbelief in Fear of Change

"I'm the way I am. I'll never change," says Lila, a 34-year-old elementary schoolteacher. Exasperated at the end of the day, she often makes statements such as, "My third graders make me furious. I probably shouldn't have been a teacher with my low tolerance level." She had been raising her voice in class, losing patience, and at times had taken a child by the shoulders and harshly shaken him. As a result she is deeply distressed and frustrated at her lack of self-control.

Joe is 25 and a bright engineering student in graduate school. His fiancée is concerned about his frequent outbursts of anger and tries to talk to him about the problem. He shrugs and tells her, "I'm the way I am. Take it or leave it, I'm me. So I've got a rotten temper and when something makes me mad, I show it. I can't help it." He concludes the discussion with, "I take after my dad. He has a rotten temper and so do I."

Shirley is a patient at the Center for Christian Psychological Services and is seeing her therapist for the third time. She sits stiffly upright in the comfortable armchair. There are tears burning the edges of her eyes. She is 29 years old, overweight and her appearance says, I don't care about me. She admits between tears that she is afraid she's losing her husband. He has been accusing her of being a slob and nagging her to lose weight. She thinks he's seeing another woman.

"I'm fat and I know it," she cries. "He doesn't have to remind

115

me. If I were slim, things would be different. He'd never look around at other women."

She pauses to blow her nose. "I *can't* lose weight. He likes me to cook him fattening, rich foods. He is thin and can eat all those foods that I'm not supposed to. How am I supposed to lose weight when he's eating all the things I love? It's impossible."

Lila, Joe, and Shirley share in common several misbeliefs. Lila believes it is her third-grade class that makes her feel anger, not realizing that she alone allows herself to be angry. She believes her anger is a permanent characteristic of her personality, which is untrue. Jesus died on the cross to free us from our sins as well as permanent "low tolerance thresholds." Lila cuts off possibilities for constructive alteration in her life and insults the work the Lord did on the cross for her.

Joe is a person who believes it's perfectly permissible to indulge in temper tantrums whenever he pleases because, after all, his father has temper tantrums, too. He tells himself and other people, "I'm me. Take it or leave it." He means, "I can't (or won't) change."

Shirley puts the blame for her overweight and slovenly appearance on her husband. She tells herself she isn't responsible in the least for her life—he is. Now she fears he's going to stray and she's terrified she might have to act responsibly and exert herself with discipline and direction.

Lila, Joe, and Shirley believe the fault of the unsatisfactory conditions or circumstances in their lives is *outside of their own control.* They have avoided taking responsibility for their feelings and actions. They also believe they can't change.

Sometimes it's not hard to think you're a victim of circumstances. Look around you for a moment. How many times in your day or week do you put the responsibility for your feelings and actions on something or someone outside of your control? Have you ever tripped over your own foot and then twirled around you as if there were a loose board in the floor or a crevice in the earth that was to blame? Whose fault is it when you burn your mouth on the hot drink? Why do you glare at the cup? How many times have you accused someone *else* of *making* you angry, or *making* you frustrated, or *making* you unhappy?

116

Nobody *else* makes you experience these attitudes. You do it yourself. Nobody forces you to feel, think, and behave as you do. A man in his early thirties said, "I do drugs because all my friends do drugs. I was arrested for dealing and now I'm facing a jail term. But it's not my fault I got caught." Stop blaming other people for your problems and your sins. Nobody *makes* you do anything. Nobody makes you sin. You do it all by yourself.

Naturally, circumstances and people around you will have some influence in your life; for example, you won't feel your best if you've got the flu, or if you're married to a person who throws pineapples at you every time you clear your throat. You're going to respond differently than if he were throwing kisses. BUT what we are demonstrating to you through this book is that *you* decide *how* you will respond to events and circumstances in your life by how you *believe.* You decide if you want to do as your friends do, whether it's joining a club, taking drugs, or whatever.

It would be untrue to say, "The reason I'm so grouchy is because I've got the flu." The *truth* would be, "I am making myself grouchy and allowing myself to act in a grouchy way. The flu causes me to experience unpleasant sensations in my body and emotions, but I do not have to react in such a way as to make life difficult for others. I could decide to be cheerful if I chose to."

The misbelief in this disagreeable behavior is, "As long as I'm ill it's permissible to act unpleasantly and selfishly."

Too often we blame others for our feelings. Imagine you are a man married to a woman who throws pineapples at you. It would be untrue if you were to say, "I'm a nervous wreck because my wife throws pineapples at me."

The misbelief is: "My peace of mind depends upon the behavior of others, and I can do nothing about their behavior." The *truth* would be, "It is unpleasant to have pineapples thrown at me and I don't like it one bit"; furthermore, "if I allow her to continue the behavior, I will only be teaching her that it is okay for her to abuse me in this way."

When you hear yourself reciting misbeliefs to yourself, a buzzer ought to go off in your mind followed by the words, "Not true!" *The truth is, I'm responsible for my feelings and actions! Nobody and nothing else is. I am.*

117

Here are some misbeliefs which should activate your buzzer:

"I'm the way I am because I was born that way."

"If I had a better education, I'd be better liked."

"If I were like so-and-so I'd be a happier person."

"If I were better looking, I'd be a happier person."

"It's not what you know; it's who you know. That's why I'm not more successful."

"Children make me edgy and tense."

"My in-laws make me edgy and tense."

"You make me mad."

"If only I were younger, then I'd have more energy and I'd be happier."

"If only I lived in a better neighborhood. Then I'd be happy."

"This house depresses me."

"I know I should change but I just can't."

"The reason I drink is because of the pressures I face every day."

"The reason I curse is because everyone at the office curses."

"The reason I steal is because my boss is too cheap to give me the raise I deserve."

If you believe any of these inventions, you are identifying the wrong culprit. Your most fierce enemy is not outside yourself, but within. For the most part, you *learned* how to think, feel and act the way you do; therefore, if need be, *you can unlearn it.*

Are you blaming other people for some unhappiness you are suffering? Is there a troublesome situation in your life which you are allowing and thereby telling yourself is the cause of your stress?

UNLEARN YOUR OLD WAY OF THINKING

1. *Realize that joy comes from your relationship to God and His unchanging faithfulness.*

You don't need to live in perfect circumstances to be happy. You don't even have to be loved and appreciated by others in order to be happy. It's pleasant to be loved and appreciated, but not *vital* to your happiness.

The Bible tells how two men of God, Paul and Silas, were

brought before Roman authorities at Philippi and beaten with rods and then thrown into jail. Bleeding and pain-wracked, they lay on the cold, dark prison floor with their feet fastened in stocks. But did Paul and Silas moan and complain, "If it weren't for the cruelty of the unbelievers, we wouldn't be wounded and bleeding and we'd be happy!'"?

Did they howl in agony, "Those unjust, unfair, rotten heathen! Look what they've done to us!'"? Suppose it were you or I lying on that unfriendly dirt floor with rats and insects skittering across our own blood in the dirt? Would we grieve, "This life as an evangelist stinks. It's nothing but abuse and suffering! Who needs it? Nobody cares, nobody helps, nobody wants to hear the Good News. Here I am, half dead and for what? Who knows if God even cares?"

Paul and Silas had strong beliefs that transcended circumstances, events, people, feelings; it even transcended pain. That belief was in the person, power, and presence of Jesus Christ. They believed their suffering wasn't as important as the message they carried,

So at midnight instead of writhing and groaning in pain, they prayed and sang praises unto God. They did not complain, blaming someone else for their physical agony, and they did not agonize in silence, biting their lips and despairing that God allowed such an awful fate to befall them. Instead, they sang so loudly their voices were heard throughout the prison! And not only that, God heard them and opened the prison doors for them. Their happiness came from the belief in Jesus Christ within them and not from circumstances around them.

2. *You are in control of your happiness or unhappiness.*

You make the choice to be happy. *You* make the choice to think true thoughts about yourself and others. You are the one who chooses not to blame the rest of the world for your misfortunes; *you* choose to stop excusing your improper behavior and putting the blame for your actions elsewhere. You face yourself as you are right now, taking responsibility for your thoughts, feelings, and attitudes.

People don't make you angry, sad, sick, etc. You *allow* yourself to be angry, sad, sick or whatever the negative feeling is you

119

are experiencing. Indulging in temper tantrums is learned behavior. You learned to throw temper tantrums and you can learn to stop. It is utter fakery to believe you cannot change your behavior.

MISBELIEF	TRUTH
1. The things you say to me make me angry!	I make myself angry at the things you say to me.
2. It makes me very upset when you don't have dinner ready on time.	I upset myself when dinner isn't ready when I expect it.

You are not so much disturbed by things—external events—but by the view you take of them—the beliefs you have about them.

A Christian should never live a life dominated by outside circumstances. Much of our suffering is because we lack the skills necessary for sound and happy living as the Bible teaches: "I have learned in whatsoever state I am in therewith to be content." We continue to believe love and joy depend upon other people, circumstances, events, material blessings, success, achievement, abilities, and other such things.

You may be unhappy because you are looking in the wrong place for happiness.

YOU CAN CHANGE!

Being "content in whatever circumstances I am" does not necessarily mean suffering in silence. It means to understand that your joy does not lie in your circumstances, but joy comes from within you. With Jesus Christ living within you by the power of His Holy Spirit, you are able to realize joy and contentment in *Him*.

Many circumstances are within your power to change. Suffering in silence is no sign of virtue (although there are times when the Lord leads us to hush and wait on Him even though we are going through a particularly difficult period). But oftentimes it can be more destructive to silently pine away in anguish than it is to rise up and do something about it. Many people do nothing

120

about their suffering because they are afraid to. Fear of other people may be the major reason.

Shirley tells herself, "My husband may get angry with me if I tell him I want him to stop bringing home ice cream and pizza when I'm trying to diet. Therefore, I won't say anything and I'll eat the stuff. Sure, I'll continue to gain weight, but it's not my fault. It's his."

Lila says, "I don't dare let the other teachers see I'm having problems with my class. They'll think I'm an inferior teacher."

Joe's dad believes a man should be gruff and hostile, especially toward women, so rather than argue or reason for himself, Joe imitates his dad. It's less risky than making his own decisions and receiving the consequences of ridicule his dad would regale him with.

Not only do you change your behavior, you change your attitudes about the consequences of your change. Shirley can stop eating the pizza and ice cream her husband brings home when she realizes she is the only person on earth with the power to make herself fat or thin. If her husband disapproves of her change, Shirley can handle it by preparing herself for negative consequences.

She tells herself, "It's okay for my husband to disapprove of my new diet. I don't crave approval for my decisions. In time he'll respect me for not eating the fattening foods. I *can* change!"

Lila changes her attitudes toward her third-grade class by realizing she makes herself angry, nobody else. She begins to learn *personal* management skills along with classroom management skills. She realizes her frustration and anger have to do with more than her job; but as she gains power over the decisions in her emotional life, she is better equipped to tackle the misbeliefs of anger and frustration. "It's okay not to be perfect," she tells herself. "I am not permanently lacking self-control. I *can* change and I *am* changing!"

WHEN YOU DECIDE TO CHANGE

1. Write in your notebook the number of times each day you attribute your feelings to external events.

2. Write your negative verbal expressions in your notebook as

121

soon as you can after you've said them.

3. Write a *better* way to handle things as we've outlined in this book.

Some notebook entries might look like this:

	Misbelief	*Truth*
8:00 a.m.	Felt lousy because of the rain.	I can be happy when it's raining if I choose to be.
10:30 a.m.	Said to Jimmy, "Your nagging makes me climb the walls!"	I make myself want to climb the walls when Jimmy nags.
2:00 p.m.	Felt it's the committee's fault that I'm overworked. They let me do all the work.	I permit myself to be overworked. By suffering silently I invite more of the same.
10:00 p.m.	Was irritated at neighbors and felt like moving, although I didn't let them know about my feelings.	I allow myself to feel irritated and to suffer in silence. I can assert my feelings in a non-accusing way.

---

4. Make time in your day to correct the irrational thinking. Make it a definite time—lunch time, coffee break time, before bed, or whatever time is best for you. This is important. Knowing and recognizing irrational thinking is the first vital point. Secondly, knowing how to change those wrong thoughts is necessary. And lastly, *do* it—take action!

"The committee is not overworking me. I am allowing myself to be overworked. On Thursday at the meeting I am going to request some of my responsibilities be delegated to others."

"I allow myself to be upset at Jimmy's nagging. Nagging is

learned behavior. I will start rewarding Jimmy for not nagging and for behaving in ways which are pleasing."

Admit to yourself that your negative thinking causes unhappiness. Take hold of the promise that the Lord gives to His people: *I will put a new spirit within you,* and allow your thinking to be dominated by the Holy Spirit. When you do this you will find that *consciously choosing* to change old falsehoods is more than a self-help notion; it's being strong in the Lord and in the power of His might.

You *can* change. The Bible is brimming with stories of changed lives through the power of God. Faith puts you in touch with the power of God. Nobody else can give you faith. You're the only one who can take the life of faith. You either take faith and believe in Jesus Christ and who you are in Him, or you wander along through life, a victim of circumstances, people, events, and situations you can't control.

Some people whose lives were radically changed by faith in God are Job (who insisted through his intense sufferings that God was still sovereign); Moses (who chose against being a ruler in the house of Egypt and joined the Jewish slaves to lead them out of slavery); Jacob (who waited and labored for a total of 14 years in order that he might marry Rachel); Joseph (who spent several years in prison for a crime he didn't commit); David (who spent years running from the wrath of King Saul); to name only a few. It would be safe to say that every man, woman and child who encounters and receives Jesus Christ as Savior and Lord of their lives experiences change. That change is conversion and regeneration of their souls as their spirits become alive, "which were born, not of blood, nor of the will of the flesh, nor of the will of man, but of God." [1]

Therefore if any man be in Christ, he is a new creature; old things are passed away; behold, all things are become new. [2]

CHANGING YOUR CIRCUMSTANCES

Nothing in this chapter or this book implies that you should not attempt to change your circumstances where it's appro-

123

priate. We are not teaching simple quiescence and passivity in saying that where disparity between you and the circumstances exists, it is always and inflexibly the rule to work at changing yourself only.

At times you will want to alter your circumstances rather than to stay in them and concentrate on changing your self-talk. This includes asking other people to change behaviors that create problems for you.

When Jesus was preaching to the people of His divinity, He was almost stoned by the outraged Jews. "If I do not the works of my Father, believe me not," He told them. "But if I do, though ye believe not me, believe the works, that ye may know and believe that the Father is in me, and I in him." These words really infuriated them and they physically charged Him. Jesus got out of their way and escaped out of their hand. Then He went away beyond Jordan and lived at the place where John had baptized Him.[3]

He changed the circumstances.

At times you will want to alter your circumstances rather than to stay in them. You can change circumstances by asking other people to change behaviors that are especially troublesome, hurtful, or harmful. It is not true that you must remain in all painful situations and accept them as your lot in life. Often it is far more godly to change the situation than to bravely but needlessly continue to suffer.

You possess a precious and wonderful ability called choice.

God is not satisfied to let us continue living in the old fleshly ways that brought destruction, sickness, confusion, and suffering. He tells us, "A new heart also will I give you, and a new spirit will I put within you: and I will take away the stony heart out of your flesh, and I will give you an heart of flesh." [4]

And to the new person, the person who takes a stand against misbeliefs that deny the power and glory of God, He gives His blessing. "And he shall be like a tree planted by the rivers of water, that bringeth forth his fruit in his season; his leaf also shall not wither; and whatsoever he doeth shall prosper." [5]

"Repent ye therefore, and be converted [changed], that your sins may be blotted out, when the times of refreshing shall come from the presence of the Lord." [6]

If the cold-hearted Philippian jailer could change, so can you. If the woman of Samaria with her questionable reputation could change and become an evangel of truth, you too can change. If the blood-thirsty Saul, persecutor of the Jews, could change and become the tender-hearted Saint Paul, loving writer of 13 books in the New Testament, you too can change.

Your attitudes, choices, and beliefs make you what you are.

---

1. John 1:13.
2. 2 Corinthians 5:17.
3. John 10:31-42.
4. Ezekiel 36:26.
5. Psalm 1:3.
6. Acts 3:19.

CHAPTER TEN

Misbelief in Never Taking a Chance

When people believe they should never take a chance, they commonly misbelieve a number of related lies, such as:

1. One of life's most crucial objectives is to prevent getting hurt. No matter what, I shouldn't get hurt.
2. Taking chances could lead to calamity. I could get hurt if I take chances in life.
3. Being safe is of utmost importance. It is terrible to be in any kind of danger.
4. It's terrible to make a wrong decision.
5. If I take chances in life, I could lose vital things like money, friends, approval, time, security.
6. I should never lose anything. Losing something is terrible.
7. I don't dare make mistakes. Mistakes are terrible.
8. I must always think ahead and try to foresee every possible trouble and woe.
9. I must intricately plan all of my actions as well as the words I say in order to prevent loss, pain, and disgrace.
10. God doesn't approve of risk-taking behavior.

Roland arrives twenty minutes early for his first clinic appointment and, determined to make good use of his time, picks up a religious magazine in the waiting room. He has to force himself to read it, but such clenched-jaw determination is not unusual for him.

"I've been so tense and nervous lately I can hardly force my-self to go to work," he explains as his interview begins. His smile is formed from the sheer obedience of lip muscles drawn back over bared teeth. There is nothing to smile about and no laughter shines in his eyes.

"It really doesn't bother me that much, but last month a guy who worked under me was promoted over me." He pauses, in-hales, continues. "Ever since, I've been nervous about going to work." As the interview progresses it becomes apparent that Roland saw his job as he saw life: an obstacle course of tempta-tions to risk-taking. His object: to get through the obstacles with-out taking risks or trying something new.

The man who got the promotion was someone who was willing to take what Roland regarded as totally unjustified chances with the company's capital and reputation. Suspecting what was go-ing on behind his boss' closed door filled Roland with anxiety. In his opinion, the risks that were being taken were outrageous and dangerous.

Roland had never been responsible for a bad decision. He couldn't understand how other people who made risky decisions with the company's money and good name could get the major promotions while he sat in the background going nowhere. He thought his good reputation for doing what was best for the com-pany should count for something.

At church he was on the board of deacons. The other board members often experienced friction at the meetings because of Roland's refusal to accept changes. When an effort was made to move the church in new directions or to change, Roland reacted in one of two ways: he vociferously objected or he retreated sul-lenly into silence.

Roland's wife presented additional anxieties. Just when they had paid off the mortgages on both their cars, she began to talk about buying a new home. To Roland this meant nothing more than a larger mortgage with no assurance they would ever have it paid off.

"I don't understand why other people don't recognize the soundness of my judgments," Roland complains.

Here's a man who rarely makes mistakes. He has nearly al-

127

ways played it safe and has bluntly refused to act if there were the slightest doubt about the consequences of his decisions. He was proud that he could look back on his life devoid of mistakes. He believed making positive choices was a skill.

Unfortunately, Roland didn't see that he actually made many mistakes and most of them serious ones. They weren't errors of judgment such as a person who behaves impulsively might make; they were quite different.

They were errors of omission.

"Roland, are you convinced that you would be seriously in the wrong if you were to take a chance in some situation?"

"I do believe that. And might I point out that because of my convictions I have a home almost paid off, a decent savings account, two paid-for cars . . . "

As he talks it becomes clear that his misbeliefs cause him intense anxiety. He defends his refusal to take risks, but doesn't understand why other people don't understand and appreciate his wisdom.

As a result of his misbeliefs, he has repeatedly avoided making decisions with an unpredictable outcome. He has chosen, instead, to do nothing or say nothing if the situation looks as if a risk may be involved. He takes the safest position possible on all points. Because of his safety seeking, he has failed to act responsibly on a number of occasions and failed to reap the rewards which people who are willing to take risks receive.

Roland's misbeliefs include:

1. God is definitely on the side of those who check and recheck to assure themselves of the safety of their choices.
2. It is unthinkable, even sinful, to make a decision which could eventuate in the loss of anything.
3. If a person makes a decision which turns out in retrospect to have been the wrong one, he then is stupid and guilty.
4. If a person makes a decision without absolute certainty of its outcome, it is sloppy and careless behavior.
5. God doesn't bless mistakes.
6. Protecting oneself and playing it safe, foreseeing and guarding against possible harm, is the aim and object of living.

In his attempts to avoid anxiety, Roland taught himself to be anxious. Avoiding anxiety meant contentment to Roland, but he never seemed to reach a place in his life where anxiety didn't exist.

Julia is a 57-year-old widow. Her doctor has advised her to move from the upper midwest of the United States to a warmer climate in the south, but the idea frightens her.

"I have roots here," she mumbles. "And I won't know anyone in a new town—everything will be so strange." Her eyes blink as she fights tears. She is very unhappy in her present home and her health is rapidly failing. If she doesn't get to a warmer, drier climate, she may die. But the idea of change is so threatening to her that she sees it as catastrophic. Suppose she makes a mistake? Suppose the town she moves to proves unfriendly and unwelcoming? Suppose she is lonely in the new place? Suppose, suppose, suppose? The anxiety is beyond endurance. She pulls a handkerchief from her sleeve and gives herself to sobs.

"Suppose you *do* make a mistake, Julia? What then?"

"What then? Why, there I'd be in a strange place, not knowing anyone. I'd be alone; oh, it would be dreadful!"

"Are you so very happy where you now live?"

"Oh, goodness, no! I'm very unhappy. My husband is gone, my children live in other parts of the country, I'm ill most of the time and I haven't much to do—"

But she still insists she couldn't make a move like the one the doctor advises. Too risky. She has taught herself not to take chances, even though she is now endangering her life by not following her doctor's orders.

Some people would actually rather die than change or take a chance. Paradoxically, the very thing they fear is what occurs by *not* taking the chance. It is not wisdom that causes a person to refuse risk. It is fear—fear of losing health, security, safety, familiarity, comfort, predictability, control, power. These are threats too great to risk.

Roland's feelings of frustration had increased to the point where he believed the whole world was falling apart. He felt threatened and unhappy at work after losing the promotion he felt he deserved, and he was frustrated and threatened at home

by his wife's talking about buying a new home. The children offered new threats as they grew older and made decisions of their
own, decisions Roland couldn't control or make conform to his
fear-related demands. He was beleaguered and discomforted
about so many things: the neighbors who bought a camper he
knew they couldn't afford, the church's decision to buy property
for a summer campground, the new tax laws, the weather, the
price of gasoline, his son's desire to be a musician, his mother
who refuses to go to a nursing home where she'd be safer but less
happy than at home. He couldn't understand why people did the
unreasonable things they did.

As Roland continued his therapy sessions, he began an in-
quisitive review of his habits. With help he was able to note situations where he had told himself paralyzing lies about taking
risks.

It was painful for him to talk about his teen years. "I remember how unhappy I always felt—I was so lonely. If I wanted to call
someone up or just hang around someone, I couldn't do it. If
there was a group of kids standing together, I'd be afraid to walk
over and join them. I was always afraid I'd be rejected, I guess.
When I was younger, my mother used to make the calls for me.
You know, like on Boy Scout night she'd call some other mother
and make sure I had a ride, and she'd invite friends of hers over
who had sons my age. She knew all the kids on the block and invited them over for special events she'd dream up—and somehow
or another I got along all right. But when I got into my teens it
seems as if everything just fell apart. I hated school even though
everybody told me I was so smart. I wouldn't ask anyone to do
anything with me. I wouldn't intentionally go up to someone and
just start walking with them and talking, you know, the way the
kids all did—"

"Do you know what made you behave this way?"

"Well, I think I was just terrified that they'd turn me down.
You know, I'd call some kid up and ask him to come over to go
somewhere and he'd say no. Good grief, I was so bound up and
scared. Just thinking about it now makes me feel bad. Why is
that?"

"Several reasons. For example, calling a friend would be taking a big chance, wouldn't it?"

"Yes. He might turn me down."

Roland's agitation mounted. He shredded his styrofoam coffee cup as he talked. "I knew I could do as well as the other kids in so many things, but I just didn't go out for them. Things like the debate team, sports—I just couldn't force myself to join in. It was so—so *lonely*. I was very angry, too. I had these fantasies about shooting people. Sometimes when I get frustrated and angry even now I find myself thinking about getting out a gun and standing in the middle of the lobby at work and firing."

Roland's misbeliefs had a strong hold over his thinking and his actions. Although chances are he would never actually act out his shooting fantasy, he was unhappy that he would think such thoughts. "I'm a Christian!" he cries. "How can such thoughts even enter my mind?"

When something is painful to us, we automatically want to get rid of it, whether that painful thing is a thought, action, event, situation or physical stimulus. "Mommy, make the ouchie go away!" the child cries. Mommy kisses the ouchie, strokes the child, coos, prays and the child is assuaged. The adult feels pain and cries, "Help! Something! Somebody! Help!" When there is no answer and the pain still persists, he reaches into his bag of previously used coping devices. One of those devices to wipe out pain may be to wipe out the people who cause pain. It also may be to wipe out the presence of happy people who only remind him of his losses and pain. That's why we often feel relieved when we read about others who are suffering tragedy and loss or when we hear of someone else's failures. It somehow relieves us of our own personal anxieties. It says, "Hey, I'm not so bad off after all. Here's a guy whose house burned down and who lost his wife and four kids, and here's another guy who just went to jail for embezzling, and here's a movie star who's dead from an overdose of sleeping pills. What do you know, I'm all right after all."

Roland's desire to extinguish the pain he felt at being lonely and left out found expression in his shooting fantasies. He'd wipe out the pain by wiping out the people.

"I don't know why I was so afraid of being rejected. People were just so intimidating to me. Somebody once said if you don't try to make friends, you won't have any. Well, it's true. I stayed away by myself and nobody came out after me to try to make friends with me. I didn't look friendly. How could I? I was scared to death of everybody."

Roland's fear of risk robbed him of a happy and productive adolescence. His teen years were a muddle of sorrow and suffering because of his misbelief that it's terrible to take a risk.

He believed taking a risk could result in being rejected. Being rejected would be terrible. His misbeliefs were:

1. Nobody ought to reject me.
2. Everybody ought to be nice to me.
3. Nobody should hurt my feelings or not want to be with me.
4. It would be terrible if someone were to intentionally hurt my feelings.

LIES!

If you believe any of the above, please consider the truth for a moment.

God himself took the risk of great loss when He set out to build His kingdom. He took the greatest risk since the history of man when He sent His Son, Jesus, to the earth for our sakes. When Jesus began His ministry He risked the loss of His reputation, family, earthly security, home, popularity and friends— literally everything a person can lose—in order to do the will of His Father.

Look at the risk God took when He created man with a free will. He took the risk that man might use his will to rebel *against* God, his creator and protector. And that's just what happened.

As a result of God's risk, the very worst that could happen *did* happen. Man *did* rebel against Him and go his own way. "All we like sheep have gone astray," [1] the Word of God tells us. "All have sinned, and come short of the glory of God." [2] Yet God created man perfect, blameless, sinless, holy and "good" in His sight; He created man in His own image![3] The risk He took was a big one and look what happened.

We can't conclude that God didn't know what He was doing or that because He took a risk He acted impulsively or without judgment (as we accuse ourselves of doing when we take risks). To God the stakes were so high that the risk was worth it.

God wants us to imitate Him. "Be ye therefore imitators of God" Ephesians 5:1 reads (NAS Version). As a follower of Christ,

132

imitate Him. This includes imitating His willingness to take some risks. You can walk at times where you cannot see more than one step ahead and you can trust God for each step. You can trust God to work out consequences you cannot. You can believe risk-taking is healthy.

Faith itself is a risk. You must trust God and act in faith in order to take that step you cannot see. If you're going to walk on water, you need to be willing to *take the chance* that you might sink to the bottom.

- You can't lead a happy, peaceful life without risks.
- To gain a friend, you have to take the risk of rejection.
- To have dates with the opposite sex, you risk being turned down or disliked.
- To speak up and be heard by others you risk rebuff, correction and censure.
- To be noticed, you risk being ignored.
- To get a job, you risk having your application turned down.
- To be a leader, you risk criticism and opposition.
- To gain a promotion at your work, you risk losing out to someone else.
- To win, you risk defeat.
- These risks are not bad.

The misbelief that it is stupid or sinful to make decisions which might turn out wrong is unfounded. We're told to be wise as serpents, harmless as doves.[4] Wisdom does not mean acting in fear or cowardice.

Perfect love casts out fear[5] means to us that the love of God has wiped out the power of fear over our lives if we will use God's methods of conquering it. "Cast your fears [cares] on Me!"[6] He explains. "Give them to Me! I know what to do with them." It is in this way we are set free to take risks.

Then whether we succeed or fail is not our utmost concern. We are not enslaved by fear of negative results. We willingly allow ourselves possible failure, possible negative results. Painful fear and anxiety no longer play a dominant role in our lives.

The Christian walking by the Spirit, in the will of God, can trust that outcomes of his actions in faith are totally in the hands of the Father. The truth for the Christian is that disaster, catastrophe, or utter defeat *cannot occur*. We have no business thinking in those terms!

God never fails.

An adage that rings true for the child of God is "Nothing ventured, nothing gained." Moses, leading Israel into the desert; Abraham, leaving his home with no idea of his final destination; Daniel, continuing to pray contrary to the law of the king; the apostles who preached Jesus crucified, risen and coming again in spite of horrendous reprisals—were all *taking risks*. They ventured with the certain knowledge that if they did not venture, they could not gain.

> *I count all things but loss for the excellency of the knowledge of Christ Jesus my Lord: for whom I have suffered the loss of all things, and do count them but dung, that I may win Christ.* [7]

These words are not the words of an unfulfilled man driven with anxiety that he might lose something precious. Saint Paul here was willing to risk everything there was to risk because he knew with absolute certainty whom he belonged to, and a relationship with Jesus Christ was more important to him than his own comfort and life.

Everyone at some point or another in his life makes decisions without the benefit of knowing the consequences. Our unhappy friend, Roland, began to realize this fact, and once he did, he started identifying his own misbeliefs about taking chances. Using our three-point system, he *identified*, *argued*, and *replaced* his misbeliefs with the truth, in that order. It was not a quick process by any means.

Misbelief:
It's sinful to make a mistake.

Argument:
Mistakes are not necessarily sinful. Many mistakes result from the fact that as a human being I am not omniscient, and there is nothing wicked about that. If I make a mistake due to acting in the flesh, I have a Savior to save me from my own mistakes and to lead me in the ways of truth. I don't want to walk in

the flesh and I don't want to make mistakes due to ignorance, but to the best of my knowledge, I'm doing neither, so I now choose to act in faith, even though I know I am taking the risk of making a mistake.

Replaced with Truth:

I have put too much value on being right and being accepted at all times. It is not vital for me to be accepted and 100% right at all times. God does not fail. My faith and trust is in Him. In the past I have tried to be my own lord, but now by taking risks I give Him lordship over my life.

Roland realized it wouldn't be the end of the world if he invited a friend to go bowling or fishing and he was rejected. He realized it wasn't the end of the world if he didn't always take the safest, most sure way. "I know I don't have to play it safer than Jesus does," he reasoned. He discovered he could stand it even if he was rejected, even if his decisions didn't turn out as he wanted or expected! He could stand it!

Learning to take acceptable risks with his career and finances was more difficult for Roland to do because the stakes were higher, but he made progress here, too, by doggedly opposing misbeliefs with the truth. He then acted upon what he knew to be true.

You can help yourself to change, too. If you have harbored any of the misbeliefs about risk-taking which we have discussed in this chapter, you can work to change those beliefs and your behavior.

Check the behaviors below which you *avoid* because they seem to you to be too risky:

_____ Telling someone else your true weak points, sins or mistakes.

_____ Investing money in something which stands a good chance of paying off handsomely.

_____ Asking for a date.

_____ Accepting a date.

_____ Asking for a raise.

_____ Telling someone you like him/her very much.

_____ Telling someone you love him/her.

135

_____ Talking up to someone who has in the past intimidated you.

_____ Telling someone your wants or needs.

_____ Inviting someone to accept Jesus as Savior and Lord.

_____ Talking to a stranger in a waiting room or on a bus.

_____ Asking someone (not in your family) to spend an evening/ afternoon/morning with you.

This is not an all-inclusive list, so please ask the Lord to call to your mind areas in which you are afraid of risk-taking. Name especially those areas where God-pleasing action is required. The Holy Spirit will quicken these to your mind. Now write them out in your notebook. Write the misbeliefs about risk-taking which prevent your acting appropriately in each situation.

Here is an example from one person's notebook:

> "*Misbelief*: It's wrong to let someone know about my weak points. I am afraid of taking the risk that's involved in telling someone else about my weak points. The misbelief I keep repeating to myself is that such self-revelations are terribly personal and dangerous to reveal. If I open up to someone, he/she might turn on me and reject me one day. Then I'll wish I had never shared such deep and personal things about myself. Besides, what if he/she thinks less of me when I reveal my true feelings? That would be dreadful. I'd feel all broken up. It's just safer not to tell too much about yourself. It's safer to keep your distance."

After you have written in your notebook, compare your misbelief with the following scriptures and ask yourself these questions:

1. "But what things were gain to me, those I counted loss for Christ." [8] *Am I willing to accept loss for Jesus' sake?*
2. "Without faith it is impossible to please him: for he that cometh to God must believe that he is, and that he is a rewarder of them that diligently seek him." [9] *Am I willing to act in faith by believing in Him with my whole being?*
3. Read the parable of the talents in Matthew 25:14-30 where the Lord teaches us that He expects us to take risks. If we do not take risks, we cannot effectively put to work the precious gifts the Lord has given to us. If we don't take risks, we won't use any of the gifts of the Spirit, we won't witness

for Jesus, we won't pray for anyone's healing, won't invite someone else to pray for us, won't generously give to the house of God, won't love, forgive, worship or ask in order that it be given us. We won't move ahead in the areas the Lord calls us to. Instead, we will bury everything God has given us in the cold relentless ground just as the servant did in this parable. God clearly objects to fear of risk-taking by this parable.

LISTEN TO THE WORDS YOU TELL YOURSELF

Sometimes the words you tell yourself never form to make clear, concise sentences. They are more like impressions. Julia, the woman who refuses to move to a warmer climate for her health's sake, didn't realize what she was telling herself at first because she never actually said to herself, "I am now going to tell myself the misbelief that it would be terrible to be alone and in a strange town." It was more of an anxious feeling she experienced as she pictured herself stranded and lonely in a strange place.

But once you *identify* your misbeliefs *argue* against them. "No, it would *not* be terrible to be alone and in a strange town. God has promised me quite clearly and vividly that He would never leave nor forsake me! It's silly of me to doubt that. Besides, there are churches and wonderful Christians in every town in the country. It will be exciting to meet and make new Christian friends. It will be an adventure. I thank God that He has provided me with adventure and excitement at this stage of my life!"

Never miss an opportunity to replace a misbelief with the truth.

If you will put effort into changing, you will develop habits that will last throughout your life. Each time a misbelief enters your thought-life, you'll recognize it as such and argue against it, replacing it with the truth. JESUS CHRIST IS LORD OVER MY LIFE!

THE CHANGE

In order to work best, this technique for extinguishing your

137

fearful behavior should at first be taken in small steps. Start out by attacking the little risks that aren't paralyzing, then progress step-by-step to larger risks. The effect of such progressive risk-taking will be:

1. To teach you to *seek the Lord* for His will in situations in which you have felt fear.
2. To *trust the Lord* to act on your behalf according to His will.
3. To *obey the Lord* by following His directions for action.
4. To experience the *blessing of the Lord* by working through your anxieties with Him.

By actually doing the thing you fear, you overcome the fear of it. Make sense? It will as you gradually progress from one risk to another. If you haven't listed anything but major risks in your notebook, go back and seek the Lord to show you some smaller ones you can start to work on. From there, progress through the others, and watch the change occur in your life. You may feel, as Roland did after he signed the papers on his new house, "I'm experiencing something entirely new in my life—peace!"

---

1. Isaiah 53:6.
2. Romans 3:23.
3. Genesis 1:26.
4. Matthew 10:16.
5. 1 John 4:18.
6. 1 Peter 5:7 (paraphrased).
7. Philippians 3:8.
8. Philippians 3:7.
9. Hebrews 11:6.

CHAPTER ELEVEN

Our Relationships with Others

The distraught woman's voice is high pitched and loud. She speaks with short breaths, snapping the ends of her sentences as though she were chewing them off with her teeth.

"That husband of mine doesn't do a thing around this house! The place could fall apart for all he cares! *I'm* the one who shovels the walk, mows the lawn, fixes the broken light switch, takes out the garbage—what does he do? Nothing!"

According to this woman, her husband obviously is not fulfilling his end of the marriage bargain. She continues, "When the car dies, who calls the service station? *I* do. When the hot water heater broke last fall, who saw to it that it was fixed? *I* did. I do everything around our house. You name it."

So far in her collection of diatribes she is unjustified. Where is it written in the law that the man does the mowing, shoveling, and fixing?

"But I also do the cooking, the cleaning, the chauffeuring, the disciplining of the kids, the shopping. You name it. My husband should do the man's work."

This beleaguered woman firmly believes her husband is not fulfilling his obligations as the man of the house. "A man is supposed to do the fixing and the muscle work!"

In other words, her husband is supposed to *meet her expectations*. He falls short of her expectations and offends her personal Law of the Man's Obligations; therefore, he is in the wrong, a cad

139

and not a man—in her opinion, that is.

Wives are not the only ones with a list of expectations they insist be met. Take the husband who is horrified at the idea that his wife wants to go to work and hire a housekeeper to do his laundry and clean the house. "A woman's place is in the home!" he protests. He can't figure out how she could insult his expectations like this.

"I don't wash dishes," he stoutly maintains. "That's women's work." He's alarmed that his wife is interested not only in going to work, but there's the chance she might earn the same salary or more than he. His Law of the Woman's Obligations says she's in the wrong, unfair, not a woman.

Putting others under the law—under my own expectations—means telling myself that others owe it to me to live up to my expectations, whether I'm wrong or right. This is one of the best methods around for making yourself miserable. You'll make others miserable, too, and not even realize why.

When you dream up a list of obligations for others, you're leaving yourself wide open for disappointment. These arbitrary obligations you put others under are not in accord with the Word of God at all.

Nowhere in the Word of God does it say to the husband, "Thou shalt shovel the walk, mow the lawn and do all the repairs on the house," and nowhere in the Word does it say, "Woman, thou shalt not leave the house, nor shalt thou ever require thy husband to do the dishes."

Your life can be a nightmare network of obligations—not only the Law of Obligations you put on others, but also the obligations others place upon you.

Carrie is a woman who is always busy, one of those people who is always out of breath when she answers the telephone. You feel you're taking her time by requiring she say hello when you call her. She works harder than anyone you know, but if you ask her for a favor, she'll always comply.

She finally confessed wearily one day, "I'm pressured, overworked, always running around for other people. I feel like a wind-up toy. Just push the button and I'll do something nice."

Carrie did most of her activities out of a false sense of obligation. She cleaned her house out of obligation (I'm *supposed* to have a clean house!); she cared for her children with far more fuss than they really needed out of obligation (After all, my husband's mother sewed all her kids' clothes; I ought to, too!); she ran errands for others, helped her own parents in every way she could, served on various committees for school and church, entertained at least twice a week, served as a volunteer for the local hospital and, in addition, she resolutely and laboriously served only homemade pasta, baked only homemade breads *and* twice a week she ironed sheets and pillow cases. If she had the time, she'd do a neighbor's laundry and ironing as well.

She was a slave to obligation. Most of her busy-ness she did not choose out of desire to serve but out of a false standard of requirements.

Carrie's social life was a response to her lists of "oughts." "We *ought* to have the Ricci's over; they had us over last week." Or, "Valarie sent me a birthday card; I ought to send her one." Or, "Jimmy gave my little Artie an expensive gift at the Christmas exchange. We ought to give him an expensive gift, too."

She went out of her way to do something for others because she felt she *ought* to. She invited people to her home because she felt she *ought* to. She accepted invitations because she felt she *ought* to. She offered expressions of sympathy, congratulations, farewells and greetings because she owed them.

Carrie is only one of the never-ending stream of people whose lives are in a snarl because of the misbelief that human relationships are alliances of obligation.

There are only two basic obligations, two things we *ought* to do: "Love the Lord thy God with all thy heart, and with all thy soul, and with all thy mind . . . love thy neighbor as thyself." [1]

God is concerned with *quality* in our relationships. Quality is obtained only through love. Love says, "It's all right with me if you be you. It's all right with me if I be me, too. That means I set you free from the obligations and expectations I might contrive. I set myself free from your unrealistic obligations and expectations, too."

God is deeply interested in your relationships with others and wants to be placed in the center of them so that He becomes the focal point of your affections and cares. His heart is motivated by love.

FALSE OBLIGATION SAYS:	THE OBLIGATION OF LOVE SAYS:
"I must because I owe it."	"I will because I choose to."
"I should because it's expected of me."	"I want to because I care."
"I ought to because I'm supposed to."	"I'd like to."

It's a matter of bondage versus liberty; law versus freedom; letter and code versus Spirit and life.

For some Christians the words "I choose" are part of a strange, unheard of vocabulary! They are so enslaved to legalistic demands that the only time they feel relief from guilt is when they are saying, "I *must*." Carrie confessed that she felt the most holy when she was pressured and overworked, pursuing a battalion of "musts."

The words *I ought to* are preludes to feelings of guilt. Carrie tells herself, "I *ought* to have my mother to dinner," and then, because she doesn't really *want* to, pleading lack of time or a conflicting schedule, she doesn't have her mother to dinner. She feels guilty. "I *should have had* my mother to dinner."

If she really had wanted to have her mother to dinner, she would have done it. If she had *chosen* to, it is more than likely she would have altered her schedule. Or, as an alternative, Carrie could call her mother and invite her for next week, giving her an invitation to look forward to and giving herself good feelings about her choice.

Suppose God created us as automatons, rigidly programmed to do His will. Suppose we were wired so that we couldn't possibly do anything contrary to His commands. Would He then have people who acted in *love*? Can a machine doing its function be said to *love*?

God's love is a love of *free choice*. What wonderful words those are! True freedom is the opportunity to *choose* to act and live as you ought. We have the glorious opportunity to discover the personality of Jesus, to choose love over manipulation, guilt, and false obligation.

How happy is the marriage where the husband and wife eke out an existence amid each other's expectations? ("You're *supposed* to carry in the groceries. My father always carried in the groceries," or "You're *supposed* to fold my socks in little mounds. My mother always did.") You're supposed to—you're obligated to me!

The answer is not to learn to love everything we do for one another; it's learning to stop hurling unloving and ungodly demands at each other. If we were allowed the right to choose our acts in love, to live according to the Gospel of Christ rather than the Gospel of Each Other, we would make some amazing discoveries about ourselves and our relationships.

Your expectations hurt yourself as well as others. When you demand that others fulfill your expectations, you make yourself a target for defeat. What happens to *you* when others don't do as you want them to? What happens to *you* when others don't help you, care for you, treat you the way you think they ought to? What happens when someone says or does something to blight your expectations of him or her? Suppose someone close to you doesn't measure up to your expectations in the areas of achievement, success, education, skills, or personal happiness? What happens when these expectations you've taught yourself to have are sitting out on your window ledge, flopping in the wind—fruitless, empty, bringing no returns?

Below are non-biblical, non-spiritual demands and expectations and their results when unmet.

EXPECTATIONS	RESULTS IF NOT MET
Husbands' and wives' demands of each other.	Feeling hurt, unloved, rejected, angry, unfulfilled, depressed.
Friends' demands of each other.	Feeling hostile, unappreciated, disapproved of, unsuccessful, rejected, unworthy.
Children's demands of parents; parents' demands of children.	Feeling unloved, unwanted, unworthy, failure, anger, lost identity.

143

Picture yourself as free from obligations to others based on false premises. Picture yourself free to act in love and out of choice. You are free *from*:

1. What other people might think or say about you.
2. What other people expect you to be and do.
3. The expectations you try to bind others with which only leave you frustrated and miserable because others rarely live up to your demands.

You are free *to*:

1. Choose to be and do all that God has planned for you.
2. Love your neighbor (husband, wife, children, friends) as yourself.

Visualize yourself being moved by the Holy Spirit from within, in much the same manner as a tree is motivated to sprout leaves or bear fruit. It's natural! You *are* a loving person, made so by the new creation of Jesus and by the indwelling of His own Spirit. Look at yourself as God does. You're a person given a choice to love other people and love yourself without fear, manipulation, guilt, or obligation.

The Bible tells us that it is *love* that fulfills the law,[2] not duty or responsibility or obligation. "For he who loves his neighbor has fulfilled the law." [3]

IS "I WANT TO" BAD?

Some Christians have a deep suspicion of their own desires. They avoid saying, "I want to," and are more likely to say something like, "I think I *should*," or "I feel impressed to . . . " or "I feel led to . . . " These righteous-sounding phrases are all fine and good, but will fit together with the glory of choice only if we admit that we *want*. Which of the following would you prefer were said to you?

"I feel I *should* come over to visit you,"

or

"I *want* to come over to visit you."

How about sentences like:

"I feel impressed to ask you to dinner."

"I really would be so happy if you'd have dinner with me. I want you to. Will you?"

144

"I feel led to marry you."

"I love you and want you to marry me."

There is nothing wicked about your desires when they are in line with the Word of God. The Word of God says that God *gives* you the desires of your heart.

Delight thyself also in the LORD; and he shall give thee the desires of thine heart.[4]

Notice it says first to delight yourself in the Lord. When your delight is in Him and His ways, your desires become His desires. They are pure and honoring to Him. The lusts of the flesh are evil because they aren't God's ways. Selfish and ungodly wants and desires need to be laid at the foot of the cross.

You're a new person when you are a Christian. When the Holy Spirit of God within you guides and motivates you, you are a completely different person from the self-seeking sinner you once were.

If any man be in Christ, he is a new creature: old things are passed away; behold, all things are become new.[5]

The question is, do you really believe you're a completely new person? "According to your faith be it unto you." [6] Are you still prowling around in your old sins and false expectations and problems? Or are you being set free from them?

Here is the marvelous possibility for every Christian:

I have been crucified with Christ; it is no longer I who live, but Christ who lives in me.[7]

This new person is so identified with Jesus living within you that you have the same desires He does. And since the desires of Jesus are pure and loving, the desires of your new self can also be pure and loving.

If you do occasionally miss the mark and give in to the desires of the flesh or the suggestions of Satan, confess it immediately to God and receive His forgiveness and cleansing. That's why we need to "test everything." [8] The fellowship of other Christians will help us to test and discern when we are uncertain about choices. They can sound an alarm when we are wrong. The Scriptures and our own consciences will serve as warning systems, too,

145

helping us in the task of testing our desires.

MANIPULATION BY GUILT

How do you make your desires known to those around you? When you don't identify your desires and tell people about them clearly, you run the risk of making people feel guilty in order to get your own way. Instead of honestly and clearly making your desires known, you manipulate people by making them feel guilty to get what you want. Manipulation is a hurtful behavior and guilt is a hurtful feeling. Did you ever hear anyone say how terrific guilt feels? Probably not.

Speaking the truth is a skill you can learn, remembering to keep accusations, threats, and hostility out. Here are some examples of manipulation by guilt and speaking the truth. Which would you rather someone spoke to you?

MANIPULATION BY GUILT	SPEAKING HONESTLY
I'm so exhausted, worn out, pooped from working all day and then overtime, too. I don't mind all the overtime (a lie) because I know how you have your heart set on buying that new car. I'm glad to work the overtime (a lie) so we can buy it for you. I'm really tired, though (truth). Working so hard really gets to me. I just don't know where I'll get the energy to drive Billy to his Scout meeting tonight.	I'm tired tonight. Would you please drive Billy to his Scout meeting tonight?

Love doesn't manipulate. Love dares to tell the truth.

Sometimes a person will be so accustomed to manipulating by making people guilty, they can't recognize *love* when they see it!

146

MANIPULATION SAYS:	LOVE SAYS:
Nobody ever calls me. The phone hardly ever rings. Of course, I always call *you*. In fact, I called *you* twice last week.	You are under no obligation to me whatsoever. I love you without strings attached.
Did you know Shirley's husband brings her flowers every Friday? *He* must really love *her*. Of course, nobody ever brings me flowers.	Darling, it would make me so happy if you would buy me some flowers. I want you to bring me flowers. Will you?
I haven't got a ride to church. I walk 12 blocks in the snow and cold, but that's all right. I don't mind.	Would you mind stopping by and giving me a ride to church? No? That's all right. I do not hold you responsible for my comforts.

You stop manipulating when you come right out and state what it is you want. Manipulation plays on guilt. If you can make someone feel guilty, you can get them to do what you want. It's hardly the way of the Lord.

Mr. and Mrs. L. were tormented over their 16-year-old daughter's behavior. She was out every night, drinking and smoking, riding around with her gang and being intimate with boys. Her parents felt they had failed her terribly. They had raised their daughter with the idea that they owed her something for bringing her into the world. Mrs. L. was pregnant before her wedding to Mr. L. and they both felt guilty about that. They tried to give their daughter everything they could to make life worthwhile for her and, in a way, it was atoning. They sacrificed and scrimped on their small salaries and sent her to the best private schools, bought her expensive clothing, gave her private lessons in piano, ballet, violin, horseback riding, skiing and figure skating. They plied her with toys, games, beautiful furnishings, gave her parties, outings, summers at camp, whatever it was she wanted or expressed a desire for. They loved their girl dearly, but it was tainted with obligation and guilt.

147

By the time they sought Christian counseling, Mrs. L. had taught herself a raft of unsuccessful manipulative behaviors. She was confused and frustrated because her daugher wasn't submitting to her demands and laws of obligation. Mr. L., too, was at a loss for answers; in spite of his threats, admonitions, outbursts, tears, demands, and guilt-inducing accusations about how much he and Mrs. L. had done for her, nothing worked. Their daughter was out doing her own thing in direct defiance of their wishes.

Mr. and Mrs. L. had to learn how to release their lists of expectations and deposit them at the foot of the cross. Instead of using manipulation-by-guilt techniques, they needed to learn to speak truthfully and lovingly.

MANIPULATIVE	TRUTHFULLY
Suzie, you're rarely home lately and we sit here alone worrying about you night after night.	We want you to stay home tonight and be with us. We'll play some games and make a nice night of it.
What do you mean you don't want to be with us, your own parents? Do you realize all we've sacrificed for you and now you don't want to spend one little old evening with us—the two people on this earth who truly *love* you?	We can understand that you'd like to go out with your friends tonight, but you'll have to call it off. We want to be together as a family and have an evening together.
To think of the years of doing for you, going without, giving you everything we could to make life happy for you!	You're special. That's why we love you.

The conversation with Suzie did not end there. It took time for her to adjust to nonmanipulative behavior as well as to make some changes in her own attitudes and actions.

The Lord Jesus stands ready to lead us into all truth by the power of the Holy Spirit. He has set us free from the law of sin and death. The old law of demands, obligations, and expectations shall no more rule over us. We are now under the law of grace. We're free.

Carrie sought professional help for her problems because she thought she was losing control of her life. Her relationships were in a discouraging tangle of obligations. She told herself she owed everybody, and she rarely did anything without first convincing herself that she *must* do it. Her deep resentments and unremitting feelings of guilt had added up to a diagnosis of depressive neuroses.

She had to be shown that Jesus' perfect work of atonement had literally broken those chains of legalism in her relationships. She needed to see she didn't need chains like these to make her a good person. Her personhood depended upon what Jesus did on the cross, not what other people thought of her.

A new and loving freedom finally did replace the self-invented obligations in her relationships. She wrote a letter to her therapist some months after her therapy concluded. We'd like to share it with you:

> . . . I can actually experience the love of Jesus flowing through me to other people for the first time in my life. I am now getting up in the morning and living through each day, not because I *must* in order to repay or satisfy someone's demands, but because I *want to serve*. . . . It's wonderful. I think the happiest day in my life was the day I threw out the word *obligation* from my thinking. . . . Thanks!

Your relationships deserve your truthfulness and love. You deserve the respect and happiness such relationships bring.

---

1. Matthew 22:37-39.
2. Romans 13:10.
3. Romans 13:8 (RSV).
4. Psalm 37:4.
5. 2 Corinthians 5:17.
6. Matthew 9:29.
7. Galatians 2:20 (RSV).
8. 1 Thessalonians 5:21.

CHAPTER TWELVE

Misbelief in Being Indispensable

"I'm sorry to be telephoning you at this hour," the cheerless voice begins. You reach for the lamp by the bed. It's three in the morning. "I—uh, that's uh, all right," you mutter somewhat unintelligibly.

"You're just the only person I could turn to," the voice continues. "I suppose I woke your wife up, too, like the last time I called. I'm really sorry."

"Uh, that's all right." You look over at your wife, who is sitting upright in bed and frowning unpleasantly at the clock. The ringing of the telephone woke the baby, whose wails now fill the air. Your wife gets to her feet mumbling something about justice.

"Yes, uh, sure," you say with a slight groan. "It's—it's, uh, all right if you come over now."

Getting phone calls like this after midnight is nothing new. People invade you at all hours of the day and night if they choose to. You have been proud to say that your life is a veritable open door for those in need.

From time to time the sneaking villains of reality poke up to startle you, but you shrug them off with righteous-sounding words like, "I've got to be willing to sacrifice in order to minister to the needs of others." You tell yourself you're learning to be "dead to self," but is that what it's really called when you're blind with fatigue and your own family suffers because of it?

Consider the experience of a young minister named John. He

and his wife, Jan, had an exciting coffee house ministry with over 500 young people a week going through their doors. The energetic couple was well known and respected among the area churches and received financial support from them. Everything looked great from all standpoints.

Several of the young people helped out in the physical labors of the ministry, but the entire burden of spiritual leadership was on John and Jan's shoulders. They did all the counseling, preaching and teaching, in addition to overseeing every other aspect of the ministry. John and Jan worked day and night for a period of three years with no vacation time off and very little time to be alone together. Their recreation and relaxation always centered around and included the young people. Night after night both John and Jan burned the late hour candles counseling some young person in need.

The ministry flourished. Hundreds of young people came to know the Lord as Savior and many were helped out of deep troubles, including drug addiction, vagrancy, sexual problems, and criminal offenses.

But then suddenly and for no apparent reason, Jan became ill. She was confined to her bed unable to move her legs. In a month she was up and around, only to have a relapse in a few weeks and return to her bed. She recovered again, but in a short time was back in bed with the same symptoms. She and her husband attributed her condition to an attack of the devil who wanted to destroy their ministry.

They didn't see the weapons he was using.

They had given every breathing moment to their ministry while their marriage slowly and insidiously crumbled. No time for each other, for rest or relaxation, their personal strength all but vanished. Weariness, worry, illness, overwork, strain; then harsh words, arguments, cold silences, prayerlessness crept in— they were in big trouble long before it showed.

Their problems notwithstanding, the ministry continued on. John and Jan couldn't see what was happening. Looking back over the events that led up to the disastrous finale, they reasoned that their troubles all began at the time of Jan's first illness.

"We prayed and prayed for Jan's healing!" they said. "We

believed God would answer our prayers! But He didn't answer the way we wanted Him to."

John asked the same question over and over. "Why did the Lord allow her to get sick?"

If you'll look carefully at this situation, you'll see it's not surprising that Jan became ill. How else could she legitimately take a rest? A holiday or a vacation was out of the question. The only way her body could find relief would be to go to bed sick. Because of a weakened physical condition, overworked nerves and tired reflexes, she was just ripe for a debilitating illness like the one she got.

The only means to assure not being overworked, pressured, run-down and faced with a disintegrating marriage was to stay ill. She didn't realize what was happening, however. She didn't intentionally get sick. Her spiritual tuning fork wasn't in use—she was given to the flesh.

The Lord gives us an example of the overworked man of God in the experience of Moses in Exodus 18:1-26. Jethro, Moses' father-in-law, saw how worn out Moses was as a counselor and judge. From morning to night the poor man was listening to the complaints and troubles of the children of Israel. He was just plain worn out. Jethro wisely saw that one man cannot do the work of the Lord *alone.* Moses was a mighty man of God and one of God's greatest servants, but he was not Mr. Indispensable.

"What is this thing that you are doing for the people?" Jethro asked. "Why do you *alone* sit as judge and all the people stand about you from morning to evening?"

Now Moses was a man with a sense of duty, a man well acquainted with the pressures and demands of his calling, not one to shirk his responsibilities, no. "Because the people come to me to inquire of God," he answered simply.

That's what John and Jan thought, too. The need is great! Look at all the troubles! We must do all we can to help! We are the only ones who can do it!

Jethro was firm and wise in his reply to Moses. "*The thing you are doing is not good,*" he told him.

He continued: "*You will surely wear out, both yourself and these people who are with you, for the task is too heavy for you; you cannot do it alone*" (verse 18).

152

Notice he told him that not only would Moses wear out, but *his people* as well!

John and Jan lost their coffee house ministry, not because of Jan's illness, but because they thought they were indispensable, the *only ones* to carry the full burden for the work God had given them. Pride, ambition, desire to succeed, fear of failure, and spiritual dishonesty were rampant. They lost their spiritual eyesight and energy first and then they lost the ministry.

The devil is very clever. He will tempt the Christian worker with something that has every appearance of good. What could be more noble than the desire to help people? What could be more Christian than working night and day for the Lord? Let's look for some of the subtle signs of the crossbones that could contaminate the pure in heart.

WHEN GOOD ISN'T SO GOOD

The born-again Christian worker is not easily tempted in areas of overt, blatant sin (robbing banks, peddling drugs, becoming hit-men for the Mafia), so the devil gets us on our own turf by appealing to our *flesh* while convincing us it's the Spirit. He can skillfully and cunningly use pride, envy, greed, jealousy, anger, lust, gluttony, sloth (the Seven Deadly Sins!) as *motives* for our do-gooding and people-helping.

Howzzat? you say.

Let's elucidate.

- The man with feelings of inferiority gets saved and then takes on an attitude of superiority over the non-Christians of the world. He preaches on street corners and pigeon-holes everyone he can with the information that they are going straight to hell if they don't shape up. (Pride.)
- The minister who knows all the answers. Has all the solutions. Has all the revelation. He does not train any counselors in the church. He tells his people to come only to him with their troubles, nobody else. (Pride.)
- The prayer-group leader who spends more time eating and finding fault with others than praying. (Gluttony. Greed. Anger.)
- The Bible study leader who seethes inside every time one of

153

the more talkative members of the group takes up too much time telling her/his points-of-view. (Anger. Envy. Pride.)
- The Christian worker who bad-mouths another worker's ministry because it's more successful. (Jealousy.)
- The church elder who is easily flattered by the attention of attractive women. (Pride. Lust.)
- The church worker who throws temper tantrums at home and tells himself the world is against him. (Anger.)
- The Christian worker who is always late, undependable, overworked, tired, nervous, worried, and demanding of others. (Sloth.)

The desire to help people is a good one. The desire to serve the Lord by preaching, teaching, and counseling is certainly good. God wants us to serve Him by helping people, yet we can thwart His glorious will by a lack of spiritual wisdom and understanding—and something else, which we will talk about next.

THE GREATEST GOOD

It's possible to be a preacher, a teacher, a leader and even a martyr without giving the slightest hoot about people. You could pastor a church, lead Bible studies, travel the world preaching, or be persecuted for your faith in God without knowing anything at all about love. That's what 1 Corinthians 13 says. It says we can preach, and teach, move mountains with our faith, give all we own to the poor people, get ourselves martyred at the stake and it's all to no avail without love.

"You're the only person I can turn to," the troubled person tells you. "There's nobody else. You're the only one who can help me." You're in the position of being savior. You swallow it up; after all, you *do* love to help. You're the one with the answers and solutions, the big shot. You're like Moses.

Listen to these misbeliefs:

1. I am the Called One and the anointing to help and direct others is upon me alone.
2. I've got something special and unique from the Lord that nobody else has. It's up to me to deliver my revelation to the world.

154

3. Nobody else can do the job I do as well as I.
4. No matter what time of day or night it may be, I must always make myself available to meet all the needs of all others.
5. Jesus expects me to give up all my rights to privacy, rest and recreation if I am to serve Him fully.
6. In order to serve God with my whole heart, I must put my family second to my ministry.
7. I've given my children to the Lord so that the Holy Spirit can teach and guide them because I have no time to do this in my life as a Christian worker.
8. God has called me to help certain people and if it weren't for me, they would be in pitiful shape.
9. It's my Christian duty to provide all the answers and solutions to the people God has called me to help. If I don't, the consequences are on my head.
10. Others should recognize my calling and be of help and support to me in the work God has called me to.
11. If someone is less spiritual than I, he has no right being in the ministry; furthermore, he has no right to be more successful than I!

Are you believing any of these lies?

Your spiritual warning flag should fly high each time you hear yourself say anything at all related to "I'm indispensable." Pastor X told us how he nearly ruined his life and ministry in the early years of his work in the pastorate. "I prayed to the Lord about the number of people who came to my office daily for counseling. I could see that the needs were great, and I felt a little fearful because these people were expecting me to give them answers. I wasn't really that sure of myself. I prayed like this: 'Lord, I am going to trust you to bring me only the right number of people so I don't overwork myself. And bring me the ones I *can* help, not the ones I can't.' "

He cleared his throat and continued. "Everything went smoothly at first, and I actually had time for eight hours of sleep at night and some free time for my family, too. But then—pow! It hit. You see, I didn't allow anyone else to counsel because I didn't think anyone else was qualified. After all, *I* was the pastor. I didn't allow anyone else to preach or teach, and I oversaw all the church government decisions as well. I was overrun with work. I tried to answer everyone's problems and troubles—I wanted to be everything to everyone. I rarely had a day for my own family and I was wearing thin."

John and Jan would have benefited from the older pastor's experience. "It was about the time when I was on the verge of a nervous breakdown that the Lord showed me I was wrong. For one thing, I was binding myself to a prayer that no longer applied. I had *told* the Lord what to do and then I wondered how come what I told Him to do wasn't working out anymore. Well, it simply didn't apply anymore. So I made some changes, thank God! I delegated responsibilities to other people. I was shocked to discover how spiritual and capable my people were. I no longer did all the counseling alone. In fact, I don't think I'm as good a counselor as some of the others on my staff. I probably never was. I *thought* I was indispensable. I thought I was the only one who could help the people."

There is a time to change your unhappy situation and not remain in it. Sadly, and too often, the changes don't come soon enough. You are the only one who can make the changes. Waiting for the situation to change is not the answer.

THE TRUTH

Pastor X took a step back before it was too late. He relinquished his grandiose ideas of himself. He told himself the *truth*. Compare the following with the list of misbeliefs on pages 154 and 155.

The truth:

1. I am *not* the only called-of-God person to help and direct others.
2. I am indeed special and unique, but so are other ministers of God. My ministry is not the most important one on earth.
3. Other people can minister equally as well as I.
4. Jesus always took time out from ministering to relax and refresh himself (Matt. 14:23) and so must I.
5. Jesus does not expect me to behave compulsively and im-

156

pulsively. He expects me to serve Him with wisdom and a peaceful heart. A peaceful heart is one that finds rest in the midst of a storm.

6. In order to serve God with my whole heart, I must care for my family as He has called me to. If I neglect the precious souls He has given to me as my own kin, I neglect my first calling.

7. My children are my responsibility and I will not neglect them. God has given them to me and I will make sure I have time for them every day.

8. God has called me to help people, but God could help them without me. I rejoice that He sees fit to use me while realizing people would not be in pitiful shape without me.

9. It is an honor to be used of God. I realize, however, that I am not responsible for providing the answers and solutions to everyone's problems. He is the Savior—I am His servant. I can point to the Way, but I cannot take the steps for the people.

10. Other people have the right *not* to share my burden for my ministry.

11. I rejoice at the workers God has called to the harvest and refuse all envy and jealousy in my life. It is well with my soul.

It took John and Jan several years to learn to replace their misbeliefs with truth. They learned to love each other and to see their work through the eyes of love. They are, at this writing, starting anew as volunteers with a large national Christian youth organization. They are also doing youth work in the church they attend. They are not indispensable anymore. They are part of a great team of workers who live for God and want to see His will brought into being in the world. They've joined forces with brothers and sisters across continents and oceans and have said "Yes" to *love*, removing the driving, striving misbeliefs of pride that they were once enslaved to.

Suppose your telephone rings at 3 a.m. for the third time this week and you hear the words, "You're the *only* one I can talk to," what will you do? Will you sigh with self-importance and relinquish another night's sleep to help this troubled person? Or will you speak the *truth* to yourself?

I am NOT a person's ONLY answer. I am NOT indispensable. I will help as I can and at reasonable hours. My family is important. I am important. This troubled person is important. You pray for wisdom and discernment and then you speak without hesitation: "I know that you're troubled and your trouble is important to me. Jesus is your only answer, as He is mine. I want to see you and work with you, but not now. Please call tomorrow and make an appointment to see me and we will work hard on your problem."

The Lord is demonstrating himself through you in the glory of love and truth. You are important, unique, special and beautiful, but thank God, none of us is indispensable.

CHAPTER THIRTEEN

More Misbeliefs Guaranteed To Make You Miserable

Now that you have read this far, you have more than likely developed some skill in identifying your misbeliefs and are doing something about them.

The first step, remember, is always *identifying* the misbelief. Second, you *argue* against it, and third, you *replace* it with the TRUTH. Say you're feeling frustrated, for example. You're tense and nervous and saying things like, "I wish I had more energy. I just can't seem to get through a day anymore without wearing out about halfway through."

Now, because you have become aware of your own self-talk and the role it plays in your life, you are paying special attention to your thoughts and words. You're listening carefully because you now know that your self-talk isn't always in complete sentences. Often it's an impression, feeling, or general mood due to a belief or misbelief.

You may express nonspecific discontent and not attach *words* to your feelings. You may say things like, "I wish I could stay in bed all day and not get up." (But listen further. *What* are you telling yourself?) "I just feel like a real nothing." (Locate your misbelief!) "Two of my closest friends are getting married. I'm not getting married. I wish I were getting married." (Keep going. So far so good.) "I don't have what I want; therefore I must be a nothing." (Bull's-eye!) There's your misbelief.

THE ATTITUDES THAT ACCOMPANY MISBELIEFS

The above untruth is then implemented with other attitudes such as "Getting what I want is vital to my happiness. I must get what I want at all costs." You can recognize the slave-driving quality here: sure-fire misery.

Let's take a look at six popular misbeliefs and at the same time look at the accompanying misbelief behaviors and attitudes. If you believe you must get what you want in order to be happy, what kind of misbelief behavior will you develop to accompany it?

MISBELIEF #1

I must get what I want in order to be happy. (I want it; therefore I should have it.)

ACCOMPANYING ATTITUDES

It's terrible if I don't get what I want.

My wants are the most important thing in the world.

Doing without is intense suffering.

If other people have what I want and I don't have it, it's unfair.

I have to do all I can to get what I want.

I'm happy when I have what I want.

Other people must be as frustrated and unhappy as I am if they don't have what they want.

Other people must want the same things I do; therefore, it's depressing to me to see people in want.

160

If I don't have what I want, there must be something wrong with me as a Christian.

If I don't have what I want, God must not hear my prayers.

The truth is none of the above.

TRUTH

- God loves me and always answers my prayers!
- The Bible says that the Lord will never leave me nor forsake me; therefore, I know that everything in my life is under His watchful eye!
- It's not terrible when my every whim isn't gratified!
- It's not terrible when my every need isn't met on my terms and time schedule!
- It may be uncomfortable or inconvenient to do without certain things, but I CAN DO IT!
- It is well with my soul! I will tell myself the truth! I can do without, I can be hassled and annoyed from time to time, but I can know in the recesses of my very being that through it all, I choose it to be well with my soul!
- I give others the right to be more successful than I, to have what I want!
- I set myself free from covetousness. I refuse to be a jealous person. It is well with my soul!
- I choose to love the Lord Jesus more than my own wants, and that's why I can give my wants to Him to bestow, bless, withhold or change.

Here are some additional misbeliefs, ideally tailored to add deep wounds and hurts to your life and keep them there.

MISBELIEF #2

It's terrible to have hurt feelings.

ACCOMPANYING ATTITUDES

Therefore, I must avoid situations and people who might hurt me.

161

People who hurt me are bad.

I'm less of a person when my feelings are hurt.

Other people shouldn't have their feelings hurt, either.

I must do everything to avoid hurting other people's feelings.

People who hurt the feelings of my loved ones are bad.

I must make people treat me kindly and not hurt my feelings.

I must always try to make others happy and never cause any trouble because someone might get hurt.

I must try at all times to be "above it all." A Christian should never feel hurt.

See the nonsense? What incredible self-defeat! A person who is victimized by the above misbelief might also be like Carrie, in a previous chapter, enslaved to obligations and expectations. "If I don't do what's expected of me, I might disappoint so-and-so, and that would be terrible. She/he might say something bad to me and hurt my feelings. *I can't have my feelings hurt because that's terrible.* I had better take the safe road and try to please everybody." This way the confused person can affect a shallow "above-it-all nothing-bothers-me" posture. Francis Bacon said "Truth will sooner come out from error than from confusion." The Bible says Jesus heals both confusion *and* error.

The *truth* is, it's perfectly normal for the Christian to feel hurt once in a while. When your self-esteem is attacked, you may feel hurt or angry, depending upon the accompanying circumstances. The *truth* is, these reactions are okay because the *truth* is, you can handle it according to the Word of God and replace the phony self-talk with such statements as:

THE TRUTH

- It is not unspiritual to have hurt feelings. I can have hurt feelings and still be a spiritual person.
- It is good for me to listen to my self-talk and hear the lies I tell myself in order to replace them with the truth. It is good for me to face the misbelief I have held that it is terrible to have hurt feelings. I stand against that lie now in the name of JESUS!
- I don't have to try to be above it all. I'm filled with the Holy Spirit and He is above it all. I choose to have mercy on myself, as God does.
- The Lord is my rock and my salvation. He is my defender and my shield. I have nothing whatever to fear. My body, my spirit, mind, and emotions are His.
- I give people the right to be hurtful and be hurt. I am nobody's savior. Jesus is Savior.

You can add many more statements of truth to this list. Take a separate sheet in your notebook and write as many true statements as you can to oppose this misbelief and the ones that follow.

MISBELIEF #3

In order to be happy, I must be loved by everybody.

ACCOMPANYING ATTITUDES

I must work hard to make everybody love me.

I must flatter, manipulate and diligently endeavor to make certain I do just what people like.

If people don't love me, I can't be happy.

People who aren't loved by others must be very miserable.

People who aren't loved by others must be failures.

If people don't love me, I'm a failure.

People owe it to me to love me.

It's terrible to be unpopular.

People who are famous, popular and adored by others are successful.

If I am famous, popular and adored by others I will be successful.

If nobody loves me, I might as well end it all. I'm useless.

MISBELIEF #4

Things have to go right.

ACCOMPANYING ATTITUDES

I have to defend everything I think is right.

I must crusade for rightness in my home, at work, at church, in the neighborhood and everywhere else I go.

People shouldn't make mistakes.

I must not make mistakes.

If I make mistakes, I'm inept.

When things go wrong, someone is to blame and they ought
to be corrected.

MISBELIEF #5

If it's worth doing, it's worth
doing the BEST!

ACCOMPANYING
ATTITUDES

Doing a poor job of something
is terrible and unforgivable.

I can't forgive myself if I do
poorly on something.

I can't tolerate a poor job.

Not getting the best grades,
the best results, is a blot on a
person's character.

People who don't work hard or
achieve success are lazy and
inept.

Lack of success is a sign of
failure.

Lack of success is a sign of not
trying hard enough.

If my children, friends, spouse
don't agree with my demands
for achievement, there's
something wrong with them.

If you can't give your very best
to something, don't do it at
all.

Jesus expects us to do our best
at all times.

Jesus expects us to give our
all; nothing less will do.

165

Jesus is not pleased with us when we do a job poorly.

MISBELIEF #6

I should always be and act happy in spite of all hardship or trouble that comes my way.

ACCOMPANYING ATTITUDES

Feeling bad or upset is not being a good Christian.

People will find out that I'm not a good Christian if they see I'm troubled or distressed.

It would be terrible if people didn't think I'm a good Christian.

I must be admired and looked up to, no matter what.

I must maintain my perfect testimony in this dark and cruel world; otherwise God won't be pleased with me.

It's up to me to convert the world with my ever-strong and courageous attitudes and actions.

There's something wrong with me if I don't receive trouble and hardship with a thankful heart.

I should be *happy* when trouble comes my way.

It's sinful to cry or feel sorry for myself. I must never let anyone know I do these things. They'll think less of me.

Nobody must ever find out what a sinner I am. I must hide my feelings and "Put on a Happy Face" like the song says.

The foregoing six misbeliefs are somewhat related to one another in that as a result of your slavery to them, you can wind up hiding out in a hospital somewhere being terribly sick (avoidance behavior. The accompanying anxieties are just too much), or you can be depressed, frustrated, suicidal, or angry, in the throes of furiously flung assaults of doubt at God.

Words like, "I can't take this Christian way of life any longer! It's too hard! I just can't live up to what I'm supposed to be!"

Or, "Nobody loves me. If I stuck my head in the oven tonight and turned on the gas, nobody would even care. Why go on at all?"

Or, ' What do you mean you didn't get the raise at work? What's the matter with you? Didn't you try hard enough?"

"I got a C on the exam. There must be something wrong with me."

These propagandizing habits need to be replaced with the *truth.* Truth is the unity in which Jesus Christ is the organizing principal and center. The smallest truth of everyday life is part and parcel of that one great *truth* which holds the universe together by the One who is *above* all, *through* all, and *in* all.

A Christian is not a person who is dominated by outside forces of the world, not one whose happiness or unhappiness depends upon situations, circumstances, or attending events. The Christian's happiness comes through his/her knowledge of Jesus and the power of God within. The indwelling Holy Spirit permeates every attitude, belief, dream, hope and thought. "I am complete in Him!" is his triumphant and *true* self-talk.

This doesn't mean you must never change an unpleasant situation! Please know that this book is not telling you to passively accept all suffering and pain without attempting to change it. When it is appropriate and within your power to remove the pain by changing the situation, *not* to do it would be destructive and downright silly. Example: A young man with a college degree in art takes a job as an insurance salesman even though there have been job openings in the field for which he qualified. He doesn't like the job he has and is unhappy and unsatisfied in it. In spite of this, he stays where he is while telling himself it's okay to suffer. Foolishness, right?

You don't become genuinely happy and fulfilled by some quirk of luck or accident. Everlasting joy is not a state of being that comes flying across the airwaves bringing with it peace and gladness just because things "go right," or somebody else decides you're a worthwhile person, or the right job just happens to fall into your lap.

During the years when World War II was raging in Europe, the small villages of Yugoslavia were hard hit with bombs, gunfire, reprisals, and hardships of every kind. The Nazis dropped bombs from overhead, the Partisan army fired the guns, the Italians fired the guns, the Ustase army fired the guns, the Cetniks fired the guns—the villagers hardly knew which flag to wave when soldiers marched down their battleworn roads. But there was one family by the name of Kovac who clung to their faith in God even though it looked as though the whole world was going to pieces. Death and destruction were everywhere with no end in sight.

Jozeca Kovac was a young wife and mother who had made a commitment to Jesus with her whole heart, and she and her husband gave their lives to Him for better or worse. It certainly looked as though this war was the worst, even worse than the one preceding, World War I. One day Jozeca was thrown into jail with several other women. The following is a portion from the book about the Kovac family, *Of Whom the World Was Not Worthy*:

"The cells, which were hardly big enough for one person, held eight women in each. There were two pallets to sleep on and two blankets. There was a drain in the middle of the floor and one window near the ceiling with bars across it.

" 'I shall not shed another tear,' she vowed, and she kept that vow for the next thirty days spent in that cell.

168

"They received their first meal the next afternoon. The guard threw it on the floor by the drain which also served as their toilet. The pot of gray liquid had fish scales floating in it.

" 'Ah, stew!' exclaimed Jozeca. 'Come on, girls, let us eat.'

"But the smell was so pungent they could not lift the cup to the chin without wincing.

" 'Rotten fish!' one of the girls wept. 'They are feeding us rotten fish!'

" 'Do they call this food! This is food for the pigs!'

" 'It is garbage!'

"Jozeca's eyes flashed. 'And we will get down on our knees and thank God for it!'

"Jozeca held the cup in front of her mouth and kissed it. 'Thank you, Lord,' she prayed, 'for this food which will keep us alive.' The others got on their knees also and they ate the stinking soup without another word." [1]

Later Jozeca prays and tells the girls that the Holy Book says if God's people will obey His commandments and follow His ways, He will pour out His blessings upon them. A thin, gray-haired woman winces angrily.

"What means this, *blessing*?" she askes incredulously.

Jozeca answers with assurance, "Why, to know *Him*," she says. "There is only one blessing—the blessing of knowing Him!"

Jozeca's joy did not depend on happy circumstances, did not depend upon the approval of others, did not depend upon pleasant surroundings, comfort, personal advantages, salubrious conditions or even answered prayer!

Happy is something you teach yourself to be.

You *teach* yourself to be happy no matter what circumstances, events or situations you face. You teach yourself to be contented because YOU have decided you are a worthwhile person. You know you are a worthwhile person because *God* says so! "For the Lord will not forsake his people; he will not abandon his heritage." [2] "The Lord is your keeper; the Lord is your shade on your right hand. The sun shall not smite you by day, nor the moon by night." [3]

169

Fear not, for I have redeemed you; I have called you by name, you are mine. When you pass through the waters I will be with you; and through the rivers, they shall not overwhelm you; when you walk through fire you shall not be burned, and the flame shall not consume you.[4]

Who says you're worthwhile? *God* does! ("If God is for us, who is against us?" says Romans 8:31. If God is for you, don't YOU be against you.)

How do you "be against" you? Which of the following do you tell yourself the most? Be honest.

I am dumb. ☐	Thank you, Lord, for giving me intelligence. ☐
I am unattractive. ☐	Thank you, Lord, for making me attractive. ☐
I can't—(whatever) ☐	I *can* with your help, Lord! ☐
Most people are happier than I. ☐	Thank you, Lord, for the happiness in my life. ☐
I'm poor. ☐	Thank you, Lord, for prospering me. ☐
People don't like me. ☐	Thank you, Lord, for making me likable. ☐
I have no talents. ☐	Thank you, Lord, for the talents you've given me! ☐
I'm miserable. ☐	Thank you, Lord, for the power to overcome. ☐
I'm lonely. ☐	Thank you, Lord, for being my faithful and dearest companion. ☐

Did you check more sentences on the left than on the right? Those sentences on the left are, for the most part, sheer hogwash. The sentences on the right are words of truth. Look at the sentences on the left and tell yourself, "Keep thy tongue from evil, and thy lips from speaking guile. Depart from evil, and do good; seek peace, and pursue it." [5]

Now, read out loud the list of *truths* on the right. Read them and rejoice. Jesus died on the cross to save you from deceit and false notions. He died to save you from the words in the left-hand column. You can add your own lies to that list. How many more have you been defaming yourself with?

The words you tell yourself have power over your life. If you tell yourself something often enough, eventually you'll believe it. Those little jokes you tell about how dumb or inept you are aren't jokes at all, they're more like curses. If you tell yourself enough times that you can't do anything right, you'll start believing it. Then, when something goes against your plans or you make a mistake, your previous lying self-talk becomes a conviction. You may say, "It figures that I'd do something stupid like that. I'm such a jerk."

Listen to the words you tell yourself. Are you building a tar baby? If you are, you can begin building castles and treasures in the kingdom of God by speaking the *truth*. Speak the promises of God in the Word of God. Speak these words to yourself *daily*!

[I] am more than a conqueror through him who loved [me]. For I am sure that neither death, nor life, nor angels, nor principalities, nor things present, nor things to come, nor powers, nor height, nor depth, nor anything else in all creation, will be able to separate [me] from the love of God in Christ Jesus [my] Lord. [6]

Now that you're really moving along with the truth, add some more to it, like this:

I am sure that neither lying self-talk nor vain lies about myself, nor attacks of the devil on my thoughts, nor my misbeliefs of the present, past or future, nor the ways of the world, nor positive thinking (which takes my mind away from GOD THINKING), nor any other ridiculous lie of the devil will be able to separate me from the love of God in Christ Jesus my Lord.

Remember, "A wholesome tongue is a tree of life: but perverseness therein is a breach in the Spirit." [7]

You're no dummy. You've come against the misbeliefs that have held you captive. Yours is now the tongue of the wise, and "the tongue of the wise is health."

Welcome home.

1. *Of Whom the World Was Not Worthy* by Marie Chapian, Bethany Fellowship, 1978.
2. Psalm 94:14 (RSV).
3. Psalm 121:5, 6 (RSV).
4. Isaiah 43:1-2 (RSV).
5. Psalm 34:13.
6. Romans 8:37-39 (RSV).
7. Proverbs 15:4.

CHAPTER FOURTEEN

What Must I Do To Be Miserable?

Or,

When the Truth Does Not Set Us Free

You can tell Esther is seriously disturbed from the moment she enters the waiting room. She huddles close to her tall, gaunt husband and stares across the row of comfortable chairs at the paintings on the wall. She wears the masklike expression every clinician comes to associate with either severe depression or schizophrenia.

Has Jesus not given a promise that holds true forever and all time, that the truth would have the power to set people free?

In the counseling room she speaks slowly and in a monotone voice. She looks at no one in particular and takes long pauses as she speaks.

Other Christian counselors and friends have told Esther that she has nothing to be depressed about. It's all in her head. They have told her she should be smiling and happy; after all, Jesus has given her His joy. They have advised her to pray more, praise more, give more and do more, and these well-intentioned words have only served to depress her further. She is now plunged into a black hole of despair that nobody has been able to penetrate.

The advice the counselors and friends gave Esther was true enough, but it made her feel guilty and condemned. The truth didn't set her free. Why? What was wrong?

173

Throughout this first interview she exhibits confusion, disorientation and delusional thinking. The struggle for her happiness will be all-out war with the devil of lies. She is diagnosed as suffering acute severe depression, and she will be treated without medication. The therapeutic tool will be *truth*.

Many times people who think counseling is simple cause more guilt and anxiety than they resolve. Esther had been devastated by the counseling she received, even though the words were true enough.

Imagine you are the client in the following dialogue. You have gone to someone you respect seeking advice and counsel because you can't shake the depression you're experiencing.

> *YOU:* I've been feeling depressed lately. I can't seem to pick myself up. I don't know what's wrong with me.
>
> *COUNSELOR:* Why are you feeling so bad?
>
> *YOU:* I don't know. I can't figure it out.
>
> *COUNSELOR:* Is there some sin in your life you haven't confessed?
>
> *YOU:* I don't think so, but I'll gladly confess anything at all if you think I should.
>
> *COUNSELOR:* Someone you haven't forgiven?
>
> *YOU:* I don't think so, but I'll gladly pray if you think I should.
>
> *COUNSELOR:* We need to pray for the healing of your memories. (At this point you pray with the counselor.)
>
> (After praying) You know, friend, you have to realize you are a child of God. Shame on you for these feelings. Jesus died to take away sadness and gloom, and the Scriptures tell us to "rejoice in the Lord always."

YOU: Yes, I know you're right. I feel so terrible about being depressed. I don't do much rejoicing.

COUNSELOR: You probably don't praise the Lord either! Do you praise the Lord every day?

YOU: Oh, I guess I don't really. I mean, especially when I'm feeling depressed like this . . .

COUNSELOR: When a Christian is truly walking in the Spirit, the Word says he will experience life and peace! Your feelings of depression are in the flesh, not the spirit. You're not praising and you're not walking in the Spirit.

YOU: I'm sure you're right. My wife (husband/ friend) tells me the same thing. I'm told I should be an overcomer. But I'm really so depressed . . .

COUNSELOR: Just listen to the words of your mouth, will you? What you say is what you get, you know.

YOU: What I say is what I get?

COUNSELOR: That's right. You *say* you're depressed and you'll *be* depressed.

YOU: So I should say I'm *not* depressed?

COUNSELOR: The Word of God tells us that the power of life and death is in the tongue. Ask and you receive, you know.

YOU: Okay, I'm not depressed. I'm not depressed.

COUNSELOR: That's better. Now just rejoice in the Lord. Praise the Lord and you'll be over that depression in no time.

175

How would you feel after this counseling session? Probably very frustrated, and perhaps more guilty and depressed than ever.

Why did the truth not set you free?

Let's examine this dialogue to see what was going on in this counselor's mind. We would be safe to say he believed:

1. Counseling is very simple once you've become a Christian. All you have to do is know some scripture verses and some popular current teachings.

2. There is no need to listen to people since feeling bad and having unsolved problems is always a result of sin and failure to apply the Word of God.

3. Knowing scripture verses is all a counselor needs to help a person who is having problems. If a troubled person doesn't want to hear the truth, it's just too bad.

Not everything this counselor believes is false. It *is* true that the Word of God heals and cleanses ("Now ye are clean through the word which I have spoken unto you" [1]), and it *is* true that some problems are the result of sin and failure to apply the Word of God. Why, then, did this counselor's words not zero into the sting of depression and help to remove it?

Esther was told to go home and quit being upset because being so upset was sinful and self-centered. Her friends told her she was selfish to feel so depressed, and if she repented of her selfishness the Lord would cleanse her of her sins and she'd feel better again. She was not offered any means of understanding her own dynamics or any *procedures* for change. She heard only the stern demands to do what she couldn't do.

Esther was supposed to just stop feeling bad and start loving the Lord the way she ought to; after all, He had done so much for her, why wasn't she more thankful? The more times she heard those words, the more deeply she agonized over her failures and mistakes. She began to believe that she was worthless and inadequate, that maybe she wasn't even a Christian.

Sometimes the troubled person, such as Esther, will be accused of having demons. We know of one woman who was accused of being possessed with a "demon of national pride." She was from a foreign country and her strong ties to her homeland apparently displeased her accusers. Another woman explained how she was accused of demon possession. "I was told my home had a spirit of art. I was shocked to think that a demon of art lived in my house! So I burned all my paintings and gave away my collection of antique books and magazines. I didn't want to be out of the Lord's will and so I stripped the place of all the art. I tossed out thousands of dollars of precious art."

The help that doesn't help and the truth that doesn't set people free can be due to:

1. Counselors or helpers who haven't any real or genuine love for people who are hurting.
2. Failure to hear what the troubled person is really saying, and instead of listening for leads into the problems, cutting them off.
3. Not bothering to learn anything about the troubled person.
4. Using the Word of God as a club to beat them with the truth.
5. Knowing all the answers and being ready with solutions at all times.
6. The mistaken thought that the counselor is a better and more worthy person than the disturbed person.

Jesus can meet every problem a human being can have, but it takes wisdom and discernment on the part of the counselor to hear how He wants each person handled. The counselor should pray for the spiritual gifts of knowledge and discernment and the wisdom to use them effectively. Helping people's emotions to be healthy is not like handing out the same prescription for every cold and sore throat. Not everyone suffers anxiety or depression alike or for the same reasons.

There are no pat answers to emotional suffering.

There are many theories, and each theorist thinks his is the truth. The cause of trouble, according to some theories of psychopathology, is unconscious conflict, caused in its turn, by childhood interactions and events. Closely related to this is the notion that memories are the causes of current difficulties and if the memories are healed, all will be well.

Still other theories locate the causes of all behavior difficul-

177

ties in the genes, offering the dubious consolation that such things can be bred out of future generations, provided we will all mate as the scientists plan for us to; or perhaps have our genetic material altered.

Other scientists insist that chemical imbalance underlies all unwanted emotion, proposing that psychopharmacologists develop elixirs, tablets and capsules which, when ingested, will produce an anxiety and depression-free world.

Then there are the religious folk who insist emotional trouble is always due to unrepented sin and lack of faith. Other religious people may locate the cause in the spirit, under the assumption that infestation by evil spirits is inevitable, especially in cases they do not understand such as dyslogic syndrome and schizophrenia. In actuality, there may be some truth in all these theories, but none of them in themselves is sufficient explanation and cure for all disordered behavior.

The fact that improvement occasionally follows the use of these treatment methods does not mean that each by itself is "the answer."

God desires to work wholeness through measures such as prayer, laying-on of hands, anointing with oil, deliverance, counseling, diet, medication, work, play, fresh air, exercise, friends, human love and also, at times, a psychotherapeutic relationship. (When the Lord has chosen to produce desired effects through counseling, it is not an alternative to "letting God do it," but rather the means He has determined to use in the particular case.)

Esther learned how to listen to the words and thoughts in her mind. She listened to the words she was telling herself which perpetuated her negative feelings.

"I just hate getting up in the mornings," she explained in the lethargic tone of voice she had adopted. "Mornings are just rotten. I hate facing the house, the kids and the mess. I hate getting out of bed. But I hate going to bed, too. I can't sleep. I wake up a thousand times a night. I never feel rested. I just hate everything. I don't see a thing good in anything."

"Esther, when you wake up in the morning and sit on the edge of the bed, what are your first *thoughts*?"

178

"I don't know if I think anything. I just *feel* rotten. I feel like I wish I could just die." She pauses, stares at the lamp on the desk, then says, "I tell myself I can't handle it—I can't handle any of it."

Another long pause. She pushes her mouth downward into a pout. "Nothing I do is right. That's what I tell myself."

Esther believed God made impossible demands on her, life made impossible demands of her. She thought she couldn't meet up with expectations made of her and now she lacked the strength to try to live up to her own expectations. She wasn't far from the truth. It was all just too much.

She had made her life the way it was. She dreamed of being married, of being the perfect wife. She dreamed of the day when she would have sweet little children around, all cute, lovable, and subservient. She dreamed of dressing them up in adorable clothes and having them near her all day for company; she'd just love motherhood. She wanted to be the *best* wife, the *best* mother, and the *best* Christian there could possibly be.

Her husband had certain expectations, too. He expected Esther to keep a neat house; teach the children obedience, manners, and respect, while loving it; have delicious meals ready when he came home from work; keep herself neat and attractive; be devoted and appreciative of him; consider his wants vitally important and be dependent upon him for her rewards in life.

The children demanded she be there 100% of the time to feed, diaper, amuse, clothe, care for and delight in them. She felt guilty that she didn't enjoy her noisy children and cluttered house more than she did and couldn't understand why she lost her temper during the day so often.

She compared herself with her Christian friends who seemed on top of things. She compared herself with the women on the TV commercials whose floors glistened merrily after a quick flick of the mop and whose children smelled beautiful, looked beautiful, and acted beautiful. She was familiar with the TV programs where the little wife always seemed to have it all together. She looked at herself and thought, "I dreamed of married life being like heaven and it turned out to be like purgatory."

Expectations too great to meet, demands too impossible to

179

achieve, where was God in all this?

Her church was active with some program going for every day of the week. Esther started out by attending the Women's Wednesday morning Bible study plus the Sunday morning church service. Gradually, she joined the Missionary Society which met on Fridays, the intercessory prayer group which met Tuesday mornings, and she volunteered to help in the nursery for the Sunday night services. She attended the Sunday School Workers' Brunches once a month.

People liked her and appreciated her eagerness to help. She thought they expected her to be energetic, giving, concerned, and involved at all times. "The world is watching you," her pastor expounded from the pulpit on Sunday morning. "Always bear in mind that the world has got its eye on the Christian! It's up to you to be a good witness!"

A good witness, a good wife, a good mother, a good Christian, a good person, a good cook, a good church worker—demands, pressures, expectations! Esther forged ahead, struggling, trying, laboring to be "good," the "best," until she failed so often and felt so guilty, she started feeling depressed.

Then came the demands to rise above her depressed feelings. "You're supposed to be an overcomer!" "Depression is sin!" "But you ought to be victorious!"

Esther's ideas of the perfect wife, mother, and Christian flew out of her grasp like paper streamers in the wind. With nothing to replace these false ideals, she felt worthless, defeated, devoid of a dream, useless, and sinful.

BUT THE TRUTH DOES SET US FREE!

A frequent cause of disordered behavior is a person's failure to examine his/her beliefs (attitudes, ideas, thoughts, self-talk) and the concomitant tendency not to question them, though they be painful, cruel, and UNtrue. Locating and identifying pain-causing fabrications plus learning the factual reality-based *truth* was the therapeutic "miracle" which began Esther's dramatic recovery.

180

Let's repeat the Three-Point Misbelief Therapy Outline:

1. *Locate and identify the misbelief in your thinking and self-talk.*

(Esther's misbelief, at least in part, was: "I'm a failure at life because I'm not the wife or mother I thought I'd be and being married isn't what it's cracked up to be at all.")

2. *Argue against the misbelief.*

("I'm not a failure just because I didn't meet expectations that were unrealistic in the first place. Marriage may not be what I dreamed it would be, that's true, but there are some things about it that aren't all that bad.")

3. *Replace the misbelief with the TRUTH.*

("In spite of the unpleasantness, disappointments and daily trials I experience, I *can* carry on. The demands that I be joyful and energetic at all times are unrealistic, and Jesus died on the cross so I can be unashamed to be real. I'm not a failure because I feel bad at times. I am a born-again child of God with a Savior who saves me from my own demands and expectations of myself and others.")

"I can change the situations in my life that need changing without fearing I'm making a mistake. I am no longer intimidated by the demands of others."

"Furthermore," Esther told herself, "I *can* get through unpleasant feelings and admit that I occasionally have them even though I have believed the fable that other people are happy all the time. I *can* be content even if things aren't as I would like them to be. I *can* get through discomfort because *I can do all things through Christ which strengtheneth me.*[2] "

Jesus taught that the *truth* has freeing power. God looks for and wants *truth* to be present in our innermost being. "Behold, thou desirest truth in the inward parts: and in the hidden part thou shalt make me to know wisdom"[3] is our prayer.

Whether we are the ones suffering or whether we are counseling someone else who is suffering, our task is to communicate the *truth* which frees the inward parts, our souls, where our emotions live.

Esther made rapid improvements when she realized many of her misbeliefs. She taught herself to replace lies with the truth in

181

her life. She taught herself to have mercy on herself, also. She taught herself to discuss her feelings with her husband and to let him know if his demands of her were unrealistic.

Living up to others' expectations will wear down the best of us and cause us to lose our own sense of self-worth to the all-prevailing menace of others-worth.

It's through the power of truth we find our personhood, making it the very foundation of our lives. Telling ourselves the truth sets us free to be the dynamic, loving, altogether whole people God meant us to be.

As a Christian, that same spirit that raised Christ from the dead dwells in you. You're His child and you are never alone as you spend the rest of your life, and indeed all of eternity, telling yourself the truth.

---

1. John 15:3.
2. Philippians 4:13.
3. Psalm 51:6.

If this book has helped you, you will want to read *Teaching Your Children to Tell Themselves the Truth,* by the same authors. It provides parents with a simple, easy-to-follow plan to help their children learn the truth and use it to shape their lives.

TELLING
EACH OTHER
THE TRUTH

To Candy

Table of Contents

INTRODUCTION

"Two Hundred Lies a Day"

You don't need a book to teach you to tell the truth, right?

That's what Joel thought about himself, too. He believed he was a truthful man—well, for the most part. And he certainly wouldn't have traced his current difficulties to untruthfulness. He knew he was a good doctor, too. Then why was he risking everything? Why was he putting it on the line in exchange for nothing?

He knew he was taking an enormous risk. If arrested he would be ruined. His practice would go down the drain. He might even lose his medical license. Julie would leave him—he knew that for certain. And his family would never recover from the shock and mortification.

Yet Joel continued walking toward the bar. He seemed driven. The familiar pattern of intense pressure from marital disharmony and professional responsibility seemed more than he could bear. Always at such times of stress his mind dangled before him the excitement of the forbidden—and the pressure always persisted until he gave in.

He knew what the end would be, yet he told himself that this time he would not go that far. He would only stop and watch the strippers for a few hours, have a couple of drinks, and then go home. Perhaps that would be enough. It would have to be enough. He had promised God he would clean up his act.

Home. Joel did not allow his mind to dwell on home. How shocked his patients would be if they knew what his life with

187

Julie had been like! Most of his patients viewed him as almost divine. What would they think if they knew he and Julie weren't talking, that they seldom got along well enough to sleep in the same bed? What would they think if they knew of the feelings (Were they angry feelings?) he had locked inside himself?

How would Julie react if she knew? He failed to notice a quick thrill of satisfaction at the thought of Julie discovering his secret. It would hurt her, and she deserved to be hurt. But he would never tell. She mustn't find out. Still, he knew dimly that in some curious way he was getting even, taunting her, punishing her, rubbing her nose in her coldness, acting out his anger at her this very moment.

She would never know. She *must* not find out. For he knew the course he was on would not stop with a couple of drinks and a show. It would end as it had always ended. He would find a prostitute and go home with her. It was his act of "communication" directed at the Julie he carried in his mind. The real Julie must not know.

Here was communication gone so awry that it never communicated at all! Julie would also never know that he was angry. He wouldn't tell her. He didn't know how. And if he did tell her, she wouldn't know how to answer. So instead of telling each other the truth, this couple had learned to "stuff it." And the result was Joel's gross, sinful, pathological, guilt-ridden misbehavior. Joel, like most people, did not think he needed to learn how to tell Julie the truth about himself and the needs and feelings he harbored.

Most people who are likely to read this book were taught long ago not to lie. The lesson usually comes early in life. The first time a child makes up a story to avoid parental wrath, he may discover that the penalty for his inventive genius is worse than if he had truthfully admitted his trespass.

If you are fortunate enough to have been reared by parents whose compassion, love, and respect for morality were consistent, you will have acquired the truth habit to the point where you wouldn't dream of lying—in most situations. You will hardly believe you need a book to teach you to speak the truth.

Nonetheless, most people, even most moral people—like us— slip around the truth without even realizing it. Yes, we have learned the difference between truth and lies. But to an extent we don't fully realize, the culture desensitizes us to falsehood, immunizes us to its evils, simmers us in a broth of untruth, and numbs us to the uncounted lies we hear each day. So we eventually take certain untruths for granted and hear them without amazement or shock.

Someone calculated that each of us tells 200 lies each day! Yet we believe ourselves to be honest, truthful folk. In fact, we'd swear to it—and chances are, we'd be swearing to an untruth. It's so much easier to "call in sick" than to go to work when relatives we like are visiting. Few people think twice before insisting to the arresting officer that they were not driving as fast as he claims they were. Most errors on tax returns occur in favor of the taxpayer, attesting to our habit of nudging reality in our own direction. The marriage counselor who interviews each partner separately can hardly believe he is hearing about the same relationship—the two versions vary so sharply.

The consequences of this built-in disregard for truth dog our tracks. Most of the time we barely notice how they underscore human faithlessness. Banks can't cash checks for strangers; stores won't take merchandise returned without a sales slip; TV monitors scan the aisles to catch furtive hands; ushers on guard make sure we don't see two movies for the price of one; in the days when virtue was important, young women learned to be wary of young men with a "line"; all America knows what a dead bolt lock is; insurance against the dishonesty of others costs us hard-earned resources; dogs, alarm systems, fences, walls, vaults, lockers, safe-deposit boxes, false bottoms, secret pockets, chains, combinations, bars, bolts, padlocks, polygraphs, voice analyzers, bloodhounds—all provide some of the most obvious signs of everyday falsehood.

LIES AND HUMAN MISERY

But the less obvious markers of lies at work need attention. Untruths devastate our plans, corrupt our characters, disrupt our relationships, shred our spirits, and putrify our sweetest daydreams.

We become insensitive to the lies because our daily life has

189

inured us to noise. It comes pouring at us from a hundred loud-speakers during nearly every waking moment. What we hear is often false; worse, we take falsehood for granted.

Falsehoods are sung, shouted and whispered to us. False-hoods hypnotize and cajole us to buy soap, magazines, tomb-stones, dish detergent, condominiums, books, fly spray, laxa-tives, scuba lessons, medical care, beer, vacation cruises, and dating services. But even more insidious, we are sold false *ideas*; we are told what to think, and are thus seduced into believing false notions about who we are, what we must have, where we really came from, what life is all about, and how we ought to live. Much that is offered on the idea market consists of lies.

Here is how those lies affect us: Perhaps we are not happy. Ask most of us why we are miserable and we will tell you that the problem lies outside ourselves; or if it lies within ourselves we will blame it on the lack of something within, some attribute which leads to happiness. "God," we whine, "why don't you just give me that one thing I lack. Then I'll be happy." We imagine our misery exists because God won't loosen up and give a little. It would be so easy for Him! Why doesn't He?

This is perhaps the biggest lie of all. The notion that the cause of our unhappiness lies elsewhere creates precisely that state of hopelessness the enemy so fervently desires: The "I can't and God won't" situation of utter despair.

Even the secular psychologist who keeps up with his reading knows better. Cognitive psychology, pioneered by Ellis, Beck, Mahoney, Meichenbaum, Novaco, and many other researchers, certainly knows better. For more than a decade, these psychol-ogists have found wanting the old Skinnerian behaviorism which insisted man is no different from the laboratory animal insofar as the mechanisms governing his behavior are concerned. If the laboratory rat could be taught to press a lever by rewarding him with pellets of pressed barley, then psychologists could teach man to save his soul by rewarding him for correct responses. The social learning and cognitive behavioral psychologists did not exactly repudiate Skinner's principles, they merely added something. Yet the addition was crucial. They discovered that, unlike the laboratory rat, man *thinks*. He assesses, appraises, and evaluates, supplying meaning to events.

It is the content of human thinking that makes the difference between misery and happiness. What matters is not the event, but how a person appraises and evaluates the event. What occurs outside him does not make him joyful or wretched, angry or benevolent, peaceful or turbulent. What he *believes* about the event makes all the difference.

So, by a quirk in the development of psychological thought, theoreticians and clinicians have come strikingly close to saying what the Scriptures say: "As he thinketh in his heart, so is he" (Prov. 23:7), and, "According to your faith, so be it unto you" (Matt. 9:29). Psychologists now acknowledge that faith saves. But most Christians have failed to note the revolutionary implications of these biblical teachings. Therefore, as is so often the case, God had to send messengers from the secular world to open our eyes to the treasure we have.

Here's the good news: If you will learn to tell yourself the truth, learn to believe it "up front," where you live, rather than stow it in some mental file labeled "pure doctrine" (to be pulled out when you need to argue with someone), you can control your own happiness and defeat every wile of the enemy. That is why Jesus said, "The truth shall make you free" (John 8:32).

WHAT IS TRUTH?

Pontius Pilate, quoted frequently on the subject, did not know what truth is. Furthermore, he thought no one else knew either. Perhaps he was ahead of his time. One reason for the truth deficit in today's secular culture is the loss of the logical and philosophical underpinnings for truth once furnished by the Christian faith. The result is relativism. Francis Schaeffer devoted a lifetime of effort to tracing the results of this loss and advancing a powerful remedy.

Relativism, the naive notion that anybody's truth is as good as anybody else's, has gained a firm foothold among psychologists, though no psychologist could conceivably live or work in faithful adherence to it. Many studies have demonstrated that even the psychotherapist who thinks he does value-neutral therapy actually imposes his values on his patient. Such value-setting does not square well with the relativistic notion that

191

each person's truth is just fine for his own needs. After all, if the relativistic psychologist acts in harmony with his professed philosophy, he will not push his own values or his own truth. He will recognize the patient's truth and values as equal with his.

Scientific studies suggest that it's a good thing relativistic psychologists aren't consistent enough to practice their relativism, for if they did their patients wouldn't get better. Improvement seems to be associated with change in the patient's values—in the direction of the therapist's values.

In contrast to contemporary relativism, this book advances the view that truth is objective (what Schaeffer calls "true truth" to distinguish it from relativistic "truth"). Beliefs corresponding with reality are objectively true, while beliefs at variance with reality are objectively false. Truth is what corresponds to the way things are. Falsehood is what does not correspond to objective reality.

THE STARTING POINT IS GOD

God is truth, according to Scripture. He is the final reality, the ultimate ground of all other reality. As the theologian-philosopher might put it, God is a non-contingent Being, meaning He doesn't owe His reality to anything else—so that if everything else were to disappear from existence, God would still exist.

When the Bible speaks of God as true, or as "the Truth," its writers have a different meaning in mind from that of the philosophers. Hebrew thought contains no static concepts. "God is true" for Bible authors means "God comes true." They are claiming that God always brings what He says to pass. The things God says must happen. "Let there be light" spoken by God creates a reality called "light." God's promises given through the prophets must come true in the Baby finally born in a barn. What God *says* is bound to *be*. Thus it is that God is "the Truth."

"I am the . . . Truth," Jesus said of himself in one of the most breathtaking claims ever made by a non-psychotic human being. He did not mean merely that He always *told* the truth, although He certainly spoke more truth in His three years of ministry

192

than anyone who has ever set foot on the planet. What Jesus meant, as shown by careful study of the Gospel of John, is that He is *God coming true*. He is the concrete reality God promised through all the prophets. In Him the God who is Truth comes true. Every one of God's promises takes on concrete reality in the person of Jesus. When we look at Him we are looking at God's Word made concrete reality. So Jesus is "the Truth."

Even as God himself is Truth, as Jesus is the Truth of God come true, God's Word—what God says—*must*, absolutely must, be true and come to pass. His Word never asserts anything contrary to reality because reality must line up with whatever God's Word says.

Although God has spoken often to us, the essence of God's message to man is found in the Judeo-Christian Scriptures. These books are the very words given by God through inspired writers. Therefore what they tell us must be so. They are truth in the se se that they cannot possibly tell us anything contrary to final reality. What they say must either be reality already or must come to pass in the future.

If the biblical record is absolute truth, the Bible is utterly reliable. With it, according to Paul in 2 Timothy 3:16, 17, we can profitably use the Bible to correct our wrong notions about reality. With the Bible as a guide, we can learn to tell ourselves the truth about ultimate reality, truth we could not know in any other way.

TRUTH THROUGH REASON AND THE EVIDENCE OF OUR SENSES

According to the Bible, the God who made the universe also constructed our eyes, ears and other senses. He invented our reasoning brain, too. He designed all these tools specifically to fit His created reality. In other words, He who made the universe also made our reason and our senses to convey truth about the universe to our minds. That is why we can trust observation, experiment, mathematics, and science as guides to truth.

The truth we are discussing includes the sort of everyday truth that is exemplified by the statement, "I am now reading a book." It includes the sort of everyday truth which reports, reliably, to another person, "What you just said hurt my feelings," or, "I love you," or, "It's snowing outside."

One important note: This empirical and rational truth must remain subject to correction by God's revealed Word. This kind of truth gains its validity by God's revelation and therefore cannot sit in judgment on that revelation. When man tries to use his senses and reasoning to judge God's Word, he becomes hopelessly lost in a quagmire of misbelief—a quagmire in which some contemporary theology is stuck. A fascinating book on this subject, *The Suicide of Christian Theology* by John Warwick Montgomery (Bethany House Publishers, 1970), may help you understand in what way theology which enthrones reason has lost the truth.

FIRST, TELL YOURSELF THE TRUTH

Some readers will not yet have come to terms with the untruths they are daily communicating to themselves. God desires "truth in the inward parts" (i.e., He wants you to learn to speak truth to yourself). Moreover, you can become contented and happy only by tasting the freedom truth can bring to your innermost parts. You can discover more about speaking truth to yourself by studying two other books: *Telling Yourself the Truth* and *Why Do I Do What I Don't Want To Do?*—both by Marie Chapian and me (published by Bethany House Publishers).

THE POWER OF TRUTH BETWEEN PEOPLE

This book, also about the power and effectiveness of truth, demonstrates the application of truth in *relationships*. Just as the truth, properly believed and used, has power to create emotional health within the individual, truth can also heal relationships. Truth heals what hurts *between* people as well as what hurts *inside* them.

See how our customs of speech frequently skirt the truth! We say, "I'd love to have you come," when we don't want the other person to come at all. We say, "Your wishes are all that matter to me," and then get angry when the other person tells us honestly what he wants. We hide what we really want and then act cross when others fail to discern our heart's desires. We fear honest refusals, so we agree to things we dislike. We explain to others why we simply *must* do something when the truth is we *want* to do it—and there is no *must* to it. We manipulate others with expressions intended to arouse guilt before God, when our real motive is to control their behavior.

Is it any wonder our relationships often hang by a thread? Or that our attempts at communication don't work? Is it any wonder nobody really knows us? Or that we can't be as close to other human beings as we can to our dogs and cats? The truth can set relationships free, as it can set the individual free. This book is an instruction manual to help us make a beginning. From it we can learn to embed the truth in our everyday utterances. Not harsh truth, but truth spoken in love.

LIVING RESULTS OF TRUTH BETWEEN PEOPLE[1]

I have seen truth heal living relationships between living people. Sometimes I have an opportunity to introduce one party in a troubled relationship to the art of telling the truth in love. Before long, reports of improvement trickle in: "She has noticed the change in the way I behave, and she likes it! What's really amazing is that she's changing too." "I think my husband may want to come in. I told him I had been seeing you and he didn't hit the ceiling. He thought something had happened to make me different. Well, Doctor, I'll tell you something: he's changed too. He doesn't stay in his silent moods for days at a time anymore. And it's been weeks since he lost his temper and swore at me."

At first, these reports astonished me. I chalked them up to coincidence. Why? Because it is a truism in the therapy business that the therapist must have both people in front of him to effect change in a relationship. Marriages are not supposed

---

[1]A very important note about cases cited in this book: Every psychotherapist could create a fascinating book by merely publishing his case records. However, he owes his clients strict confidentiality. Conversations in the consulting room are privileged, and must not be revealed to anyone. For this reason, although the case materials in these are true-to-life, they are composites rather than specific cases. Identifying features have been changed, details have been merged, histories have been blended, with the result that all are beyond recognition.

to be helped much when the therapist works with only one partner.

I therefore always stipulate at the outset that our target for change will be the behavior of the patient. I deliberately avoid shooting for major changes in the behavior of someone who is not present in the sessions. Instead, I concentrate on the patient, aim at altering the patient's behavior by substituting truth-in-love in place of the old, misbelief-based behavior. The patient and I agree at the outset to consider our work successful if he changes in ways which satisfy him. We will never gauge improvement on the basis of whether or not the absent partner changes, but only on positive improvement in the patient.

But experience has proven otherwise. In spite of this careful focus on the patient, reports of change in the absent partner keep coming in. In case after case, not only does my patient report that he is doing better and feeling better, but also that the behavior of the *other* person in the troubled relationship has improved!

The principles taught in this book can improve relationships. I urge you, however, as I urge my clients, to aim strictly at improving your own speech and actions, recognizing that the other person's behavior is his own responsibility, and changing it is God's business. This ends the effort to control that person, and thus relieves you of a great burden. If you focus on bringing your own words and deeds into line with loving truth, you will be gratified with success, whether or not your spouse or friend shapes up according to your wishes.

THE IMPORTANCE OF EFFORT

Reading a book is, for some people, a struggle. They are apt to think, therefore, that reading alone will generate osmotic pressure sufficient to soak change into their tissues. Not so.

This attitude resembles what many people think when they visit a professional counselor. They arrive at their first clinical appointment believing their own effort ends at that point. "Now the doctor will fix me up," they tell themselves as they relax into the deep recliner (which most of my clients choose). Not so. One of the first things a client must learn if he is to get well is

196

that change comes hard. He must work at it. If he doesn't want to work, he will have to anyhow, since I don't know how to help anyone who won't work.

You will often read instructions in this book for changing something. Plan to work hard at following those instructions. Make the effort to keep logs, teach yourself new responses, seek out opportunities, and put the instructions into practice. If you merely read, not much will change. If you read and *work,* putting your new information into practice, you will change the bad habits of a lifetime and success will be yours.

Your goal may seem too modest. Perhaps changing someone else would seem a much more worthy accomplishment to you. It won't work. Focus rather on changing the one person in the world whose behavior you can control: *yourself.*

Work with this book to develop the habit of truthful speech in all your relationships. The payoff for this will be the satisfaction of seeing the change in your dialogue with others. If others change, too, so much the better. And, in my experience, contrary to what I was taught to expect, others do change at times. But even if they don't, *you* can. And there is great satisfaction in knowing that you are acting as God would want you to act.

That is the goal: Conforming to the clear life standard of God's Word. May the Spirit of Truth take you by the hand and guide you over each exciting step on the path toward truthful, loving speech.

William Backus
Forest Lake, Minnesota
Christmas, 1984

CHAPTER ONE

Say What You Want to Say

"You wanna know what I shoulda told him?"

Pauline's face was livid, her fury obvious. She then recited the speech she wished she'd made to the garage foreman. She was sure he had cheated her. But she made the speech to her friend, Judy.

To the foreman she'd muttered only, "Are you sure this is right?" He said he was. She thought otherwise, but she only clamped her lips together as she silently wrote out her check for the repair bill. Her rage infused her acting with real conviction—but it was only acting. Furthermore, if she had told the foreman what she "shoulda," it would have been an angry blast pushing him to retaliate in kind.

But if she had given it more thought, Pauline would have concluded what most of us have decided in our sober moments: Better to speak simple, straightforward truth than to stuff your feelings and say nothing or to let your anger fly.

WHAT'S THE SECRET?

What makes a relationship between people good? A heart hungry for closeness to other human beings? Is it enough just to want closeness?

Is the secret hidden in something mysterious called "personality"? Or can you make a lot of close friends if you just read a great deal, have more information than the *Encyclopedia Britannica*, and spout it off at every opportunity?

199

Do you try to make it by being smarter than everyone else and showing people how well you've succeeded? Do you try to get along better with people by stuffing your anger and always being Mr. Nice Guy? So why do you sometimes feel as though you can't get along with *anybody*?

Does it seem that the more you give in and go along, the harder it is to have solid, positive relationships? Do you find that your explosions only blow right back in your face? Has the whole business of relationships seemed such a mystery you've thrown in the sponge and given up?

How do you break into a group and become a part of it? How do you talk to someone you've never met before when all you want to do is socialize? How do you ask others for what you want? Should you forget it, keep quiet, and hope they'll guess? When others are doing what you don't want them to do, are you stymied because you don't know how to tell them what you feel?

The secret is *truth talk*—telling each other the truth, as the title of this book suggests. And we will pay attention to an important qualification: The truth must be told in love.

TRUTH TALK

Truth talk is what this book is all about. If you will work through these pages with the aim of learning the skills of truth talk, you will earn rich dividends on your investment. You will experience closeness and new freedom in your relationships. One person alone can improve many relationships by mastering the skills and the spiritual depth of truth talk. If two people practice truth talk together, their relationship will achieve remarkable unity. Such relationships reward rather than punish, release rather than bind, and relax rather than stress. Most people have to acquire the skills of truth talk late in life, since these skills usually have not been taught to children. But once learned, truth talk proves its worth.

To get yourself off to a good start, study the fourth chapter of Ephesians. There you will discover the principle underlying this book. Truth spoken in love keeps interactions between people smooth and rewarding. In this chapter Paul describes the Body of Christ. He says Christians, members of that body, are connected to one another by joints. If those joints are arthritic so that contacts between members are abrasive and poorly lubricated, the body itself will creak and falter. When the joints are working smoothly, the body's movements will be effective and efficient. In this brilliant chapter, Paul shows that telling each other the truth is what makes the members relate smoothly. He calls it "speaking the truth in love." Truth is the oil which lubricates the joints in the Body of Christ.

Paul wants his readers to understand the vital importance of truthful and loving speech:

> Therefore, putting away falsehood, let every one speak the truth with his neighbor, for we are members one of another. Be angry but do not sin; do not let the sun go down on your anger, and give no opportunity to the devil. . . . Let no evil talk come out of your mouths, but only such as is good for edifying, as fits the occasion, that it may impart grace to those who hear. . . . Let all bitterness and wrath and anger and clamor and slander be put away from you with all malice, and be kind to one another, tenderhearted, forgiving one another, as God in Christ forgave you. (Eph. 4:25–32, RSV)

CARRIE AND ROGER

When I first saw Carrie, she complained, "My husband and I have nothing between us but trouble." I asked Roger to come in with her, and we three took a good look at some of the patterns in their talk with one another. Their relationship could have been aptly described as a creaky, arthritic joint in the Body of Christ.

Experience has taught me that a relationship in trouble is a relationship in which people aren't telling each other the truth. And what they are telling each other is often not said in love. Thus, the joint between them, unlubricated, grinds and squeaks, and may even bring the relationship to a painful halt. In any kind of relationship, people are often guarded and protective about themselves, fearful of revealing their inner reality to others. Instead of revealing the truth inside their hearts, they stick to safe platitudes about weather and politics. Some people seldom reveal anything of themselves, even after considerable familiarity in a relationship. These same folks rarely guess the reason for the inevitable consequences: When others don't show much liking for them, it is often because others have been given very little to like, very little to know.

In cases such as that of Carrie and Roger, people frequently think they've been telling each other unvarnished truth. As this troubled couple discovered, however, they have not been doing so. They've just been throwing unvarnished barbs. Inhibitions, misdirected training, and unrealistic guilt keep them from saying simply and truthfully what they want, like, don't want, and don't like. They find it hard to admit they are hurt or angry, or to ask one another directly to change something. It's beyond them to give a positive word or to receive a word of correction—or even to receive a compliment!

After a few sessions it became clear that Carrie and Roger had developed patterns of speech which substituted indirect statements for straightforward truth. This damaged their feelings and wounded their relationship. When, together, we observed closely the way they dealt with disagreements, we saw that, instead of simple truth, they used devices such as these:

1. Their dealings with each other were nearly always indirect. They seldom "came right out and said" what they meant.
2. They often used questions rather than statements when statements would have been more truthful—because they were not really seeking information, but rather trying to impart it. Example: "Wouldn't you like to get some counseling for our problems?" is the way Carrie asked Roger to attend counseling sessions with her.
3. They both said "you" when they meant "I." "Do *you* want to go to the movies?" meant, in both of their mouths, "*I* want to go to the movies."
4. They both tried to change each other's plans or actions by generating guilt. Example: "You never ask me what I'd like for dinner and then you expect me to be grateful to you for fixing it!" or, "Can't you, once in a while, consider my feelings?"
5. They regularly resorted to put-downs and labels. Example: "You are just thoughtless—that's all there is to it."
6. They often used language (inappropriately) implying obli-

gation and even moral necessity rather than simple requests. Example: "You should . . ." or, "You ought to . . ." rather than the simple, "I want you to . . ." which would have been true.

7. They almost never expressed heartfelt positive feelings toward one another, seldom gave each other compliments, and rarely expressed appreciation and gratitude. They never thought of going out of their way to perform acts of love for one another.

8. Sometimes they didn't talk at all and communicated only with actions. Carrie would slam doors or bang things around as she worked. Roger would fall silent. The old saying that actions speak louder than words may be so, but they don't speak as accurately!

People routinely substitute these devices for truthful communication in troubled relationships, especially in stressed marriages or between roommates and friends. Some people have never communicated truthfully with their parents or their children. Even so, most people seem to believe firmly they already tell each other the truth. Few realize the extent to which the meanings of their words are left to be guessed at and to which their desires are veiled behind indirection and ambiguity. They live without integrity.

INTEGRITY

In a relationship without integrity, people leave each other to guess what the truth is. They play games with each other, then they rationalize these games by telling themselves, "If he loved me, he would be sensitive to my needs and I wouldn't have to tell him what they are."

If you have a relationship you would like to test for integrity, try a device I sometimes employ in the clinic. You and the other person first list the things you most want from each other. Then make a second list of your guesses as to what the other's list contains. Quite often the lists will be surprisingly different. If they are, the point I am making will be driven home: People don't tell each other their true wants and needs.

203

Roger, for instance, thought Carrie wanted him to make more money and get a promotion. These things didn't appear anywhere on Carrie's list of her desires. Carrie thought Roger would say he wanted her to leave him alone. Instead, Roger revealed his deep desire for Carrie's companionship and closeness.

Most of us know more about ourselves than we allow anyone else to discover. A few succeed in hiding nearly everything from others. According to international law, prisoners of war are required to give only name, rank, and serial number when they are captured. That's about all some of us allow others to know about us. We have had a breakdown of integrity.

Integrity is a word seldom encountered these days, except perhaps among politicians trying to persuade you to vote for them. But it is a big word in the Bible. We need to recover what integrity stands for: "A righteous man who walks in his integrity—blessed are his sons after him!" (Prov. 20:7, RSV).

The word integrity occurs, among other places, in Psalm 7:8: ". . . judge me, O LORD . . . according to the integrity that is in me." There and elsewhere in the Bible, it stands for manifesting in life and words the truth a person knows and possesses in his heart. When he knows the truth about what he is within and then allows that truth to surface, he has integrity.

The word integrity comes from the Latin *integer*, meaning a whole number, not a fraction. The concept behind personal integrity is wholeness. When a person is the same without as within, when what others know about him is the same truth he knows about himself, he has integrity.

When someone knows the truth about himself and tries to hide it from others, he lacks integrity. The person hiding what he really is becomes a fraction, not a whole number. Some people make a habit of hiding themselves from others. They, like prisoners of war, give only what they must give—no more than name, rank, and serial number.

I sometimes discover the level of a person's integrity by administering a psychological test. The MMPI (Minnesota Multiphasic Personality Inventory), my favorite clinical psychological test, has several validity scales designed to reveal to the psychologist when a person taking the test is trying to hide what he truly knows himself to be. A high score on some of these scales may point to lack of integrity. When I interview a client who has scored high on the validity scales, I can witness for myself his reluctance to reveal much of anything about himself. Instead of telling me of his own pain and misery, he will concentrate on describing how others cause him grief and trouble.

Carrie and Roger had the same difficulty with each other. Their interpersonal troubles were caused by things they believed which were actually untrue. These beliefs were destroying their integrity and their marriage.

They had both been raised in similar environments. They had been taught that it is critically important to look good. Their parents had told them repeatedly, "You must always appear before others with your best foot forward," and, "Watch your public image, it's your most important possession." Carrie and Roger had even been told that their Christian witness would be ineffective unless they always appeared positive, happy, and perfectly righteous—even when they felt just the opposite inside.

Their learned, habitual social behaviors robbed them of integrity and turned them into straw people, hollow shells whose dealings with others amounted to "faking it" much of the time. Nobody knew them and they did not know each other. They were duped by a grand *misbelief*:[1]

"I must always appear perfect on the outside, even when I am very different on the inside."

I had to work hard to convince Roger and Carrie that learning the truth about themselves and revealing that truth to others was not contrary to God's will, for they had long believed

---

[1]Misbelief: A belief which is contrary to Christian truth or everyday fact, planted in our minds by the devil, nurtured by our sinful old man, and repeated over and over to ourselves. Misbeliefs lead to neurosis, bad behavior, and misery. Readers unacquainted with the term should consult *Telling Yourself the Truth* by Marie Chapian and William Backus, published by Bethany House Publishers.

that God wanted them to put up a front—they called it "giving a positive witness." This is exactly what God *doesn't* want. Paul wrote that life among Christians should be marked by speaking the truth, not by speaking pleasantries that others may want to hear. He certainly didn't mean that the merely innocuous is all that should come out of our mouths.

"BEING A GOOD SPORT" VS. TELLING THE TRUTH

Roger had been making little "humorous" remarks about Carrie; remarks which hurt. She, however, wanted to appear as a person who "can take a joke" so she didn't tell her husband how unfunny his wisecracks appeared to her. When Carrie broached the subject in their next counseling session, Roger seemed surprised. "I was just trying to have a little fun with you," he explained lamely. As we talked together, however, Roger began to reveal that anger at Carrie lay festering under the surface and had been bubbling up in his "humorous" cracks.

When Roger's resentment was finally exposed, everything made sense. It seems Carrie had been reading a novel that afternoon, while Roger raced against the clock to finish the long list of household chores he had been saving for Saturday. And though it was irritating to be so much busier than Carrie, he tried to be a "good sport" about it all, squelch his anger, and say nothing. For her part, Carrie squelched her negative feelings about his hostile wisecracks. Both had been trying to look perfect, calm, and serene when inside they were hurt and angry. Another misbelief:

> **"It is more important to look good than to speak the truth in love."**

By learning to tell one another the truth, to own up honestly to their negative feelings, they became able—with little or no misery—to resolve such situations. By being willing to show one another something besides pleasantries, they began to avoid long range unpleasantness. Carrie and Roger had to work hard to acquire the new habits of integrity set forth in this book. But as they began to tell each other the truth about themselves, they also began to discover a real relationship growing out of their increasing integrity. And they began to prize and appreciate the power of the truth to deepen love and create closeness.

You can also use the material presented in this book to discover your communication habits, and to determine when and where they depart from the scriptural norm of truth-telling. If you work on changing those miscommunication habits, you can improve your relationships with others in marriage, friendships, and everyday interactions with other human beings— especially fellow Christians. Members of the Body of Christ can actually experience closeness and oneness if they will allow the Spirit of Truth to work truth into their lives and conversations.

Do you sometimes put other considerations ahead of telling others the truth? Below is a checklist of common misbeliefs used by people veiling, hiding, or distorting the truth. You might find some of your own self-talk sentences among them.

CHECKLIST OF REASONS FOR HIDING THE TRUTH

_____ I can't tell Myrtle I don't want to go to the movies with her. It might hurt her feelings.

_____ I can't tell John his interrupting bothers me. He might get offended.

_____ I'll tell Mother we have other plans. We don't, but we can't tell her the truth: we're just too tired to have her visit right now. That would upset her because she wouldn't think the reason is good enough.

_____ I can't tell them I'm a Christian. They'd think that's weird!

_____ I can't tell them I'm busy praying and can't talk to them now. They'd think I'm trying to be super-spiritual or something.

_____ I don't want to date Harold, so I'll tell him I'm going to be out of town. Then I won't make him feel so bad.

_____ I can't tell Nick I put off answering his letter, so I need to make up some reasons for my delay.

_____ I'll say I feel fine because Christians aren't supposed to be as depressed as I am right now.

_____ I can't admit that I'm angry because Christians are al-

207

ways supposed to be in control.

_____ I can't tell Ed I don't like his talking to others about me because he'll come up with something he doesn't like about me—and I can't stand that.

_____ I can't say what I really think to my wife because we'd get into a fight and I want peace at home.

This list, of course, is not exhaustive. You may be able to add other examples of the kind of rationalizing misbelief that truth-veilers use to support their not speaking truth in love.

FOR REVIEW, PRAYER AND DISCUSSION

1. Study Psalm 5 carefully. Note the references to those who speak lies, are deceitful, and have no truth in their mouths. Note how they flatter with their tongues, and pay attention to what is said about the relationship between such people and the Lord.
2. How can learning to tell others the truth result in new freedom in relationships for you?
3. Do you think the skills of truth talk typically have been taught to children? Why do you think this? Do you think these skills should be taught to children?
4. What, according to Ephesians 4, is the place of truth in the Body of Christ?
5. What was the basic cause of the trouble between Carrie and Roger?
6. What are some kinds of things that are hard for people like Carrie and Roger to say?
7. What does "Wouldn't you like to. . . ?" really mean in the mouths of Carrie and Roger?
8. Give an example of a person saying "you" when he means "I."
9. Devise a typical guilt-generating statement which might be used by a husband or wife.
10. Explain what integrity is.
11. Give a misbelief which mars integrity.

CHAPTER TWO

Nothing's Wrong with Saying "I"

Sometime during my formative years I learned that the pronoun "I" should be avoided. I should talk about others, not about myself. And if discourse about myself can't be avoided, I should use circumlocutions instead of the personal pronoun, first person singular, nominative case.

It is especially important, insisted one of my mentors of long ago, to avoid saying "I" in written material such as letters. So I resorted to expressions such as, "The movie, *Thin Ice*, was attended last Saturday afternoon with friends. Bikes were ridden to the theater. It was all much enjoyed." I was careful to write that way, instead of saying, "Last Saturday I went to a movie with my friends. I rode my bike and enjoyed the picture a lot." Somehow people consider it egotistical, vain, self-centered and unchristian to use the pronoun created especially to stand, in the subject of an English sentence, in place of the speaker's name.

Others must have been taught similarly. I have found my clergy friends frequently avoiding "I" by saying "we" instead: "We love you all very much and we are delighted to be back in the pulpit today," or, "We had a fine holiday, but we are glad to be back at our desk again, serving in your midst." What are they trying to do? Use the plural of majesty? I don't think so. It's simply that they have the creepy feeling that using "I" would bring the rejection and judgment of others. They were probably taught that the pronoun "I" is a no-no. This is a misbelief if I ever heard one.

This studied avoidance of a perfectly good word, for which there is no satisfactory substitute, seems to me to be silly. Frequently, however, this habit is knit together with a number of similar devices which serve to conceal the truth in our communication. We might call them devices for miscommunication. They arise out of misbeliefs, sincerely held, no doubt, from childhood; but wrong, nonetheless.

SINCERELY WRONG MISBELIEVING

I have found through hours of conversation with others, much of it dealing with problems which arise from miscommunication, that most people sincerely believe the following untrue notions:

- I must not say what I feel unless it is positive and pleasing to others.
- I must never say "I'm hurt."
- I must never say "I'm angry."
- I must never say "I'm full of doubt."
- I must never say "I don't trust you."
- I must never reveal my sense of inadequacy. Rather, I should hide it from others at all costs.
- If others knew my innermost feelings, they might dislike or reject me, or even punish me in some way for having feelings they don't like or respect.
- I'm the only one who has feelings like these.
- I must not use the word "I" because using that word is self-centered and wrong.
- Revealing myself is self-centered and wrong since people should never talk about themselves.

A CASE OF CHURCH PHOBIA

"Thump-bumpety-bump-bump-bump" went Carla's heart. The accelerated pounding frightened her. And it happened every time she went to church these days. She would sit down hopefully, trying her best to believe that today would be the day she'd be rid of her anxious feelings. But before long, the tension would steal over her, and all the discomfort and fear would return.

Carla felt like walking out. She was afraid of the feelings which came over her when she sat still. But Carla was even more afraid of leaving in the middle of the service. She was terrified that someone else might notice and guess that she was hurting inside. So the tension and anxiety would increase until Carla began to believe she would surely pass out or perhaps even drop dead.

I suggested that she could easily get up and walk out of the service if she chose, then return when she felt better.

"Oh, dear! I couldn't do that! Why, that would be awful!" said Carla. Her face wore an expression of shock.

"Why?" I asked, though I thought I knew what the answer would be.

"Because everyone would know."

"Know what?"

"Know that something is wrong with me—something awful. And that would be more than I could bear."

Carla was convinced she had to keep all other people believing she was calm, serene, adequate, stable, unruffled—in short, perfectly controlled. And not merely most of the time, but at *all* times. And it was this belief in the necessity of non-communication that made her relationships with others frequently tense and anxious.

The point I am making by telling you Carla's story is this: *Many people sincerely believe they must exert great effort to conceal what they really are, rather than reveal themselves to others. Furthermore, they believe that the result of revealing themselves to anyone else will always be disastrous.*

NOT "PIGGING OUT" ON ATTENTION

Nothing in this book should be interpreted to mean that people must talk endlessly about nothing but themselves. It is not a special virtue to focus attention on self. Self-revelation is not an exercise to boost the ego. I am not advocating that the subject of all conversation should be self, nor am I suggesting that self-adulation and self-glorification ought to make a comeback in Christian circles. The sort of conversation exemplified below is *not* what we're after:

I'm the kind of guy when I get my feathers ruffled I don't mince words. So when this cop stopped me, I said, "And what's the problem?"

And he said, "Sir," (he definitely called me "Sir") "you were going over the speed limit."

"Well," I told him, "I was driving at exactly the same speed as the other traffic, so I'll take the matter to court if you try to give me a ticket."

He could see I meant business—when I say something like that it's not an empty threat. I have a lawyer friend who told me, "Tom, any time you need me, just call. I'm great in traffic court, and I do know several people . . ." Anyway, I had this cop completely buffaloed. I knew it when he backed off and just gave me a warning. I don't take any guff from these guys.

We can hear similar boastful, attention-demanding "I's" in nearly any group having an ordinary conversation. The Christian, however, dead to self through the cross of Christ, has put aside such self-centered "pigging out" on attention. He now has a renewed self. He can still enjoy recognition and attention and find them reinforcing (as psychologists would put it), but he doesn't crave them desperately and they are not the aim of his life's activities.

It is no crime to say "I." It can even be valuable and loving to reveal the truth about your thoughts, beliefs, attitudes, opinions, and feelings to others. It is often very courageous and considerate to let someone else discover your innermost thoughts and feelings, and it is distortion (of truth and relationship) to be always on guard lest your true self be seen. It would be hard to find fault with such expressions as these:

"I was greatly helped by the teaching you gave in our Bible study."

"I have to admit that there are times when my anger gets away from me. I think it would help if you would pray with me."

"I didn't like it when you lost your temper the other

day during our discussion."

"I love you."

"I really appreciate what you did for me."

"I seldom enjoy TV, but there was a show on last night that moved me so deeply I'd like to watch it again."

A COUPLE AVOIDING "I"

Let us tune in on a couple in dialogue. In this conversation both people show their fear of direct and truthful communication. Notice how frequently they substitute a question for a straight statement of the truth, and how hard both persons work to avoid saying "I."

Lara: Don't you think you ought to spend some time with the kids? They haven't seen their father for two weeks!

Bill: What's wrong with your eyes? Can't you see me having dinner with them every night? And what did I do Saturday afternoon—*all* afternoon?

Lara: Do you call taking Johnny to the dentist spending time with him? Don't you ever want to play ball with him like other fathers do with their sons?

Bill: What about two nights ago? You didn't see the shape George, next door, was in when he got home, did you? Would you rather have a husband like him? You want me to stop off for a few drinks after work like he does? He's one of those "other fathers" you think are so wonderful!

Lara: Speaking of getting home late, when are you going to start calling me when you work overtime? The other night you. . .

Not surprisingly, this discussion didn't get anywhere. By the time they reached this point, both Lara and Bill had forgotten the issue they were discussing and were busy firing salvos at each other, each trying to win the battle by annihilating the other. This couple's greatest hindrance to progress was, among other things, their studied avoidance of "I."

PRACTICE USING "I"

As people learn not to avoid the personal pronoun, "I," their speech usually becomes more direct and truthful. This chapter has shown that avoiding "I" is occasionally the result of a misbelief that the use of this word is somehow selfish and wrong. In fact, truthful expression about what a person wants and expects from others is often less selfish and more loving than circumlocutions.

Set yourself a goal for increasing the number of "I" statements in your conversation. Begin by noticing what sorts of substitutes you habitually use for "I" sentences. Do you say, "Don't you like detective stories?" when you really mean, "I like detective stories"? Perhaps you say, "You probably think. . ." when you mean, "I think. . ." Below are some more examples. Try changing them. Practice making "I" sentences out of them.

"Don't you think we're going to have a change in the weather?"

"Look at all the work we got done today."

"It would be nice if someone would consider me once in a while."

"That red coat doesn't look very good on you."

"After four years, college was finally completed and a job was found."

"It was fun being with you."

When you locate flaws such as these in your own conversation, practice changing your speech. Record how many simple, direct "I" statements you make in the next three days. Then try to double that number in the following three days. Soon, you will find your speech becoming more direct and truthful. Of course, you will want to guard against glorifying or glamorizing yourself while you are learning to use the word "I" more often. Remember, your purpose is telling the truth. You want to use the word "I" when that is what you really mean and when it is the legitimate, appropriate way to say what you really mean.

FOR REVIEW, PRAYER AND DISCUSSION

1. Why do some people avoid the use of the pronoun "I" whenever possible?
2. Did Jesus avoid this pronoun? See Matthew 3:14; 5:17ff.; Mark 13:30; Luke 21:3; John 17:24 as examples; there are many, many others.
3. Did Jesus avoid expressing his needs and wishes? See the passages listed above.
4. Did Jesus avoid expressing negative feelings? See Matthew 26:38; Mark 3:5; John 11:35.
5. Why do you think Carla (in this chapter) was so afraid to let others know she had a problem with anxiety?
6. Why do we want to learn the unabashed use of the pronoun "I"?
7. In what circumstances would it be most important to use "I" to reveal to another your thoughts and feelings?
8. Can you think of some bad consequences which might follow from not revealing your thoughts and feelings in some circumstances?

CHAPTER THREE

Attacking and Defending vs. Speaking the Truth in Love

Carlo never did keep his second appointment, or make any further effort to continue seeing a psychologist. In a sense, the referral by his physician was virtually certain to fail, since people with Carlo's set of symptoms never believe they need psychological help. With all their might they fight against believing it—because they *want* their illness.

Carlo was seeking abdominal surgery, and with consummate skill he made himself appear to have appendicitis. The attack he staged appeared critical. But his physician's skill was even greater than Carlo's ability as an actor. Noticing scars from previous surgeries, and being unable to find objective evidence of appendicitis, the physician carefully uncovered Carlo's bizarre medical history.

Carlo was diagnosed as having a *chronic factitious disorder* (an imaginary disease). Such a patient, though in perfect health, is often able to lie effectively enough to convince physicians that he is ill. The result is that he spends his entire life either in the hospital or trying to get admitted. And from his point of view, seeing a psychologist would only spell the defeat of his deepest desire—the desire to live out his life as a surgical patient.

Carlo and others with this very rare diagnosis want only to avoid the truth. They want to dodge the truth to such an extent that they are willing to risk all life's opportunities, expose

216

themselves to hazardous surgical procedures and potent medications, and even mutilate their bodies—all in order to avoid the truth that they are healthy.

The disorder is sometimes called *Munchausen's syndrome* after a fabled character in German folklore, Baron Munchausen, the world's greatest liar. Munchausen, like these poor patients, loved to lie so much that he actually avoided the truth whenever he could. Shamming is a way of life for these folks.

Many people need to learn truthful speech for precisely the same reason: Shamming has become a way of life. They have learned to sham with their tongues so well they do it without thinking. They live with relationships horribly contorted by their avoidance of truth, and, like Carlo, think nothing of it. And, like Carlo, they frequently find themselves not wanting to change.

Perhaps reading the previous chapters has already convinced you that many of us need to change the way we talk; that, when compared with the standards of truth set forth in Scripture, our speech appears littered with devices for avoiding truth. While we are working at repentance and change in the particulars already discussed in this book, we can go on to identify a few more common devices most of us use to communicate while bypassing the truth.

DEFEND AND ATTACK AND AVOID THE TRUTH

Let's listen in on Lara and Bill, whom we met before, and note how their habits of defending and attacking destroy all possibility of truthful communication:

Lara: When are you going to fix that dripping faucet? I can't stand it any more.

Bill: Well, you don't give me a spare minute. You know what you made me do yesterday, don't you?

Lara: Made you? You *offered* to take Mother home after dinner. Then you say I *made* you do it. No matter how nicely I ask you to do anything, you find a way to start a fight, don't you?

217

Bill: You call it a fight when all I'm doing is explaining why
I haven't fixed your faucet? You always expect me to do
more than I can handle.
Lara: Expecting too much? Let me tell you something, Bill.
You're not the one to talk! Look at the list of things you
expect me to do—and you never thank me for any of
them.

Once again, the original issue is forgotten. Lara and Bill
are, at this point, so involved in attacking and defending that
the dripping faucet is no longer important or even remembered.
All that counts now is winning. Perhaps the whole process is
Bill's self-rescue tactic. Since he has never learned to say, "I
don't want to fix the faucet now," defending and attacking provide a reliable device by which Bill can escape from performing
requests he doesn't know how to refuse. Truth becomes lost in
the conversations between attacker and defender. People use
attacking and defending to avoid saying what they truly mean,
and/or to avoid hearing what someone else means and wants
them to hear.

For instance, suppose that Marla, fresh from a class on
truthful speech, and eager to try some of her new truth skills,
goes home and says to Herbert, "I want you to know I didn't
like the way you kept interrupting me at the party last night."

Herbert, an inveterate attacker, is quite likely to think that
he has been attacked, and therefore must protect himself. To
preserve his pride and avoid admitting that he may have
thoughtlessly interrupted his wife at the party, he will defend
himself by going on the offensive—and he thinks he hasn't a
moment to lose.

So Marla can expect Herbert to respond like this:

"Well, if you ever got anything straight and gave people
accurate information, I wouldn't have to interrupt you. Last
night I had to clarify nearly everything you said."

How did Marla handle that? Well, if her class had progressed far enough she might have learned how to say the following truth in a loving but firm tone:

"Yes, I do understand that you thought I was inaccurate and
that you needed to clarify things. But I still want you to know
it hurt me to be interrupted. I'd like you to stop doing it."

And if Marla hadn't yet learned the rest of her lesson, she probably would have attacked right back, defending herself in the process:

"You didn't have to clarify *everything*. And while we're on the subject, you really fouled up the facts when you were telling Tom about the mileage you're getting with your new Honda. But I didn't correct you, did I?"

ATTACKING

Look at a few more examples of attack substituted for truth and love:

"I suppose you'll spend the whole day watching TV—again!"

"So you went to *another* luncheon! You do that full time, don't you?"

"This fish is cold—but I suppose I ought to be glad you cooked it at all."

As you can see from these examples, attack is untruthful because it covers up the admission that the attacker wants something. Furthermore, attack is unloving, because it invariably conveys to the other person a negative squelch. Attack says, indirectly and in ways particularly difficult to deal with, "You are bad, evil, no good, and worthless. I am upset and angry with you."

Often people attack each other when they don't know how else to express their desire for change or when they want to avoid the issue the other person is raising. Attackers believe they cannot afford to listen or admit any mistake. They believe that, no matter what, they must stave off the issue of changing their behavior. They seem to believe that to change their ways would harm them.

Herbert, instead of attacking, could, with the aid of the Spirit of God, have chosen to speak truthfully and lovingly: "You know, I did interrupt you frequently and I can understand that it didn't make you feel very good. I'm sorry I hurt your feelings." Such a loving, truthful response would have done Herbert's self-image no damage at all, while the attack he thought would rescue his pride actually led to a verbal battle which left him

219

and Marla glowering at one another and ashamed of themselves.

DEFENDING

Defending is another way of avoiding the truthful word "I" in interpersonal communication—and avoiding other truth issues as well. People commonly perceive themselves as having been attacked, even when they weren't. For instance, in the above example, Herbert thought Marla was attacking him, though she had merely told him of her hurt. So Herbert attacked back. Sometimes, retaliation is a device for personal defense when a person perceives someone else to be attacking him. And even if he doesn't necessarily think he's being attacked, he may put up a defense out of sheer habit or to avoid responding to a request he would rather not honor. Here are some examples:

She: Could we see a movie tonight?
He: I think I take you out plenty!

She: I would really like a car with more horsepower.
He: I didn't pick out this car. You did.

He: I'm so hungry I could eat a horse!
She: I certainly hope you don't expect me to go home and cook after you've made me walk all over town with you.

She: We need a new carpet in the living room. The dogs have practically ruined this one.
He: I didn't pick out those dogs, and nobody asked my opinion about the whole subject. I'm not about to buy a new carpet.

"I couldn't help it."

"You made me do it."

"Well, I wouldn't have done it that way, but I was forced into it by the children."

"What I did was perfectly reasonable, you know."

"I was just doing what you told me to do in the first place."

"Well, the other day, you did something just as bad or worse. Let me tell you about it!"

"If you think I'm bad, what about your brother? I don't think you paid any attention to the way he treated your sister-in-law, but I did! I suppose you think he's perfect!"

Like attacking, defending avoids the truth because it is usually designed to preserve the *status quo,* even at the cost of twisting the truth. The defender thinks, *Rather than work on change, I will put up a good defense for what I am or do already.* Or else, like the attacker, he seeks to preserve his pride by avoiding any admission of guilt or weakness.

Removing defensiveness from speech and replacing it with truth requires work. Truthful speech substitutes understanding and admission of fault where this is appropriate. Truthful speech omits defensive self-whitewashing. Below are some examples of truth substituted for the defenses listed earlier.

"I realize you'd enjoy seeing a movie tonight, and I know you've been in the house all day, but I don't want to go out tonight. Sorry."

"Yes, I know you'd like a more powerful automobile. Perhaps next time we buy a car we can make that one of the more important considerations."

"I'll bet you are hungry after shopping all day. I am too. But I don't want to cook dinner tonight after all this walking. I'd like to get dinner in a restaurant."

"You're right about the condition of the living room carpet— it's taken quite a beating. But I don't want to help pay for a new one. I want that to be your responsibility since you chose the dogs and they've damaged the rug."

PRACTICING TRUTH INSTEAD OF DEFENDING

In order to help you practice making truthful, loving, non-defensive responses, below are some statements—cues—to which an attacker/defender would probably respond with attack or defense. Construct a truthful and loving response for each one. And bear in mind that love does not require you to agree with the other person's notions and whims. It is perfectly all right to disagree and even to refuse his requests. Refusals can be made in truth and love. The cues may not always be models of truthful, loving speech; it is not necessary for others to be truthful and loving in order for you to learn these new skills.

1. You need a haircut.
2. I wish you'd hurry.
3. If you were a good Christian, you wouldn't talk that way.
4. I don't see why you never take me to the movies—like tonight.
5. You sure blew it when you made us move to this city.
6. This sure is a funny way you planned for us to celebrate Christmas.
7. Why on earth did you order tickets for these seats?
8. Why are we taking this route?

GROWING UP ATTACKED

I had a difficult time establishing therapeutic rapport with Becky, age 18. Her feelings seemed to get hurt no matter how carefully I avoided saying anything negative about her. For example, I ended one session without praying for her. I had prayed for her many times in previous sessions, so Becky assumed she had now done something to offend me, that I no longer cared for her, and that our relationship was probably ruined. At other times, Becky would spend entire weeks stewing over some gesture I had made—such as the raising of an eyebrow. To her, these things meant she had displeased me in some way and that I was upset with her for something she had said or done or failed to do.

Becky wanted to stop her treatment sessions, feeling she had done so badly in our relationship that I must be offended, frustrated, and angry with her. Her solution for this problem in her past relationships had been to pull out of them. Now it was crucial that she learn new ways of dealing with others. In my judgment, Becky had to stay in therapy at all costs.

222

Why did Becky think ordinary gestures, facial expressions, or inadvertent omissions meant I was attacking her or that I was irritated by her? We discovered the reason early. She had grown up being attacked.

Becky's poor mother, with so much hurt of her own to deal with, did not realize she was handling her pain by clobbering her daughter. Over the years Becky learned to expect criticism, even to interpret facial expressions and gestures as signifying criticism. Attack was her mother's stock in trade, and Becky learned to believe, unconsciously, that her behavior always irritated others and that they were therefore striking out at her for nearly everything she did.

Becky learned to avoid this pain by leaving a relationship as soon as it became uncomfortable, making excuses to the other person for avoiding the relationship. As a result of her moving away from others, she never confronted them with her feelings that she was being criticized, and never gave them an opportunity to confirm or deny her impressions that she had upset them. Meanwhile, by passively avoiding people who liked her and sought her company, she kept her fear level down, but also eventually alienated others until they did become irritated. When Becky discovered others no longer liked her, she believed her original notions had been confirmed. Thus she had shaped the course of her relationships into a vicious circle.

Sometimes people who have unusual difficulty with relationships have grown up attacked. Having a parent whose criticisms took the form of aggressive attack can create an abiding expectation that, whatever one does, it will result in attack by others and that others are going to attack sooner or later. Such persons may develop an attitude of perpetual defensiveness. Becky would often make a defense response even if she wasn't actually attacked because she always expected others to be on the attack.

DEFENDING WHEN YOU AREN'T ATTACKED

Some readers of this book may be defenders, even when not attacked. If you don't fit the bill, you may live with someone who does—or work under someone who does. Below are some examples. You may find they occur frequently in your speech or in that of someone you know.

George:	Oh, look, there's an oriole in our back yard!
Nina:	I know it's an oriole; you don't have to show off to me.

Cindy:	What movie would you like to see, honey?
Paul:	Why do you always make me pick the show?

Roommate #1:	You seem depressed. Feeling kind of down?
Roommate #2:	I can't help it! Get off my back, will you?

Janet:	Want some more pie, Rita?
Rita:	Yeah, sure, then you'll say I'm too fat!

Nina, Paul, Roommate #2, and Rita all share with Becky two underlying convictions: They believe they are being attacked because it's inevitable that others will try to put them down or show them up. They believe that they are inferior to others and that others will always act in a way to show off their superiority. They expect that any actions or words of others amount to criticism and attack, even when those actions or words appear innocuous. In addition, they believe that they must defend themselves to survive. They invariably tell themselves it is vital to defend.

Their two main misbeliefs are: (1) "I am surely being attacked," and (2) "I must always defend myself."

LEARNING THE TRUTH ABOUT ATTACK AND DEFENSE

If you are a defender, you will have difficulty in relationships because of your long-held belief that others are attacking you. Learn now to tell yourself the truth about attack, as well as about the notion, possibly learned at your mother's knee, that you must always defend yourself. In Becky's case we worked out a plan for change.

After Becky had kept records for a week, logging each instance of defensive speech, as well as each instance of feeling attacked by someone (even if she didn't respond by defending), we studied the incidents she had logged. In none of them did it appear likely that she had actually been attacked; Becky was able to grasp that truth when she examined her log carefully with my help. She could also see that her defensive responses were damaging her relationships. And finally, Becky learned she had been failing to tell herself the truth in these interactions with others. She had thus spoken to others what was not true, and spoken it in fear rather than in love.

After Becky understood her misbeliefs ("I am being attacked" and "I must always defend myself"), we proceeded to stage two of our plan. Now we devised some self-directing self-talk which Becky memorized for use in interactions with others. She was to tell herself the following:

> "Hold it, Becky. You're not being attacked. Scrap that defending response because it's based on lies and misbeliefs! Think a minute and give a response that is both truthful and loving."

In stage three Becky was to instruct herself, using her memorized speech, each time she was tempted to defend herself. She was to log the interactions in which this occurred so we would have a record of her progress.

Improvement was rapid. Becky had initially logged from eight to ten defending responses in each of her first weeks of record-keeping. After applying self-instruction, her first weekly total dropped to two defending responses. The next week, zero. And from then on, as long as we kept records, Becky was logging between zero and two defending responses per week.

Of course, Becky's relationships improved. No longer put off by her defending, other people warmed up to her as they never had before. Becky joyfully discovered trust, closeness, and deep affection. With her heart full of praise to God, Becky read and reread Ephesians 4.

After terminating her sessions, Becky entered college and

shared an apartment with roommates. It soon became evident that one of her roommates was an inveterate attacker.

One night Becky was studying her math assignment with her radio playing softly beside her. Suddenly Jo, the attacker, rose from her chair, stalked over to Becky's radio, and with evident anger and irritation shut it off.

"Do you mind?" said Jo with the sort of inflection that meant, "You really should have known that your radio was disturbing me. You're an insensitive person and you upset me."

"I was flabbergasted!" Becky told me later. "I hadn't been defending for so long, and I'd gotten so accustomed to telling myself that I wasn't being attacked, that at first I couldn't believe I was being attacked. But you'll be pleased with what I did. I told myself there was still no reason for me to defend. And I didn't.

"Instead I said, 'I can understand that my radio was disturbing you. And I don't mind a bit if you'd rather have it turned off. But from now on I would like you to tell me quietly if something I do is disturbing to you.'"

There were other similar confrontations with Jo, but Becky was able to handle most of them without defending. As a result her requests for Jo to stop attacking made an impression. Meanwhile, even on those occasions when Jo chose to attack, Becky was able to react effectively and calmly. The result was an enormous increase in Becky's feelings of adequacy and ability to cope.

KEEP A LOG

Perhaps you want to change your own untruthful speech and the misbeliefs which give rise to untruthful communication with others. You may be an attacker or a defender, or for that matter, you may discover yourself in all of the miscommunication patterns identified in this book! You may not have known before reading this book the reasons for your chronic feelings of loneliness, your persistent sense of being misunderstood and "taken the wrong way."

If you want to change, if you find yourself saying, "I can see patterns of attacking and defending in me and/or in others around me," you will find it necessary to work very hard. So begin with prayer and make a commitment to God.

Then keep a log. Write down each incident in the category of things you have decided to work on. Keep a good record of every single incident for a week. This will give you a baseline measure of how often your untruthful behavior occurs. You'll be able to gather hard evidence of change in case the devil tries to tell you later that all your efforts are fruitless and that you are a hopeless case.

After keeping your log for a week, study it to find patterns of unloving or untruthful communication. Perhaps yours will be a problem of attacking or defending or both. Perhaps you'll discover some other patterns you'd like to change as you work through this book. Note carefully the beliefs which undergird your behavior. And analyze them carefully to determine which ones are misbeliefs.

Next make up a set of self-instructions similar to Becky's and memorize them. They are now yours to use in your self-talk when episodes similar to those on your log occur in the future. You may even want to practice in your imagination. (Suppose that so-and-so has done or said such-and-such. Then give yourself your new self-instructions and invent a calm, truthful, effective response to use in reply.)

Finally, start applying your new patterns in actual relationships. This set of very basic steps can bring about enormous changes in your interpersonal behavior, and lead to positive improvement in relationships. Continue keeping your log so you can tally improvement.

Be sure to pray daily during this learning process. Ask especially that the Spirit of Truth will reveal to you the truth for each situation, as well as the truth you need to express to others. Just as important, pray for the gift of love to keep your truthful behavior focused toward the other person's good.

LIKE CARLO

The attacker or defender is very much like Carlo, the man you met at the beginning of this chapter. His Munchausen's syndrome, though very rarely encountered in medical practice, resembles conditions found much more frequently in daily life. Their habit patterns are like Carlo's in that they distort the truth.

The attacker is hiding the truth behind his attack. The truth he hates to speak out simply and plainly is his request, his wish, his straightforward statement of what he wants or how he feels. Similarly, the defender is too busy covering his supposed fault or weakness. He thus fails to notice or tell the truth about his reaction to the attack—whether real or imagined. Unlike Carlo, however, many who have these engrained habits and others like them are able to recognize what the truth is and to work on change.

Perhaps as you read on, you will discover other patterns of miscommunication which have crept into your repertoire. If you do, you may want to work toward change, toward the goal of this book: that you and other readers will tell each other the truth.

FOR REVIEW, PRAYER AND DISCUSSION

1. What is *chronic factitious disorder* and why does it resemble the miscommunicating speech of many people?
2. Make up three everyday examples of attacking and/or defending speech.
3. What does attack speech cover up? (What makes it untruthful?)
4. Now invent attacking/defending replies to the examples you created in question 2.
5. Finally, invent new and truthful self-instructions and then devise loving and truthful speeches to replace the examples you made up for questions 2 and 4.
6. Why do people sometimes erroneously perceive themselves being attacked?
7. Besides not telling the truth, both attackers and defenders are often trying to avoid having to _____ .
8. List the steps Becky went through to change her speech habits.
9. Would you like to change any of your own speech habits? If so, in prayer make a commitment to work systematically. Now begin by starting to keep your log.

CHAPTER FOUR

Manipulation by Guilt

Which of the following is sometimes—even slightly—true of you?

_____ Occasionally I enjoy giving orders.

_____ I feel good when I can talk someone else into following my example.

_____ Once in a while I like to know that *my* ideas are being carried out.

_____ I like to give advice.

_____ I wish my spouse (or relatives or close friends) would more often consider what I want.

_____ People should listen to me, and if they did, things would go better.

_____ I like to persuade my friends to do the same things I do— buy the same make of automobile, for example.

If you checked any of the items above, or (it happens quite often) if you checked nearly all of them, you will want to develop a better way of telling others what you desire, and at the same time learn to recognize their freedom to decide. You will want to learn to tell others the truth. If you denied all or most of the inventory items, you are probably hiding from yourself the fleshly pride of authority.[1] The flesh loves to run things. Of course, some people are so shy and diffident they never try di-

---

[1]See chapter four of *Why Do I Do What I Don't Want to Do* by William Backus and Marie Chapian, published by Bethany House Publishers, 1984.

rectly to tell others what to do, but even the shy and diffident would *like* to get their way. When they fear making a direct request, they will often resort to indirect methods for getting others to do what they want.

MANIPULATION

"Manipulate: to control or play upon by artful, unfair, or insidious means."[2] According to this Webster's definition manipulation is morally wrong. We are manipulating when we use these techniques to influence others.

Notice this does not mean it's wrong to get others to do something by saying, directly, what you want done. Neither does this mean no one should ever attempt to change others or persuade them to do things he wishes them to do. But manipulation, going beyond merely saying what is wanted, or beyond trying to persuade someone to change, is wrong. The manipulator thinks, *I can't just come right out and say what I want. John would never agree. So I have to figure out a way to make John do what I want him to do without directly stating what I desire.* Manipulation is usually fleshly and sinful because it is an attempt to control others without honesty or proper God-given authority.

Some people who use guilt to manipulate others also use guilt to control themselves, thus manipulating themselves as well. Those who are easily manipulated by others may also, in their self-talk, manipulate themselves. And they may be the more likely to try manipulating others by the same guilt-producing tactics. This chapter will show how telling the truth in love can help those who manipulate by guilt to become more straightforward by telling the truth.

"SHOULDS"

Do you have any friends who, without being asked, tell you their ideas about what you "should" do? Have you ever asked yourself what they really mean by all those "shoulds"? Maybe

---

[2]*Webster's New Collegiate Dictionary*

the following list will refresh your memory.

"You really should take your vacation in January. We do."
"You should get a better stereo; you ought to have one like ours."
"You should whack your kid once in a while. He'd behave better."
"You shouldn't refuse my requests unless you have a good reason."
"You shouldn't go anywhere without me."
"Know what you should do? You should get another car, then you'd have a second car when you need it."

On they go, "shoulding" you about everything.

Do you dislike it when people talk to you that way? Probably so, though you may not know exactly what it is that irritates you until you analyze what's actually happening.

OBLIGATION STATEMENTS

"Should" sentences put people under obligation. They are often used where no real obligation exists. Obligation statements are phrases which, by their structure, make someone feel under compulsion to do or feel something. If he doesn't do what he is obligated to do he feels guilt. When obligation statements are used and there is no actual obligation, he may feel guilty anyway, just because of the way the words affect him. People often use such statements—usually unintentionally—to make others do what they desire. They may thus be using guilt to manipulate people.

Here are more samples of obligation statements:

"You *should* read the editorial page more and the sports page less."
"You *ought* to bring home some flowers."
"You *must* try harder to remember when I ask you to stop at the grocery store."

All of the above sentences imply that the listener owes something, and therefore it is imperative that he does what the speaker wishes.

231

Though the Word of God says, "Owe no man anything, but to love one another" (Rom. 13:8), most people are easy targets for the feelings of guilt and obligation these "should" statements generate. They seem to forget they are freed from the law by the cross of Jesus Christ. This freedom from rules invented by men extends even to "laws" concocted by relatives or friends who are trying to manipulate.

JORDAN

Jordan is a person who was manipulated by the "shoulds" and "oughts" of others. A sitting duck for guilt blasts fired by others, he also shot himself full of guilt with "shoulds."

Jordan's conversations with me were larded with guilt-producing phrases: "I ought to have mowed the lawn on Friday, but I waited until Sunday. I am a lazy procrastinator," or, "I should have repaired the roof three months ago, but I kept letting it go. I don't know what's wrong with me!"

Not too surprisingly, Jordan was complaining of depression, nervousness, worrying, and a kind of psychological paralysis. He just couldn't get going. People with this feeling of leaden sluggishness are often full of obligation misbeliefs.

Soon it became clear that Jordan was simply reiterating the very same phrases his wife was using to control him. He made this easy for her because he was convinced he was an awful person, a "lazy, no good procrastinator." But under the surface, nestled right next to the wad of guilt in his heart, Jordan kept another wad of livid fury.

Jordan was out of touch with his anger which was hidden under guilt, but even though he was hiding it from himself, Jordan was paralyzed with rage. He was frustrated at being manipulated by obligation statements. And he did not know how to claim and live in the freedom he had in Jesus because he never recognized that he was free. So he was powerless to deal with the bondages of obligation with which others held him.

Jordan's log included the following obligation statements:

"You really ought to call your mother today. She hasn't heard from you for two days."

232

"You really must get a haircut—you look terrible."

"You've got to plaster that damaged spot in the bathroom ceiling, and you've got to do it this week."

"You must get that lawn mowed today."

"You should take Nancy to the park."

"Remember what you said to Joe this afternoon? The way you put it, he's probably going to be hurt. You shouldn't have used the words you used."

No one likes to be steered into doing things out of guilt and obligation. Yet people have frequently been trained to believe the notions Jordan harbored. That is why they try to manipulate others with "shoulds." And it is why they control others with the same tactics.

Often this sort of talk works all too well to produce guilt and behavior changes (superficial though they are) in others. This will often arouse anger in the person being manipulated. It also may produce compliance, yes, but somewhere inside himself the recipient will resent the attempt to manipulate him.

THE LEGALISTIC MISBELIEF

Obligation language results in miscommunication because it rises from the *legalistic misbelief*: "My life and most of my behaviors are a matter of obligation; of obeying laws, rules, and norms. There is little room for desires, wishes, and free choices. In fact, my desires are probably very bad, and it is selfish to have wishes."

The Apostle Paul, in his letter to the Galatians, teaches that the exact opposite is the truth: We are not under the law, but under the Spirit. Under the Holy Spirit we receive new desires from God who dwells within us. If we follow these God-generated desires we exhibit behaviors which are the fruit of the Spirit. Our fruit-bearing behavior grows freely out of our new nature as children of God, and does not occur as a result of telling ourselves, "I must, I should, I have to . . ."

AN EXERCISE

Keep a log for several days of all the obligation statements others make to you. Stop when you hear someone tell you, "You

233

ought to, you should, you must . . ." Make a note of what it is you are supposedly obligated to do. Or, if you are a person who uses such statements on yourself and others (and unfortunately, most of us are), keep in your log a record of your own "should" statements. Maybe you will want to record both the obligation statements others make to you and those you make to yourself and others. Unless you make this kind of effort you will have a difficult time changing behaviors which have become second nature to you.

Be sure to notice what you are obligating others or yourself to do. Notice also what others are binding you to do. You will often be startled when you observe the sorts of things we human beings thoughtlessly try to make ourselves or others to do as sacred duty and moral obligation.

One fact will probably surprise you: The examples in your log deal with things which are, most often, matters of liberty. No commands from God compel us to do them.

"SHOULDING" ONE ANOTHER

Often, two people will engage in mutual obligating. Their talk sounds like quotations from a rule book. Here is a sample:

She: Don't you think you should write to my mother and thank her for the cuff links she sent you?

He: I think you should do it—she's your mother. I write my folks—you should write yours.

She: Your parents have never sent me anything. I think they should give us personal gifts as my folks do—not all that junk for the house.

He: You should be glad my mom thinks of the things we need as a couple. Your folks never do. At least my folks realize I'm not made of money.

She: You certainly aren't! I guess my folks think you're earning a decent living so we can afford our own eggbeater. Shouldn't you turn off that TV for a while? It'll ruin your eyes.

He: Now that you mention it, I think we could buy our own

eggbeater if you weren't throwing money away on other things. You should spend less for groceries. Clothes, too. And stop running around so much. And, while we're talking about eyes, how about yours? I'm still paying for your old glasses, and now you want new ones!

TEN[10] COMMANDMENTS

God gave ten commandments. But we human beings have discovered how to multiply them—by using obligation statements inappropriately to put ourselves and others under the law. These statements make our wishes sound like God's commandments, putting others under obligation to perform for us. We create a social climate in which people are chafing under the burden of, not ten commandments made by God for our good, but ten-to-the-tenth-power commandments cooked up by others—with a lot more where those came from.

Study your log. Notice that most of the obligation statements are untrue. That is, there is no actual law on the books of heaven or earth which prescribes the actions urged on you— or those you have urged on others.

Look again at Jordan's log recorded earlier in this chapter. Not one of the ten commandments prescribes the duty of telephoning one's mother at least once every three days. Nor do the law books of government at any level reveal such an obligation. A moment's reflection on the fourth commandment shows no such requirement, since there are many, many ways a person might honor his parents without making daily phone calls. If Jordan's log were truthful, laws would exist somewhere demanding frequent haircuts, plastering, letter writing, lawn mowing, and visits to the park.

And even if such laws existed, obligation would not be the basic motive for Christian behavior. Remember, those who are in Christ have died to the law ("For I through the law died to the law, that I might live to God," Gal. 2:19, RSV). The person alive to God does what his new self loves to do because he desires only what pleases his Lord, not because he constantly thinks about rules, laws, requirements, and obligations. He doesn't lay such things on others, either.

235

Look again at your log of obligation statements. Write out for each one the words which make it untruthful for you, a person who in Christ Jesus is free from the law. Willingly extend the same freedom to others as well.

Incidentally, some of the things you have called "shoulds" might be good ideas for you to consider. They won't often be utterly "off the wall." Only the legalistic tone and the guilt motivation make them harmful and inappropriate.

REVISING OBLIGATION STATEMENTS

When you have finished keeping your log for several days, and reviewed it to note how obligation sentences are usually untrue, try rewriting them. Make them say something true. Replace the shoulds, oughts, and musts with words that do not imply that the behaviors involved are commanded by God.

Your rewritten sentences will sound very different from the old ones. They may resemble these:

"I would really appreciate it if you could fix the ceiling some time this week."

"Nancy has been asking to go to the park and I would like you to take her. Do you think you'd be willing to?"

"I want the lawn to look good for our company tomorrow and I'd like you to mow it today. Will you?"

"I want to call Mom and let her know how much I care about her. It's been a couple of weeks since she's heard from me, and I don't want her to worry."

Notice that "I want you to," "I would like you to," "I want," and "I like" replace the obligation statements. That is because the truth behind most obligation statements is really a wish or desire of the speaker. Obligation statements cloak these desires in the guise of requirements or commandments.

Telling each other the truth means admitting we are merely voicing our wishes, not the eternal will of God, when we make everyday requests of one another. It may also mean translating the obligation statements of others so that we don't let them trap us into a network of guilt.

Below is a table of "should" statements paired with their

236

truthful revisions. Practice revising your "should" statements in the same way.

UNTRUE "SHOULDS"	TRUE "WISHES" AND "WANTS"
1. You should take the time to thank me once in a while for all I do for you.	1. I would really feel good if you were to tell me you appreciate some of the things I do for you.
2. You must get ready now; we just can't be late again.	2. I want to be at this party on time; will you please be ready by a quarter to five?
3. You ought to brush your teeth two or three times a day to keep your breath fresh.	3. I don't like to kiss you when your breath isn't fresh. I wish you would brush your teeth more often. Would you be willing to?
4. You ought to turn off that TV and get outside and rake those leaves up. Randy, next door, finished his lawn this morning!	4. Our lawn is covered with leaves and I don't like the way it looks. I feel embarrassed because our neighbor's lawn is clean and ours isn't. It would really please me if you'd rake them up today. Will you?

Notice how frequently the word "I" is used in the above statements. If you are going to tell others the truth, you will have to admit it when the purpose of your speaking is to gratify a wish or desire of your own. And, despite what you may have been led to believe, there is nothing wrong with having and expressing wishes. There is, however, something wrong with cloaking them in the guise of laws and commandments, as if heavenly authority were always on your side.

There is a need for "should" language. It is perfectly appropriate when it refers to true duty and obligation. If God has commanded something it is usually truthful, straightforward, and loving to say such things as:

237

"You should love your neighbor as yourself."
"You must obey the traffic light."
"You must not steal your neighbor's peaches."
"You ought not get drunk and drive a car."

But notice that these statements are not mere disguises for some friend's wishes. They are true obligations, leveled by God or by God-instituted authority.

FREEDOM FROM MANIPULATION

If you have a problem with easily-aroused guilt, you will want to use this chapter to gain freedom from the bondage of being readily manipulated. Do others "lay a guilt trip" on you rather easily and thereby manipulate you or, failing that, leave you feeling guilty, frustrated, and angry? Claim your freedom in Christ, the freedom expressed in Romans 13:8 ("Owe no man anything, but to love one another"), and tell yourself the truth about the real meaning of most of the obligation statements others direct toward you. Remind yourself repeatedly, "That person is really only expressing his wishes and desires, and I am not obligated to fulfill them!"

Perhaps you are frequently nagged by a person who tries to put you under guilt and obligation with such phrases as, "You know, you really should hang up your own towel and washcloth instead of expecting me to do it for you." If so, you will want to learn to translate the speaker's "shoulds" into more appropriate language and rephrase his request for him. Even if he just acknowledges your way of saying it, communication between you will be improved.

Here is an example of "translating":

Obligator: Don't you think you should rake the lawn this afternoon? We're having company tomorrow, you know.

You: You're saying you'd like me to rake the lawn so you'll feel good about the way our house looks when the guests come tomorrow?

Obligator: Yeah, well—yeah. I would appreciate it.

Once the other person's obligation statement has been translated into an expression of his wishes, you are free to express your wishes in the matter too, and together you can work out a solution if your desires conflict. Such a resolution is hardly possible if one person insists that his desires are tantamount to the law of God.

Remember, in Christ you are free from the law. And so is the other guy! Count on the truth-telling help of the Spirit of God!

In this chapter we have focused on the guilt-producing use of "shoulds, oughts, and musts." There are many other common devices for generating guilt and manipulating by means of guilt, and in future chapters we will learn about them and how to deal with them, as well as how to stop using these tactics.

FOR REVIEW, PRAYER AND DISCUSSION

1. Is it wrong to want, sometimes, to change another person's behavior?
2. What is manipulation?
3. Differentiate between manipulation and legitimate efforts to get another person to change.
4. What three words are often used by manipulators to generate guilt motivation?
5. Why are those words usually not appropriate?
6. Amy, a young college student, thought she was obligated to do anything anyone else wanted her to do. What would you say to that? (See Romans 13:8.)
7. Why do you think Jordan, in this chapter, was complaining of painful feelings?
8. What is the legalistic misbelief?
9. Now give the truth to counter the misbelief in question eight.
10. When are obligation terms appropriate?
11. The truthful rephrasing of most obligation statements begins with "I want you to . . ." or "I would like you to . . ." Make up an obligation statement and then rephrase it in truthful terms, beginning with one of these phrases.
12. What is one suggested way to deal with another person who habitually uses obligation statements instead of statements expressing his wishes (which would be the truth)?

CHAPTER FIVE

Ask and It Shall Be Given You—How to Make Requests

"The situation is so desperate I'm willing to try anything!"

Dawn could hardly pull herself together to tell me what she was weeping about. She had come to the psychologist without believing he could do much; but shaken down to the soles of her feet, she was willing to play a long shot.

"I thought my marriage was solid!" she sobbed, tearing sheet after sheet out of the tissue box and daubing at her tears with long, inaccurate swipes.

Just four days before Dawn's first visit her husband, Trent, had told her he no longer loved her. He was taking extraordinary delight in talking to a woman who worked at the desk next to his. In fact, Trent suspected he might be in love with the other woman. She was, he said, especially warm and understanding in a way he had never before experienced.

Trent's announcement had almost destroyed Dawn. Though there had been no physical affection between Trent and the other woman, his relationship with her seemed closer and more mutually empathetic than his relationship with Dawn had ever been.

A fresh flood of tears and some more blotting provided an opening for me to ask, "What did you say when Trent told you about his feelings?"

"I asked him how he could possibly do such an awful thing and then *tell* me about it." Dawn pulled herself together so she could continue the interview.

"You asked him questions?"

"Of course! I asked him how he could dream of treating me this way. I asked him what I had done to deserve it. I asked him what fault he could find with anything in our marriage."

"Were you satisfied with Trent's answers?"

"What do you mean?"

"Did Trent's answers to your questions help to resolve the problem between you? And did you feel relieved?"

"Of course not! I just felt more angry and upset every time he opened his mouth!"

"Sometimes we ask questions when it would really be more truthful and appropriate to express our own feelings and desires," I replied. "It sounds, Dawn, as if you never even thought of telling Trent how you felt and what you wanted him to do under the circumstances. Instead, you asked questions."

"That's ridiculous! He knows how I feel—or he ought to. If he had any sensitivity whatever, he'd realize how upset all this was bound to make me."

Dawn was becoming irritated. She seemed incredulous that I should even suggest she could do something far more effective in her communication with Trent. She thought it logical to subject her erring husband to a battery of questions.

A HOME WHERE NOBODY MADE REQUESTS

It gradually became clear that Dawn had been raised in a home where conversations typically contained more questions than a quiz show. Sometimes the people in her home conversed without questions. Occasionally they narrated experiences and shared some feelings about life outside the home. But, when it came to their feelings about one another, Dawn's family resorted to questions. And when it came to communicating their own wishes to one another, they scored zero. They used questions and circumlocutions instead. They talked around the subject, hoping others would "get the hint"—or else ask one another for explanations.

So Dawn did what she had learned to do: She communicated indirectly. Rather than tell others her needs, she asked questions and dropped hints.

241

When the first interview had ended I knew what had blocked the way to closeness between Dawn and Trent. I wasn't sure yet how Trent dealt with the truth about his own needs and wants, but it was clear as a sunny day in January that Dawn rarely said what she wanted. Like most of us, she had learned much from the role models she had grown up with—her parents. Because they had always avoided direct communication about their wishes, she too avoided telling others the truth about her desires. She used the tactics of questioning and hinting. Such tactics produced many negative byproducts destructive to Dawn's marriage. Dawn needed to learn to tell the truth about her wishes, to make requests.

I formulated quickly the treatment plan for Dawn. I was to provide her with a new role model, and to teach her to express her wants. Over and over we role-played conversations. Dawn learned not to say things such as, "Why don't you ever tell me you love me?" She learned how to say, instead, "I want you to tell me you love me more often, please."

With effort Dawn changed her behavior. She learned to express her wishes and desires to Trent openly and directly.

Admittedly, there were some discussions between Dawn and me about the appropriateness of all this. I encourage clients to discuss their thoughts, feelings, and wishes for their therapy. Dawn did just that.

Like many other people, Dawn had (erroneously) come to believe it was somehow wrong to say the words, "I want . . . I want you to . . . I don't want . . . I don't want you to . . . I would like . . . I wouldn't like. . . ." To Dawn, such expressions were transparent evidence that the speaker was selfish.

Dawn believed that a truly spiritual person would never give any expression to his own wants, but would, instead, be interested only in the wants, needs and feelings of others. I had to show her that this notion was both unbiblical and unreasonable, a tactic of the enemy to fog human communication and produce trouble. Finally she began to see that this distortion of the meaning of selfishness and self-giving was playing a major role in the deterioration of her relationship with Trent.

Trent was now ready to come in at my request. He expressed interest in working on his marriage when he discovered that the procedure would involve, not long hours of recounting every detail out of the past history of the relationship, but training in how to be close and honest with the woman he had married.

I wasn't surprised to learn that Trent routinely avoided telling Dawn or anyone else what he wanted them to do. After both Trent and Dawn were taught to express their wishes directly and to handle each other's direct expressions, they were given six sessions of training in solving their problems with the truth.

Trent discontinued his conversations with the other woman, preferring to develop closeness with Dawn. Today, their marriage is solid because they learned how to reach one another with the truth.

IS IT WRONG TO SAY, "I WANT"?

A session of family therapy was in progress. The topic, raised by Harry, was family efforts to cope with Beverly's premenstrual syndrome (pms) behavior.

I asked Beverly a few questions about her tolerance for medications which her physician had suggested. Suddenly she burst into tears and shouted, "Why is the problem always me? Why are we talking about me all the time? Why can't we once in a while talk about somebody else? I can't stand this!"

Everyone in the room was startled, including me.

"Beverly," I asked, "do you want us to stop discussing your pms now?"

"I don't see why I'm always made to take the blame for everything!" Beverly shouted through her tears, as she worked up to a real tantrum.

"Just tell us your wishes, Beverly," I said, "and please do it without shouting."

Beverly continued to yell for a while, then finally calmed down and allowed the session to progress. She had made one thing startlingly clear: She found it easier to lose her cool, cry, and shout generalities than simply to say, "I want you to stop talking about my pms for now."

Beverly, like many readers of this book, had been taught it is not nice to say, "I want." She was sure that to directly express her wishes and likes was somehow selfish. As a result, she had

243

developed a habit of getting what she wanted by temper tantrums. Though she was ashamed of them and felt defeated after each one, they enabled her to avoid saying, "I want." Until this key was found, she had prayed and made resolutions to no avail. The tantrums seemed bigger than she was. After she learned to express her wants truthfully, she gained victory over the tantrums.

Those who never say, "I would like you to . . ." or "I want . . ." usually learn some other, more destructive tactics for obtaining fulfillment of their wishes and needs. Temper tantrums, putdowns, hinting, questioning, generating guilt, door slamming, and pouting—all are methods for getting one's way without saying, "I want."

I DON'T WANT TO *MAKE* HIM DO IT

Some people believe that the mere expression of a direct wish to another person "forces" that person to comply. When I first try to teach them to make a direct request they argue, "I don't want him to feel he *has* to do it for me." Of course it would be evil and selfish to force or manipulate another against his will. But does speaking the truth actually involve the use of force? Of course not. No one is forced or compelled by a simple request. We all have as much right to refuse requests as to make them.

NOTE: Later this book will discuss the need most people have to learn to refuse requests, to say no. If a person is free to make his requests known to another, he is also free to turn another down. The person who automatically does whatever another person asks must learn to discriminate. Love and the Holy Spirit are the keys to knowing when the right response is to honor a request and when to say no. But clearly, no one is forced or compelled by a request.

Dawn objected to the idea that she should "come right out and ask" directly for what she wanted. "I thought the desires and wants we have come from the sinful old self and are supposed to be crucified," she argued.

She was partially right, "For you have died, and your life is hid with Christ in God." However, ". . . if any one is in Christ, he is a new creation; the old has passed away, behold, the new has come" (Col. 3:3; 2 Cor. 5:17, RSV). "New" includes new desires. But the enemy has a demonic program for trying to return a believer to his old selfish ways. A Christian certainly has the capacity to be selfish, but he is now free to be unselfish. And the new nature does have desires which can be fulfilled unselfishly.

Many wants and desires are basic needs (e.g., Jesus' thirst at the well in Samaria), or even Spirit-given drives, wishes, and feelings of the new man. Normally, therefore, it is truthful (and loving) for a person to say plainly what he wants from another. By developing discernment a person will be able to hear the Word of God and the Spirit of Truth so he can sift out selfish wants from legitimate desires.

Some people don't speak directly of their wants because they avoid the pronoun "I." (See chapter 2.) They believe it is selfish or in bad taste to speak of themselves. They may even avoid saying "I" to God! But there is a huge difference between using the personal pronoun to express legitimate wishes and loading conversation with "I's" all meant to laud self and give glory to the ego.

If you avoid using the word "I," especially to express your wants and wishes directly, you can set a goal to increase your awareness of your own speech habits and to increase your directness and honesty. Set a week-long goal of deliberately saying to someone, in at least three instances per day, "I want you to . . ." or "I would like you to . . ." or "I don't want . . ." or "I don't like. . . ." In each instance write down what you said, what the other person said in response, and what the result was.

At the end of the week look over the log you have kept and evaluate it in the light of Scripture. You should discover that your truthful speech is less selfish and sinful than the old devices you substituted for truthfulness. You might want to set another goal for subsequent weeks, continuing until the new speech pattern feels natural to you.

THE TROUBLE IS YOU DON'T ASK

The principle of asking directly is well-established in Scripture. Jesus taught, "Ask, and it will be given you; seek, and you will find; knock, and it will be opened to you. For every one who asks receives, and he who seeks finds, and to him who knocks it will be opened" (Luke 11:9, 10).

Paul, like Jesus, advocates direct requests to God. He exhorts the Philippians, "Have no anxiety about anything, but in everything by prayer and supplication with thanksgiving let your requests be made known to God" (Phil. 4:6, RSV).

The letter of James in the New Testament could be used as a textbook for a course in Christian communication. "You do not have, because you do not ask" (James 4:2, RSV), states the case succinctly. Although in this verse James is referring to communication with the Heavenly Father, he is also discussing troubled relationships. And he is saying that some of the troubles in his readers' relationships with God are due to failure to ask directly for things. In the same way that people need to speak openly to God they need to deal openly with one another.

If direct, honest expression enhances a person's relationship with the Holy Creator of heaven and earth, it is bound to enhance his relationships with brothers and sisters in the family of God. So, when someone does not receive from others the consideration, the love, the help, and the cooperation he deems appropriate, it is often the case that "he does not have because he does not ask."

Jesus expressed His wants directly. Consider the following examples:

"[I want you to] follow me and I will make you become fishers of men" (Mark 1:17, RSV).

"I will [I want to]; be clean" (Mark 1:41, RSV).

"If anyone says to you, 'Why are you doing this?' say, 'The Lord has need of [wants] it. . .' " (Mark 11:3, RSV).

"[I want you to] Give me a drink" (John 4:7, RSV).

"Father, I desire [want]; that they also, whom thou hast given me, may be with me where I am. . ." (John 17:24, RSV).

I am not saying that every whim should be expressed to other persons. There are times when it is not appropriate to ask. Sometimes ordinary politeness and good etiquette govern whether or not to ask. For instance, if someone is invited to dinner and his host serves hamburger, it would not be especially cool or appropriate to say, "Pardon me, but if it wouldn't be too much trouble for you, I'd like you to prepare a T-bone steak for me." Neither would it be right to ask another person to do wrong: "I want you to commit larceny with me," or "Let's commit adultery together," are obviously wrong requests.

James and John's mother, Salome, brought a wrong request to Jesus: "I want my boys to be top men (next to you, of course, Lord) when you come into the kingdom. I just want them to be first." Jesus rebuked her and the boys for asking such a thing (but He did not rebuke them for making a direct request), then taught them what true greatness in the Kingdom would mean—sacrifice and service for others, even to the point of death. Greatness is not, as they had thought, holding powerful, honor-laden positions.

WHAT PEOPLE DO INSTEAD OF ASKING

What do people do instead of coming right out and asking for what they want? Some prefer to do just about *anything*. They are so bent on avoiding direct requests, they will simply go without rather than ask. It's rather common to hear words such as these:

> "I'm not going to ask him for it. He should know that it's important to me. If he loved me, he would do it automatically. What an insensitive person he is, not to have noticed! No sir, Doc, I'd rather forget about it than come right out and ask a klutz like him!"

There is a problem with those who say, "I'd rather do without than ask." They most often don't merely do without. They instead become frustrated. Or irritated. When the other person doesn't automatically sense and anticipate their desires they feel aggravated. They may try to hide their feelings, but generally that doesn't work and they resort to indirect measures to get even.

Those measures often consist of *passive-aggressive tactics*. Showing anger and disappointment through procrastination, stubbornness, dawdling, inefficiency, and "forgetfulness" is passive and ineffective. He keeps forgetting to fix her favorite chair. She burns the beans she knows he loves. He forgets to pick up her package at the drug store. She neglects putting enough starch in his shirts. All these are pretty worthless communication devices, yet people use them to tell others they are upset because they did not get what they wanted—but wouldn't ask for.

A common passive-aggressive measure is *crying*. Although genuine tears are a normal emotional outlet, some crying is an indirect expression of bitterness or anger. Crying is a common symptom among those who pride themselves in doing without rather than asking for what they want. The following example demonstrates this.

Dave often finds Nelda weeping softly. Over the years they have developed their routine so that what happens next is as clear to Dave as if they were reading a script. He is to ask what is wrong. The script calls for her to shrug her shoulders and sob, "Nothing!"

With that answer Dave knows what he has suspected: There is trouble. He has done something. *What,* he wonders, *could it be?* He probes again and Nelda runs from the room to throw herself onto her bed. Dave follows her, begging. All he wants to know is what on earth he has done.

After Nelda determines that Dave has suffered almost enough she reveals the reason for her tears. Punctuating her narrative with sobs, Nelda tells how she has noticed from her kitchen window that Lew, across the street, brings home flowers every Friday afternoon. To her the conclusion is inescapable: Lew must genuinely love his wife.

"But—" she shrieks, "as long as we've been married, you've never brought me flowers unless it was some special occasion!" Nelda wants flowers but won't ask because she has persuaded herself that Dave must bring them spontaneously if the flowers are to prove he truly loves her.

Dave soon becomes irritated and a full-scale battle erupts, ruining the weekend for this couple. But even worse, Nelda's substitution of passive-aggression for direct asking becomes more frequent. And unless the process is checked it will result in Dave's developing a wary approach to life. He will walk, uncomfortably, on eggs, around his wife. He will believe that he simply cannot afford the punishment he would receive if he were to be truly honest with her. And she will feel even more closed out and unloved.

Such tactics merely destroy. Men and women who pride themselves on not asking, meanwhile substituting anger and self-deception, need to see clearly that the "anger of man does not work the righteousness of God" (James 1:20, RSV), nor does it lead to improved relationships. Rather the "anger of man," repeatedly and chronically substituted for plain asking, kills human closeness and love.

Some people who would rather "do without" resort to *hinting*. Look at the following examples:

"Don't you think it's a little cold in here?" means "Please close the window."

"What would you like for dinner, hot dogs?" means "I'm hungry for hot dogs and I'd like you to get some for dinner tonight."

"Don't you think your hair is a little long?" means "I'd like for you to get a haircut today."

"Don't you just feel like redecorating the living room with completely new wallpaper and furniture—a fresh color scheme?" means "I want to buy new wallpaper and furniture for the living room. What do you say to that?"

"Not one person at church has ever offered to pray with me!" may mean "I would like for you to pray with me."

A patient was, unavoidably, kept waiting until fifteen minutes after the hour of his appointment. When he was finally ushered into the consulting room, he pointed to his watch before sitting down, a frozen smile on his face, and said, "It's two-fifteen."

"So what?" the therapist replied, hoping the patient would express his feelings and wishes directly.

"It's a quarter after two," the client replied, his face still frozen in a smile which bared his teeth. This man was still hoping that his hinting, his indirect communication, would bring the therapist to apologize for keeping him waiting. He wanted all this to occur without his having to express himself directly. But the therapist wouldn't buy it.

"What of it?" asked the therapist.

Finally, the patient had no choice but to say directly that he was angry and upset because he believed he would not get the time he had paid for.

"You'll get all the time you paid for," the therapist replied. "But you'll get more than that. I want to teach you how to deal with me and others when you want something. If you will learn today how to do that, then start practicing it, you won't feel as helpless, upset and angry as you felt just now. And you will be able to do something effective when you are bothered by the actions of others."

For the remainder of that hour, the therapist modeled and the patient imitated. He learned, among other things, how he could come into the consulting room, sit down, and say, "I want to ask you to give me the fifty minutes I have coming. I notice we are fifteen minutes late getting started, and I don't want to miss out on that much of our time together." He also learned to wear a serious expression rather than a meaningless grin when he wanted to deal with something seriously.

Building on this single episode, the patient began to practice dealing with other people by expressing himself directly. He drew closer to people with whom he worked. His perpetual frustration and resentment toward others diminished. His formerly high blood pressure readings approached normal. He began to spend his hours in bed sleeping instead of tossing and thinking about what he should have said to others or how he could get even with them.

"HE SHOULD DO IT WITHOUT BEING TOLD"

Rather than make direct requests of others, some people tell themselves that others should do the things expected of them without being told. They believe others should automatically perform according to their expectations. They insist that the world should conform to their notions of what ought to be. Thus they seek to impose a burden of legalistic obligation on others just so they won't have to take the trouble to ask directly.

Remember Dawn, whose problem was described at the beginning of this chapter? When I first tried to get her to tell Trent what she wanted, she argued vehemently: "Trent should know, without being told, that a woman needs affection and not just sex. And he should work out little ways to show his love for me without my having to spell them out for him. That spoils it. Other men take their wives out—and not just to prayer meetings either. I don't see why Trent couldn't think of such things himself. He really should!"

Dawn was eloquent on the subject of her belief about what Trent should do if he wanted to be a first-class husband. In a way she was right—it is awfully nice when somebody spontaneously brings gifts, does favors, goes out of his way to show affection, and exerts himself to please. Just because it's nice, however, doesn't make it obligatory. Yet many people exhibit a set of misbeliefs which far exceed this. For instance:

> "Because it's nice when people do things I like, and especially nice if they do them spontaneously, it follows that others must please me, and must do so without being asked."

> "If I have to tell another person what I want, getting it can't be worthwhile."

> "To signify genuine love for me, others should change the way I want them to—but it should not be necessary for me to request the change. If I have to ask, our relationship is clearly awful and the other person obviously doesn't love me."

These statements reflect the Spontaneity Misbelief:

Spontaneity Misbelief:
"I shouldn't have to ask. If I have to ask it ruins everything."

If such beliefs are allowed to flourish and govern behavior

in relationships, they will destroy closeness and prevent genuine progress. Therefore it is important to learn to make requests.

Here are some reasons for learning to make requests:

1. *Making a sincere request is speaking the truth in love.* To ask, "Are you cold?" when you really mean, "I would like you to close the window" is indirect and beside the point. And because, through such communication, others are hurt, relationships are damaged, families are broken, and strife is generated, indirection can be unloving as well as untruthful.

2. *If you want a close relationship, learn to make requests.* No relationship can be close where significant desires are perpetually hidden. Two people may be close in physical distance, but the habit of not making requests erects a barrier to closeness of relationship.

3. *When another person's behavior bothers you, it is important to make requests.* Acting stoic may seem at first to be the Christian way. But a stiff upper lip when you seriously suffer from what someone else is doing may only make you cross and angry in the long run. Jesus spoke up when He was hurt by someone else. At His trial He was struck in the face. He did not quietly accept this, but spoke up, saying, in essence, "Please stop striking me or bring a witness to testify that I deserve punishment. Your behavior is violating my rights and I want it to stop" (John 18:22, 23). (You may think I am taking liberties with the text, but I believe this is the precise meaning of Jesus' words to the guard who struck him, as reported by the evangelist. Apparently there was no further trouble with this guard.)

Sometimes such simple requests are more effective than you think they will be. A professor, known for his sharp, sarcastic lashing out had his college classes frozen with fear. He was known for an acid tongue with which he etched emotional scars on hapless students. One day he began verbally immolating a young woman, right in front of the class. She interrupted with a calm "Please talk to me nicely." What could the professor do? He could not complain that she had been impertinent, and she certainly wasn't weakly inviting more scorn. For the remainder

252

of the quarter he carefully refrained from lambasting the girl who had the courage to make a simple, truthful, dignified request. In fact, the man's demeanor improved toward the entire class.

4. *When you stop construing your requests as obligations you will be more comfortable making requests of others.* A young woman said, "Marge asked me to go to the movies last night. I couldn't think of an excuse, so I had to go." Repeatedly people tell me, "I didn't come right out and ask him because I didn't want to make him feel he had to do it." Aside from our duty to obey God-ordained authorities, we are free to deny or assent to the requests of others. Christian liberty means that we "owe no man any thing" (Rom. 13:8). Love may react to a request with compliance, refusal, or an alternative offer.

LEARNING TO MAKE REQUESTS

Here are the phrases you have to become comfortable with:
"I want."
"I don't want."
"I like."
"I don't like."
"I would like you to."
"I would not like you to."
"I would like."
"I would not like."
"Will you please?"
"Would you be willing to?"
Read the above phrases aloud several times until you become comfortable saying them. Many people have spent a lifetime avoiding such expressions. They need to become desensitized to them with practice.

Now rework the following statements, changing them into sentences which use the word "I" appropriately to express wishes:

Don't you think you should wipe your feet before you step on my clean floor?

253

Why don't you ever take me with you to your church?
Wouldn't you rather see a movie than go to a play?
You always have to make me wait for you or you're
not happy!
Would you like to go for a walk with me?
Can't you quit insulting me?
It sure is cold in here since you opened that window.
You could pass the food to somebody else instead of
just sitting there stuffing your face!

Begin introducing the above phrases into your conversation
by taking the following steps:

Step 1: During the next three days, keep a log of your use of
the direct request phrases in conversations. Don't try
yet to increase their frequency, just note them down
and note when and with whom you use them. If you
should find yourself using any other phrases with iden-
tical meaning, log them too (e.g., "It would please me
very much if you were to . . .").
After three days of careful tracking and logging, total
up the number of occasions on which you used any of
these phrases and divide by three. That will give you
an average daily rate. This is sometimes called a base
rate. If your base rate is three it means you use direct
request phrases three times a day.

Step 2: Determine that over the following three days, you will
increase your base rate. You may decide to increase it
by one or two, or even more. Deliberately create opportunities to use request phrases. Keep careful notes on
when and with whom and with what results you made
your requests.

Step 3: Continue practicing these phrases, gradually training
yourself always to make direct requests. Be sensitive
to your old habits of indirection trying to come back.
Remind yourself of the truth and combat your misbeliefs when they crop up.
Be sure to note changes in your own feelings and in the
improvement in quality of your relationships. Look for
increased freedom and joy, greater closeness to others

254

in the Body of Christ, decreased anger in yourself, less friction and abrasiveness between yourself and others.

You may find it difficult to practice these principles. "I'd rather take a beating than ask," some people say. But by facing your fear and reluctance, and by patient practice, you can learn to ask in truth and love.

SOME EXAMPLES: RIGHT AND WRONG

Here are some examples from conversations in everyday situations. In each one you will find a concrete instance in which requests are made. You may want to use these examples as models for your own program of change.

Example 1: A Secretary Makes a Request. Imagine you are a secretary. You have just squirmed through a staff meeting in which your boss criticized you in front of the entire office staff. The criticism was sarcastic, caustic. You want to do something because this pattern has been occurring frequently. How will you handle your problem?

The *wrong* way to handle the problem:

You: I'll type this letter the best I can. I have had a lot of pressure lately.
Boss: Pressure's part of life. Get that out by noon, will you?
You: If I can.
Boss: I don't know what's wrong with you. Your attitude had better improve.
You: Well, if there were a little more appreciation and a little less criticism in this office—
Boss: If you don't like it here, you can look for another job, you know.
You: I know. Maybe I will.

The *right* way to handle the problem (after making an appointment to talk):

You: I'm having some problems with my feelings about the staff meeting yesterday—I was very embarrassed when

255

you made a point of discussing my typing errors in front of everyone.

Boss: I didn't mean to embarrass you. It's just that so many errors bother me.

You: I know you like letters typed perfectly, and I don't blame you. I'm going to take extra trouble to proofread. But I would like you to tell me privately if you have criticisms. It would help me a lot.

Boss: Sure, I can do that. I guess I wouldn't like to be chewed out in public either. Thanks for talking to me about it.

Example 2: Making a Request of a Teen-ager. Angie, age 15, has been leaving her room a mess. Her mother wants her to keep it clean. Angie has just come down for breakfast before school.

The *wrong* way to handle the problem:

Mom: You're getting up later every day. You have to take time to eat your breakfast. Now you eat every bit of that oatmeal before the bus comes!

Angie: I don't like oatmeal. And I'm in a hurry.

Mom: You're always in a hurry. And that room of yours! What a pig pen! I don't know how you can stand the mess.

Angie: Get off my case, Mom, will you? I cleaned my room Saturday. And anyway, what about Buz? Have you looked at his room lately? Why don't you ever bug him? It's always me you pick on.

Mom: Buz has a paper route—he can't always clean his room.

Angie: You always stick up for him.

Mom: No, I don't!

The *right* way to handle the problem:

Mom: Good morning, Angie!

Angie: Hi.

Mom: I'd like to discuss something with you. It might take about ten minutes. Is this a good time for you?

Angie: No, Mom, it isn't. I have to eat and run. How about after school?

Mom: Fine. Will you be home about four o'clock?

(Later that afternoon they sit together in the kitchen.)

Mom: I want to work out something with you about keeping your room clean. I'm really uncomfortable when your bed isn't made and clothes are lying all over the floor. I'd like you to plan a way to keep it clean.

Angie: I can understand it bugs you when my room is a mess. You want me to make the bed every morning?

Mom: And pick up your clothes. Then once a week, I'd like you to dust and vacuum your room, change the bed, and wash, dry, and put away your sheets. Could you work that out?

Angie: I'd have to get up five minutes earlier. I've been meaning to do that anyway. Sure, Mom, I can give it a try.

GUARD YOUR MOTIVES

The goal of this chapter is learning to make requests, *not getting your way*. Other people may refuse your requests. Often, this is their right. Nothing in this chapter is meant to teach ways of making others do things they don't want to do. The test of success with truth talk is not that other people do what you ask, but that you ask honestly, lovingly and directly. The proof of success is when the Heavenly Father says "Well done!" to you.

We fail to receive what He has for us because we fail to ask. The same is true of our human relationships. We frequently are robbed of richness and closeness because we do not ask. Often people have been taught not to ask, for fear that others are obligated to perform whatever is requested. This is not so. Others omit asking because of a mistaken but long-held belief that asking is selfish and wrong. Many grow up in homes where no one asks directly, and consequently they have poor models from whom to learn. Passive-aggressive tactics are sometimes employed to get others to become aware of your needs, but they come from anger and cause anxiety and resentment, poisoning relationships. We learned how to make requests and how to introduce the habit of direct asking into daily speech.

FOR REVIEW, PRAYER AND DISCUSSION

1. Make up a plausible dialogue between a husband and wife, with each using nothing but questions. What's wrong with this?
2. List several ways in which people communicate indirectly.
3. Give some reasons why people resist learning to express their wants directly to others.
4. What is often the relationship between temper tantrums and failure to make direct requests?
5. Show why requests don't "force" others to comply.
6. Show why requests are not in themselves selfish.
7. Give examples showing that Jesus expressed His wants and needs directly.
8. Give five or six examples of people trying to communicate without making direct requests.
9. What do James and Paul in the New Testament write about the importance of asking?
10. What are passive-aggressive tactics? Give some examples.
11. Give some examples of hinting.
12. What is the spontaneity misbelief?
13. Repeat the most common phrases used in making direct requests.

CHAPTER SIX

Free to Say No

Has something like this ever happened at your front door?

Salesman: I want to ask you a few questions. Do you ever peel and cut vegetables?

You: (Warily) Yes.

Salesman: Then you know how odious it can be, especially with an ordinary kitchen knife. How often do you serve vegetables you prepare yourself? Once a day, at least, I'll bet.

You: Every night—almost—unless we have something like spaghetti.

Salesman: If you're using a knife now I can show you how you can make one very easy change and save enormous amounts of time and money. Are you interested in saving money and time?

You: Well, of course, but—

Salesman: Yes, isn't everybody? If you'll just let me step into your kitchen, I can show you some things that will astound you.

You: Well, all right, come on in.

The salesman demonstrates his gadget and you are impressed.

Salesman: You really can't afford not to own one. Tell you what I'll do: I'll let you have a Vegowhiz for 30% off the regular price—today only, of course. And you can't buy these in any store. It's a great opportunity. I'll just write it all up and show you what it comes to.

259

Let's see, here. Twelve ninety-five. And if you'll give me your check right now I'll leave you two extra blades.

You: Well, I don't know . . .

Salesman: Your time is worth money! Just think how much you are going to save. You just can't afford to turn this down.

You: Well, all right. Let me get my checkbook.

Did you really want the Vegowhiz? Of course not. Nor did you want to spend your time talking to the salesman and watching his demonstration. Your marshmallow-textured sales resistance could have been due in part to your deep reluctance to using the word "no."

Many people hate to refuse anyone requesting anything. They have a fear of telling others no! Their "no-phobia" creates situations in which others take advantage of them and of their inability to refuse. Salesmen have a heyday with them. Unscrupulous doctors may perform unneeded surgeries. Politicians have their votes just for the asking. Clerks can make them buy two bottles of aspirin instead of one, merely by asking, "Two bottles or three?" Wives, husbands, children, friends, and relatives find it easy to manipulate them.

As a result, these "no-phobics" feel abused and frequently bewildered at just how they managed to get themselves into the binds they are in. They get into those binds by agreeing to what someone else has pushed on them, and then wishing, too late, they hadn't been so quick to assent.

CREATIVE EXCUSES

The most creative activity "no-phobics" engage in is inventing excuses. When they can't think of an excuse, they're stuck. Take Jerry, for example. As Jerry left the house he told his wife, "I'm going to a meeting at the church. I don't know exactly what it's for, but Jason invited me and I couldn't think of an excuse—so I had to agree to go." Instead of refusing the other person's request point blank, people like Jerry do their best to fabricate or latch on to one or more seemingly solid barriers to their fulfilling the unwanted proposal. Phrases such as "I can't because. . . ," "We'd love to, but. . . ," and "I would, except that . . ." act as little fences, protecting them from having to issue outright refusals.

Sometimes an excuse can backfire, as in Wanda's situation. Her Aunt Marge asked Wanda to let her visit sometime during August.

"I could visit you for a week or so any time during that month," she assured Wanda.

Wanda didn't mind her aunt's visits, though they did tend to prolong themselves. But Wanda knew her husband Drew would be miserable. So she searched her mind for an excuse.

"We're going camping some time during August and I'm not sure exactly when," Wanda replied with relief. "It depends on when Drew can get off."

"Oh, that's all right," answered Aunt Marge, undaunted. "I'll just keep August open and as soon as you find out when you'll be home, let me know, and I'll just pop in for a nice visit."

"That will be fine, Aunt Marge," said Wanda, trying not to show the helpless anger she felt. Wanda felt powerless. Aunt Marge would visit, despite the fact that her visit was inconvenient for Drew and Wanda. And, it seemed, there was absolutely nothing Wanda could do to control her own schedule.

This episode exemplifies one of the problems created by trying to substitute excuse-making for no-saying. Often, very often, excuses don't work. Persistent people will take another's excuses and work around them. Of course, there are times when a person can't think of an excuse. Since he doesn't want to lie, and his imagination isn't running in high gear, he is stuck. From his vantage point, he can't do a thing about it. Frustration and resentment, all carefully hidden from the other person, taint and damage what might have been a positive, love-filled relationship.

Are you the sort of "no-phobic" who simply must have an excuse, any excuse, if you don't want to grant someone else's request? Do you believe it inexcusably selfish to refuse any request from anyone just because you don't want to grant it, even if it isn't the will of the Lord for you right now? Do you always employ one of the following phrases when you would

261

rather not do something suggested by someone else?
- "I'd love to, but I have a headache."
- "I can't. Mike said he might come over."
- "I have some work I have to do around the house."
- "My wife wants me home."
- "We can't come. My husband doesn't like things like that."
- "I can't get a baby sitter."
- "I have to do homework."

Is it vital that a person give other people reasons why he chooses to refuse their requests? Does he owe others an explanation? No!

An excellent example of this truth is the story told by Jesus of the laborers in the vineyard. The owner of the vineyard paid those who had worked only the last hour of the day the same amount as those who had harvested grapes for almost twelve hours. When the day-long workers complained he replied, "Am I not allowed to do what I choose with what belongs to me?" (Matt. 20:15, RSV). He didn't feel compelled to offer them reasons, to explain and excuse himself. And that, on a divine level, was the point Jesus was making in this parable!

If you have been brought up to believe you *must* make an excuse, that you *owe* others a list of reasons for every choice you make, particularly when you refuse a request, look again at Jesus' words. You are entitled to do what you choose with what belongs to you, so long as your choice is prompted by God's Spirit at work in your spirit. The grape grower in Jesus' parable offered no reasons for his peculiar decision except "I choose." Neither are you obligated to offer other people reasons (or excuses) when you choose to deny their requests.

Of course, you may *want* another person to know the reasons that prompted your decision. If you do, you may give those reasons. But no law of God or man requires you to do so. Instead, you may simply say things such as those below. (If you read over this list and feel butterflies in your stomach as you imagine yourself saying such things, you probably are "no-phobic.")
- "No, that won't work out for me. I'm sorry."
- "I won't be coming to that meeting. Thank you for asking me, though."
- "I don't want to do that. Sorry. Perhaps another time."

262

- "I won't be over next weekend. Please ask me again, will you? I really do want to come."
- "It's not a good time for you to visit. Let me get back to you when it will work out better for us."
- "I don't want to lend out my rototiller. Sorry."
- "I don't want to give to that particular cause. Sorry."
- "I really don't care to go to that restaurant. Could we choose another one?"
- "I can see you are in a difficult bind, but it won't work out for me to baby-sit for you."

WHY WE AVOID SAYING "NO"

Why do people fear and avoid refusing others' requests? I have asked many of my patients why they fear refusing others. Here are some of their answers:

"The other person might feel hurt."
"I might never be asked again."
"She might not like me."
"I might lose his love."
"I might make them angry by not going along with them."
"I feel obligated."
"I feel that I should consent."
"I know I'll feel guilty if I refuse."
"I just have the feeling that I ought to do what they ask."

These notions and feelings are so pervasive, a best-selling book, published in 1975, still attracts readers who identify with its title, *When I Say No, I Feel Guilty.*[1]

The habit of saying yes by compulsion is usually formed early. From the punitive or shaming reactions of parents or authority figures the child quickly learns that no is often, if not always, a "no-no" and that the best way to get along is to agree, whether you want to or not. Adolescents fear ostracism for saying no to their peers, and as a result many do what they don't

[1]Smith, Manuel J., Ph.D , *When I Say No, I Feel Guilty.* New York, Bantam Books, 1975.

really want to do, going along with the crowd to disobey God, parents, and teachers.

The habit of agreeing, of going along with whatever others ask or demand, becomes an iron cage for many. They hate to disappoint others, or see others as authorities to whom they dare not risk saying no. They believe the opposite of Romans 13:8 ("Owe no man any thing, but to love one another"). Their version reads, "You owe everyone who makes a request, because you are under the law and obligated never to refuse anyone anything." This was Vernon's problem. "I feel like such a wimp," Vernon said, wincing as he finally brought himself to get the words out. "I'm nothing but a yes-man. Gene, a guy who works with me, has me wrapped around his finger. I choke up with tension whenever I see him coming."

"Wrapped around his finger?" I asked, prying for an example.

"Yeah—like at the soda machine. He hits me for quarters just about every day. He must owe me fifty bucks by now just for the change I've loaned him."

"You give the money to him?"

"Sure. What else can I do? He follows me when I go to the machine during break. And he always pats his pockets, snaps his fingers, and says he happens to have no change right now and would I lend him a couple of quarters. I give it to him, he thanks me, and tells me he'll pay me back tomorrow. But he hasn't paid me a penny yet. Meanwhile, I'm mad enough to hit him. But mostly I'm mad at me. Why do I let myself get taken like that?"

Vernon had to be convinced it is not always and everywhere wicked to refuse anybody requesting anything. He learned he had a duty to discern and discriminate between those requests God wanted him to fulfill and those not in harmony with God's desires for him and other people. In the instance of Gene, Vernon came to see that God did not want him to encourage and foster Gene's indiscriminate borrowing, in part because it strengthened Gene's sinful disregard for the property of others.

Vernon learned to say no to Gene and to experience his freedom to refuse others in various situations.

"No, Gene," Vernon said next morning at the soda machine.

"I won't be lending you the money for your soda today because you haven't repaid the money I've already loaned you. I'm not going to keep buying your soda for you, and I'd like you to stop asking me for loans."

This wasn't easy to do, and Gene didn't like it very well. But Vernon certainly felt better. His gloom lifted, his depression cleared, and as the knot in his stomach gradually unwound, he began to feel like a person with some backbone.

THE CONSEQUENCES OF NEVER REFUSING

You may be one of those whose pain results from never refusing anyone anything. If you are, it will take special courage for you to recognize it, and take steps to learn to say no. Since refusing is frightening for you, you will try every method to avoid facing the fact that there is no other way than to go through the hard discipline of learning to turn others down.

Do you find, on examination, that your life is burdened with one or more of the following kinds of unwanted situations?

- Engaging in activities you know, in your heart, to be contrary to God's will for you, but feeling you can't control your life.
- Putting up with long and inconvenient visits from friends and relatives.
- Paying for work on your car that you didn't order.
- Talking to salesmen when you really don't want to.
- Spending hours on the phone with people you can't get away from.
- Buying things you can't use.
- Doing favors against your conscience (e.g., "I know you won't mind buying this appliance for me on your employee's discount. Nobody will ever know.")
- Going to bed with people you're not married to because they insist, though you know it's wrong.
- Accepting invitations you'd like to refuse.
- Making up "reasons" for avoiding any of the above because you don't have any other way to get yourself free.

Then you're feeling irritated, frustrated, and guilty much

of the time. Irritated and frustrated because you have lost control of your life (and you aren't giving it to the Lord, either!). Guilty because you are putting up a false front or making phony excuses which are not speaking the truth in love. No wonder you feel as Vernon did—like a wimp! Or a marshmallow! Or a wet noodle! Or a nonentity! You have worked yourself into a pattern of living in which you are always saying to yourself, "You don't count, what you want doesn't matter, you have nothing to say about anything, and your goals, desires, wishes, and preferences aren't worth any more than you are." No wonder you feel as if you have a "poor self-image"! You are dealing it out to yourself.

THE EXAMPLE OF JESUS

Did Jesus invariably say yes to whatever was asked of Him? You might get that impression from certain paintings which depict our Lord as a soft, sweet, effeminate type who wouldn't ever disappoint anyone no matter what He wanted. As Dorothy Sayers put it, they have "pared the claws of the Lion of Judah." But you won't find that sort of Jesus in the Bible. Consider the following sample dialogue (recorded in Luke 12:13, 14, RSV).

Man in crowd: Teacher, bid my brother divide the inheritance
with me.
Jesus: Man, who made me a judge or divider over you?

That is a point blank refusal. And Jesus didn't offer a list of excuses either. He said, in effect, "I won't do it because that's not what I'm here for."

When Peter asked Jesus to stop talking about suffering and dying, Jesus did not say, "Oh, poor Peter. He doesn't understand but his intentions are good. So I'll humor him and go along with him." Instead, He replied, "Get behind me, Satan! For you are not on the side of God, but of men" (Mark 8:33, RSV). When God has set a person on a path toward a particular goal, indiscriminate willingness to be drawn into the plans and designs of others is "not on the side of God, but of men."

Jesus, "leaving you an example, that you should follow in his steps," (1 Pet. 2:21, RSV) was certainly the Lamb of God who laid down His life in humble self-sacrifice for sinners. But He was no weak namby-pamby, no pussy cat, no milquetoast, no spineless jellyfish who lacked the backbone to refuse requests.

Certainly Jesus taught us to say yes to the needy. But He didn't mean for us to go along with everyone about everything as a kind of automatic reflex. We are not to give in just because we haven't learned how to do anything else!

Jesus' ability to say no implies He was very familiar with Proverbs 1. A portion of that chapter enlarges on how the fear of the Lord is the beginning of wisdom. According to this section (vv. 7–19), a very important part of wisdom is knowing when not to consent to the blandishments of others. The notion that a true Christian will never refuse anyone anything is certainly clobbered in these powerful verses!

HOW TO REFUSE TO BE MANIPULATED

We shall call them Jack and Jill. They were a couple who had particular difficulty making and refusing requests. Both of them, in fact, made their requests very indirectly and manipulatively. And both had difficulty refusing without either getting angry or communicating so obliquely that the refusal wasn't clearly understood and accepted. They reported the following dialogue in one of their treatment sessions.

Jill wanted to join a health spa so she could work out with her friends, and firm up and improve her figure. She needed Jack's approval, however, because they would have to take funds from some other budget item to pay her fee. Jack did not want to spend the money. Here is how they handled the problem:

Jill: Honey, I've been thinking. You need some exercise.
(Do I need to point out to you how very manipulative this opening sentence is? Instead of truthfully stating her own request, Jill tries to make Jack want a spa membership for himself, pretending to show concern for him.)

Jack: Huh? What's this all about? I get lots of exercise cutting this two acre lawn every Saturday!

Jill: But don't you think you need to exercise more often?

Three times a week, they say, is a minimum. Besides, I
need some exercise too. So why can't we join the new
health spa?

Jack: Oh, so that's it. You want to spend some more money. Do
you think I'm made of money? I get plenty of exercise
trying to earn money faster than you can spend it!
(Jack now recognizes Jill's manipulation. But his refusal
is equally indirect and manipulative. He aims at Jill's
potential for guilt feelings. The idea is to make her feel
awful for so abusing her hardworking husband.)

Jill: All you ever care about is money. You never listen to me.
You tell me we don't have the money for anything I want
and then you go spend $8,000 we don't have for a boat!
What about me? Don't I ever get anything? All I'm asking for is a membership at the health spa so I can work
out with my friends, and you're too selfish to even listen.
(Jill, too, is an expert at guilt manipulation. She, in effect, accuses her husband of selfish, grasping greed evi-
denced by his unenthusiastic response to her wish to join
the spa.)

Jack: I'm going out! (Slams door as he leaves.)

We worked on changing the way both of them approached
the matter. Jill's request was to be truthful and straightforward. Jack was to refuse with a clear statement of his own
wishes in the matter. In this instance, because he wanted a
close relationship with Jill, he was encouraged to give her reasons for his decision. Here is the way Jack and Jill learned to
work it out.

Jill: Honey, I really want to join the health spa they're building in town. Some of my friends are going to start working out there three times a week, and I'd like to join
them. Firm up some of the flab, you know.

Jack: Want to get the old bod in shape, huh?
(Notice Jack has learned to take time to listen and to
grasp exactly what Jill wants.)

Jill: Yes, I do. And I've been looking for something I can do
with friends. What I'd like you to do is help me figure
out how we can budget the membership fee.

268

Jack: You'd like a little socializing along with your workout and you want us to see if we can work it into our budget.
(Instead of rushing into a refusal, Jack takes pains to let Jill know he is attentive to what she wants and why she wants it. It is possible, too, that Jill will find a way to finance her membership without serious damage to the budget.)

Jill: I'd really appreciate that. When would be a good time for you?

Jack: Could you get the figures together by tomorrow night? Maybe you could come up with some suggestion about how we could afford it. I might join myself if we can work it out.
(Notice Jack's effort to be open to Jill's request rather than to close the issue without hearing her out completely.)

Jill: Sure, Jack. I'll see what I can come up with by tomorrow night.
The next night, after looking at the figures Jill has assembled, Jack finds he doesn't want to spend the $180 membership fee.

Jack: I can see that joining the spa is really important to you. But I don't like the idea of taking the money out of our savings or out of our tithe. You haven't been able to find any other allocation to cut it from, have you?

Jill: Well, no, but we could always increase our savings later.

Jack: That's true, we could. (Agreeing with what is true in Jill's assertion.) But I really don't want to do that. I feel insecure when we start using money we've budgeted for current expenses. So I'm afraid your plan won't work out from my point of view. I just don't want to do it now. How about trying to work it into next year's budget? I've got a raise coming in January, you know.
(Notice that Jack's refusal, when it comes, is clear, straightforward, and truthful. Jack takes the responsibility for it by saying twice, "I don't want to." Many people evade responsibility at this point by ascribing their choice to circumstances, talking as if their decision is forced upon them: "So, you see, there just isn't enough

Telling Each Other the Truth

money for you to join the spa." Jack doesn't do that. And you shouldn't either.)

Jill: Well, I'm disappointed. You know how I hate to wait. But I guess I can hold off for a while. I want the things we spend money for to be agreed on by both of us.

Refusal in an intimate relationship such as that between husband and wife will involve many more self-revealing statements than refusal in a relationship which is not particularly close such as Jerry's in the next example.

Remember Jerry who thought he had to go to a church meeting to which Jason had invited him because he "couldn't think of an excuse"? Jerry eventually learned how to be comfortable saying no without giving reasons or making excuses. Watch him in action below.

Jason: Jerry, what have you got on for Wednesday night?
(You may recognize the manipulative tactic. Jason tries to get Jerry to tell him that the evening is free before he makes his proposal because he believes it will be harder for Jerry to turn him down once he has admitted he has no plans.)

Jerry: What's on your mind, Jason? Do you have something to suggest?

Jason: You don't have any particular committee assignments up at church, do you, Jerry?
(Jason, an old hand at manipulation, now hopes for an admission that Jerry isn't *quite* doing his duty at church. Not holding any assignments at present, Jerry certainly can't turn this one down.)

Jerry: Sounds as if you have something in mind. Tell me about it.
(For the second time, Jerry has asked Jason to make a direct request. Meanwhile he refuses the manipulative bait dangled by his friend.)

Jason: There's a meeting of the new financial planning committee up at church on Wednesday night, and I was thinking it would be a good experience for you to come and see how you like it. Maybe you might be available to be on the committee in the future.

270

Jerry: I won't be available, Jason, and I don't want to serve on a committee right now. Sorry. Thanks for asking me. I do appreciate being considered.

Jason: It really doesn't take that much time. We meet only one evening a month, and you wouldn't have to do anything except attend the meetings—

Jerry: Even though it wouldn't take a lot of time and I would only have to attend meetings, I don't want to do it right now. Thanks, Jason. And have a good meeting!

Jason: Well, you sound as though you mean it. Maybe some other time. Thanks anyway, Jerry.

Jerry is no longer a victim of manipulation. He has learned to say no!

Connie had a desperate case of "no-phobia." The first time I saw her she told me she had been gang-raped by four young men. As we talked it became evident that Connie had known all of them. This twenty-one-year-old woman had had sex by consent with each one of them at various times. When they discovered their "common bond" with Connie, they decided to rape her. Connie's already low evaluation of herself had now sunk to zero. Connie was convinced she was utterly worthless. Almost panicky with her need to have her value affirmed by some man's love, she was distraught because of the inattention of Gil, her current boyfriend. It seemed to her to be a dismal repetition of her previous dating relationships. She believed she would never be able to hold on to a man.

Connie: Gil hasn't called me for a week. I got tired of waiting so I called him and went over to his house. His folks were gone. He wanted to have sex, so we went to bed together. Then he told me I had to get out because his folks were coming home. I think he was lying. I don't think he wants to see me as much anymore.

Backus: What do you think is wrong?

Connie: I don't know. It happens every time. They start out and can't get enough of me. Just when I think something good is going to come of it, they begin to take me for granted. It's like as soon as sex is over they want to get rid of me or something.

271

Backus: What would happen if you didn't have sex with them?

Connie: Didn't have sex? I always go to bed with them. It's like I have to or they'll lose interest. I don't seem to be able to have a guy any other way.

Backus: Do you *want* to have sex with your dates, Connie?

Connie: No, I hate it. I feel guilty too. I'm a Christian and I know it's wrong. But, like I say, the guys all expect it. It's just part of the package.

Backus: Have you ever tested your theory that you have to give in to pressure in order to hang on to a man? Have you ever refused and stuck to it to see what would happen?

Connie: I've never been able to. I always panic and give in.

Backus: Would you be willing to give it a try, just to see what will happen? You know, it's pretty nearly impossible to build a close, long-term relationship around sex alone. God meant sexual unity to be a vital part of a combination of security, commitment, love, and closeness that can occur only in a permanent, exclusive man-woman relationship—that's marriage. To try to make a relationship with sex coming first is almost to guarantee failure.

Connie: I know it's not right to have sex before marriage. And I can see I'm not any closer to having a good relationship with a man. But I just don't seem to know how to say no. I've tried, but I never succeed.

I taught Connie how to handle sexual manipulation with refusal. She was a good student and soon had the tactics down pat. She was an attractive woman and soon she came in announcing that she had been out with a man she'd met at a friend's party. Connie found Greg interesting, but she was afraid he wouldn't call her again since she'd turned down his bid for sex.

Backus: Tell me about it.

Connie: I asked him in for a cup of coffee at the end of the evening. While we were talking he put his arm around me, pulled me toward him, and put his hand on my knee. I thought, *Here it comes. I'd better speak up as I've been meaning to do.*

So I took his hand, gently but firmly, put it back on his own knee, got up and took a seat close to him but opposite him, so I could look him straight in the eye. And then I did it just the way we practiced.

I said, "Greg, I want you to know that I really like you. I had a wonderful time tonight, and I think you're really cool. But I need to tell you right now that I'm not going to bed with you. I'm a Christian, and I believe sex before marriage is wrong. I want you to know that it's not that I don't find you attractive. I do. But I'm going to try to develop a close relationship with someone based on common interests and good communication, not on sex."

He was shocked, I know. He didn't quite know what to say at first, and then he smiled and said he understood, and that at least I'd said it loud and clear. We chatted for a while, I told him again what a great evening I'd had, and he left. I'm so afraid I'll never hear from him again!

Connie did hear from Greg, the very evening after our session. He called and invited her, not to his "pad" to watch TV, but to have dinner with him. Connie was ecstatic.

Notice carefully the important steps involved in Connie's refusal.

1. She physically removed Greg's hand from her body when he began to approach physical intimacy.
2. She moved physically away, but not too far away, suggesting that she was not rejecting Greg, but only the offer of physical intimacy.
3. She looked Greg in the eye as she talked.
4. She affirmed Greg and her interest in him several times, understanding that it would be easy for Greg to feel rejected and hurt by her actions unless she did.
5. She made her refusal clear and firm.
6. She made her interest in a real relationship clear. Greg will know, not only what she doesn't want from him, but what she does want in a relationship with a man. If he, too, is interested in closeness, this will attract him. If not, he might

273

as well look elsewhere for someone who wants nothing but a sexual encounter.

Promiscuity, however, is not the only problem that a "no-phobic" can fall into. Anger is another possible by-product.

One of Tim's difficulties was with the management of anger. He came complaining about a lifelong tendency to procrastinate to the point where he had lost several excellent positions. Examination showed, however, that Tim often got angry and flew off the handle at others. I asked Tim to log all his angry episodes for a while.

As we together combed through his anger diary, several patterns emerged. One of them was an almost invariant pattern of agreeing to requests, even when Tim didn't want to comply. Then Tim would either fail to perform (procrastinate) or become angry, furious beyond reason, at the person he felt was controlling him by requests Tim seemed unable to refuse.

We worked on refusal, training Tim to say no when he didn't want to comply. One chronic source of irritation for Tim was the borrowing habit of his neighbor, Dave. After we had worked on it for a while, Dave came over to borrow Tim's rototiller. This machine was important to Tim. He kept it in top shape, babied it, and used it very carefully. He did not like lending it to Dave every spring, but had done so for the past two years. This time he made up his mind to refuse.

Here is the conversation as Tim reported it, a gleam of triumph in his eye:

Dave: Top o' the mornin' to ya, Timmy Boy. I came over to borrow the little ol' rototiller. Gonna get my garden in early!

Tim: I'm not going to lend out my tiller anymore, Dave. How about a cup of Melanie's excellent coffee?

Dave: Oh, sure, fine. Any cream? Thanks. What's this about not lending your tiller? I've been counting on it. And I'm all ready to till!

Tim: I'm sure you've expected to borrow it again this year, since I've always lent it to you whenever you've needed it. And I'm sure you're all ready to till this morning. But I'm not going to lend it out anymore.

Dave: But, Tim, I don't understand. I've always taken good care of it. I've never hurt it, have I? I'd be responsible for any damage that might accidentally occur.

Tim: You're right, you have taken good care of my tiller and you haven't damaged it. And I believe you'd take responsibility for any damage. But I'm not lending it to anyone anymore.

Dave: How come? What's happened? I've always appreciated how willing you were to lend your things to me. Have I done something? What in the world is going on?

Tim: I know you've appreciated being able to borrow things from me, Dave, and you haven't done a thing to hurt our relationship. It's just that I'm changing some things about me. One of the things I haven't liked about myself is that I agree to things I don't really want to do and then get irritated about it. I'm trying to stop doing that. One thing I've never really wanted to do is lend my rototiller. More coffee?

Dave: No thanks. I have to get going. I guess I can go down to the hardware store and rent a tiller. I'm not sure I understand this, but I'm glad to hear I haven't done anything to upset you. I'd better be going. I want to be sure to get a tiller.

Tim: Dave?

Dave: Yes?

Tim: Let's plan a fishing trip one of these days.

Dave: Okay, sure, Tim. See you later. Thanks for the coffee.

Pay particular attention to the way Tim dealt with Dave's repeated efforts to persuade him to change his decision. Time and time again, Tim (1) acknowledged Dave's points because they were correct and he wanted Dave to know that he had been heard; (2) repeated his decision not to lend his tiller; (3) revealed his motivation to his friend, Dave, even though it meant discussing his dislike for his own past behavior.

Should Tim have refused Dave? Some readers will feel Tim was wrong to refuse to lend his tiller. And there is a question of Christian love here. Would Christian love require a neighbor to lend something whether he wanted to or not?

Perhaps. We discussed that question after the fact because Tim raised it when reporting his success at being able to say no. We agreed that Christians ought to lend to those who are truly in need. Often, however, there is no real need. As the dialogue shows, Dave found it a convenience, but not a necessity, to borrow from his neighbor. He could afford to rent a tiller, but, he informed Tim, he had dismissed the idea in favor of regularly using Tim's machine. There surely are occasions of real need when the Christian will want to lend what he has out of love for his neighbor. We decided that this was not one of them and that Tim had discerned God's way in this particular situation.

Furthermore, Tim's negative, resentful feelings which had already created a problem, were made worse every time he allowed himself to be manipulated by Dave. The destructive influence of Tim's resentment ended when Tim learned to respond to Dave's requests according to the way he felt he needed to rather than with puppet-like compliance. From Tim's point of view their relationship improved to the point where Tim looked forward to their fishing trip.

PRACTICE REFUSING

Try your hand at refusing in the following situations. You may want to write dialogues using principles learned from examples given in this chapter. Or, you may want to role play with someone else, each of you taking turns playing the part of the requester/manipulator and the person refusing the request.

- Your mechanic has telephoned to say that your car, which you brought in for routine service, needs to have the radiator hoses and fan belts replaced. You don't want to do that now.
- You and your spouse have spent Christmas with your parents ever since you were married. Your children are just out of infancy and now you want to establish some home Christmas traditions of your own. You have prayed about it together and it seems right to turn down your mother's invitation to spend Christmas Eve and Christmas morn-

ing with your parents. What you want to do is spend Christmas Eve and Christmas morning at your own home and join your parents for dinner on Christmas Day. Your mother is on the phone inviting you to come over as usual. You want to refuse and to change things. Your mother tries to persuade you to continue to celebrate Christmas her way.

- Your friend wants you to go to the movies, but you want to stay home. You have no special reason except that you don't want to go out this evening. Try to turn your friend down without making excuses.
- Your little boy wants a cookie and you don't want him to have it now.
- Your parents have always dreamed you would be a doctor. You, however, have discovered the excitement of missionary work, and you don't want to study medicine. You are to tell them you won't be fulfilling their lifelong dreams for you.
- You and your friend, spouse, or co-worker are going out for dinner. The other person wants Chinese food. You don't want Chinese food tonight—or any other night, for that matter.

FOR REVIEW, PRAYER AND DISCUSSION

1. Give some reasons why we need to learn to refuse others at times.
2. Why is refusing difficult?
3. What are some of the misbeliefs of those who find refusing difficult?
4. Suggest some times when we should not refuse others.
5. What does Romans 13 say to those who always feel obligated to please everyone else and do what is asked?
6. Give some examples of Jesus refusing requests.
7. Make up a truthful response to someone who wants you to buy something for him using your employee discount privilege. (You are not supposed to use your discount for anyone but yourself.)

CHAPTER SEVEN

Dealing with Critical People[1]

Her psychological test scores were normal. What could she be doing in a clinic for troubled people? I always study test results carefully before my first visit with a new patient, but in a few cases the person seeking help has no clinically significant psychological problems. In the case of Jenny, the problem was a critical spouse.

"I know you could help us if only Carl would come in with me," she began, looking me straight in the eye, "but he refuses to get help. He says he has no problems, and that if there's a problem, it's me."

Jenny was an attractive, slim, neatly dressed woman whose appearance concealed her forty-four years. Her emotions were under control. She did not appear depressed or nervous, and her thought processes were intact.

"What do you want from me?" I asked her. Clearly she did not, like some less well-adjusted persons, expect that I could work some sort of marvelous change in her husband at her request.

"I was hoping you could help me learn how to handle Carl's criticisms. I don't know if it's possible, but I'm getting to the point where I have to try something new. What I've done all these years hasn't worked." Jenny smiled slightly and looked

[1]Much of the material in this chapter is adapted from the excellent book by Manuel Smith, *When I Say No, I Feel Guilty,* published by Bantam Books, 1975.

278

down at her hands, presumably recalling her futile attempts to turn off her husband's put-downs. Our session continued.

Backus: What have you tried so far, Jenny?

Jenny: Well, at first I tried to handle his critical comments by showing him how unreasonable he was acting. You know, he would criticize the food or some other thing I'd done.

Backus: For example?

Jenny: Let me see—well, for example, one of his perennial themes is the way I spend money. This has been a bone of contention for years. When I come home after doing the grocery shopping, if he's home, he will watch me put things in the refrigerator and say, "What'd you buy this for? We don't need it." I explain why I bought whatever it is and why I thought we needed it. But it doesn't help.

Backus: How do you mean that? What happens?

Jenny: Well, he almost never accepts my explanation, but instead he'll argue that we don't need whatever it is, and that I'm spending all his money and driving him to the poor house. I argue my side of it, and we end up angry at each other after nearly every trip to the store.

Backus: So defending your purchases doesn't help?

Jenny: Not a bit. It just makes matters worse. I don't know what to do. Then our prayer group started studying the role of women, and I got the idea that I would just be silent and try to submit. If Carl objected to something, I wouldn't do it. I even took things back to the store if he complained about them.

Backus: Did Carl stop criticizing then?

Jenny: No way! It just got worse. He seemed to get even more critical. He put me down for the way I drove, the way I cleaned the house, even the way I sewed buttons on his shirts. I just felt angrier and angrier until I could hardly look at Carl without screaming. I'm still struggling to keep from arguing with him, but I'm not managing very well.

Backus: What do you mean?

Jenny: I can't keep up the silent act. Every once in a while I
just let loose and tell him off. Then he gets his feelings
hurt and we don't speak to each other for days.

Clearly, Jenny's efforts to be gentle were producing even
more distress and anger than her previous attempts to defend
herself. She wondered how she could forgive her husband at
whom she felt almost perpetual rage.

WHY CRITICISM HURTS

Perhaps you have your own Critical Carl or Correcting Cora.
No one has escaped getting criticized altogether.

Why does it distress us so to be criticized?

Most of us have been taught to please others. Our parents,
for instance, expected us to please them. And what pleasure we
experienced when Mother or Father would say, "You did that
so well! How pleased I am with you!" And we learned very early
to experience inner pain when one or the other parent found
fault: "That was naughty! You shouldn't have done it that way."
Their judgments meant everything. They were so big and so
"always right." The bottom seemed to drop out of our world
when we failed to please them.

Many people seeking psychological healing are still allowing themselves to be wounded by the ongoing criticisms of one
parent or the other. Some have dedicated their lives to the fruitless task of somehow, some time, some way pleasing that critical parent: "How can I make Daddy love me and respect me?
I simply must find a way!" Many 30– and 40–year-olds are
investing their lives in the project of making Mom or Dad thrilled
with them. Not everyone is still trying to please Dad or Mom,
but most people are nevertheless hurt and angered by criticism
today because of habits and beliefs formed long ago.

Those who get hurt make themselves vulnerable to criticism by misbeliefs. They believe they absolutely must please
everyone else all the time. They believe that if anyone else
should become displeased with them, it would be unendurable.
"I've failed—I've totally failed," they wail when others are upset with them. They hurt when they are faulted and get angry

when others intimate that they aren't quite perfect.

For these reasons most people consider it crucial to defend themselves when they are criticized. *I can't let that go by,* they think. So they simply have to prove that the criticism is totally wrong, that they have been sadly misunderstood, that the response they made was correct and reasonable, that the other person is a poor judge who has no right to criticize anyway. So they argue, plead their case, or attack the critic: "I had these solid gold reasons for what I did. And anyway, who are you to say anything? Remember the time you. . . ?" They may also modify their behavior to try to please the critic and avoid criticism in the future.

The residue left after all this is anger, frustration, and strained relationships. Rarely do people handle criticism effectively.

WHO DOESN'T GET CRITICIZED?

Rarely does anyone escape criticism entirely. Inevitably everyone will occasionally be criticized. Here are some examples of common, everyday criticisms:

- "Your clothes look as if you slept in them!"
- "You haven't visited us for weeks and you never call. Your father and I worry about you. You should visit us more."
- "Are we having ham *again*? Can't you think of anything else to serve?"
- "It's good but you could have done a lot better."
- "I don't see why you can't spend less for clothes."
- "People get bored when you talk so much!"
- "It wasn't very nice of you to tell us we had to go to a motel instead of staying at your place."
- "You are a cold, distant person."
- "Your attitude isn't very good."
- "Your tie and socks don't match."
- "Whenever we want you to come over you say you're busy."
- "You're always late for everything."

THE TRUTH ABOUT CRITICISM

Most of us, reading through the above list of common criticisms, would experience an automatic impulse to launch into

281

an elaborate defense speech. We would explain that we *have* visited, and that it hasn't been more than four or five days since we called; that we haven't had ham *that* much; that we've *tried* our best; that our clothes were *just* pressed; that many people *are* interested in what we have to say; that we thought a motel would be *more* comfortable; that we couldn't *help* being late, and so on.

We usually presuppose that the critic is wrong, that we have been terribly misunderstood, and that we will not survive another minute unless we set things right or prove the fault-finder wrong. None of those common beliefs is true. Strange as it may seem, most criticism is correct. Not always, but often. Not entirely correct, but correct in a large measure. Occasionally, of course, the critic errs totally.

But much as it may startle you to learn it, the critic is ordinarily at least 90% right. Perhaps you *are* often late, unavoidable as this may be from your point of view. Maybe you *have* excused yourself several times when your friends wanted to come and visit you. You never did win any prizes for matching colors, so it's possible that your tie and socks really *don't* go well together. If you try, you can perhaps see some truth in the criticisms leveled at you.

Not only is criticism frequently correct, it may even be good for us. I didn't say it would *feel* good. But what doesn't feel good may still *be* good. God can use criticism, even painful, unfair criticism, to call our attention to need for change. Since He is at work through Christ Jesus to separate us from our sins and make us holy, we must not overlook the means He may choose to accomplish His work in us. Sometimes the means may be painful criticism.

Perhaps God desires also to teach something to the critic, particularly if the person habitually indulges in criticizing others. God's Word has some uncomplimentary descriptions of such people. One of the more humorous passages in Scripture compares them to the annoying "drip-drip" of water through a leaky roof! God does not want us to reinforce and reward these critical souls by giving them attention and a sense of importance when they carp. That, however, is the likely effect of defending ourselves or arguing when they criticize.

282

HOW TO RESPOND TO CRITICISM

Look in on another session with Jenny, who decided to work for a few sessions on changing her responses to Carl's critical comments. We began like this.

Backus: Jenny, you have learned that Carl's criticisms of you aren't totally false, however much they may irritate you—right?

Jenny: I don't like it but I have to admit it's often true. Carl seems to be able to swoop down on any fault or weakness I exhibit—and they really are faults and weaknesses. And even when he criticizes my actions they're always things I've really done. He doesn't just make them up.

Backus: You've also seen that defending yourself and arguing probably reinforces Carl's critical behavior.

Jenny: Well, they certainly haven't stopped it!

Backus: Are you willing to try a very different response?

Jenny: Yes, anything. What do you have in mind?

Backus: Agree with Carl.

Jenny: Agree? With the criticisms? But why? That seems like just what Carl wants.

Backus: I don't think so. I think he wants you to argue and defend. That, at least, is what happens. And he keeps coming back for more. Let's try it out. Let's pretend you are Carl and I am Jenny. You criticize me. I'll show you what I want you to do from now on. Are you willing to see for yourself how it might go?

Jenny: Sure. But what do I do? Criticize you just as if I'm Carl?

Backus: Go ahead. You be Carl now. Try to answer me as you think he would answer you in a situation such as the one we're playing.

Jenny: OK. (Playing Carl's role) Don't tell me you spent the day doing nothing but writing letters! This living room is a mess!

Backus: (Playing Jenny) You're right, the living room *is* a mess. And I *did* spend quite a bit of time writing letters.

Jenny: (Still playing Carl) You should spend more time keep-

283

Backus: (As Jenny) No question about it. The house could use more of my attention. And I could write letters while we're watching TV in the evening.

ing the house neat and write your letters while we're watching TV or something.

Jenny: (Pauses, stumped) I just don't know what Carl would say if I did that. I've never done anything but argue and defend myself before so we'd be in a royal battle by this time. He'd probably respond with something like, "Well, why don't you then?"

Backus: Then you say, "That's an idea with merit. I really will consider it." In other words, you keep right on being as agreeable as you truthfully can.

Jenny: I'll try it. I really will. I can't wait to see what will happen.

Backus: Will you please keep a diary of your interactions with Carl when he criticizes you? I want you to write out as precisely as you can what each of you says and how it turns out so we can work on refinements.

Jenny: Yes, I will. You want me to write, verbatim, what each of us says when Carl criticizes.

TRUTHFUL AGREEMENT

Before looking at Jenny's diary, please notice how truthful agreement can be employed to handle criticism. The critic, from long practice, expects a response which makes clear you have been affected emotionally by his criticism. When you defend yourself or argue, you underscore that the criticism is significant to you and that he has succeeded in getting your total attention. This provides the sort of unhealthy reassurance of his importance and significance the critic is seeking.

When you assure the critic that he is right, you signal at the same time that his criticism has not hurt or surprised you. He has not shot you down. Instead, you surprise him and give him nothing to continue arguing about. This has the effect of removing the reinforcement from willy-nilly criticism, and you can thus expect its frequency to drop.

Especially important is the truthfulness of the criticism.

You probably are concerned with telling others the truth, yet often, when criticized, you try to deny or combat the criticism, true or not. You consider it important not to let any criticism stick to your Teflon-coated self; so you deny even truthful criticisms, or, failing that, supply a supposedly good reason for acting as you did.

Now, instead of arguing, begin agreeing if the criticism is truthful. Of course, if the criticism is entirely false (and a few, a very few, are), you cannot agree with it. Nonetheless, you can find alternatives to argument. For example, if someone levels a critique containing no truth at all, you can say something like, "I can understand why you might think that is the case," or, "Yes, I know how important that is to you." You can, in other words, substitute understanding for argument.

Perhaps the criticism is only partly true. The critic, for example, says, "You are always late!" You know, for a fact, that you are often right on time, but you are also a few minutes late on many occasions. So instead of saying, "No, I'm not always late," you say might say, "It's true. I am often behind schedule, and I know it irritates you to have to wait." You thus combine partial agreement with understanding.

ADDING TO CRITICISM

If you really want to stop the critic in his tracks, *add your own self-criticism to his,* and therefore take whatever wind is left out of the critic's sails. Surprisingly, it can make you feel good about the process of criticism. But more than all that, it will cause critical people to decrease the frequency with which they criticize you and will lead to more constructive ways of dealing with disagreements.

Suppose someone finds fault with you for talking too much at a party. You can add to the criticism yourself by saying, "I did talk quite a bit, didn't I? (Agreeing.) Not only that, but I probably told everybody more than they wanted to know about cars! (Adding to criticism.)"

Imagine someone tells you the meat you are serving for dinner is overcooked. You say, "It is quite well-done, for sure. (Agreeing.) It's not very tender either. (Adding to criticism.)"

285

Someone tells you your lawn needs mowing. You say, "It certainly is long. (Agreeing.) And what's more, the hedge needs trimming too. (Adding to criticism.)"

Remember that adding to criticism is not for the purpose of lowering yourself, but to avoid argument and not allowing the critic the satisfaction of making you defensive. And, of course, you must never add untrue criticism. Your goal must always be truth.

ASKING FOR MORE

One other truth-seeking tactic: When you have agreed with the critic and added to the criticism, *ask for more*. Try, "Was there anything else about my behavior at the party that wasn't quite the way it ought to be?" or, "What else can you tell me about this dinner that isn't up to par?" or, "What other things should be improved in my front yard?"

You may be afraid to try all these techniques for fear you'll look more vulnerable than ever. But once you do these things you'll likely discover, as Jenny did, that you have taken the rewards out of criticizing for people who are habitually on your back with faultfinding and carping. More than that, you will discover a new freedom from the devastating effects of criticism. Knowing how to handle it, you will find yourself less fearful and defensive about the critical remarks of others.

A SPECIAL CASE

One kind of criticism deserves special treatment here. Occasionally another person will tell you of some flaw in your personality. He is generally (though not always) a well-meaning individual who is not very clear about what he means. So he phrases his critique in terms so vague you have no idea what he is talking about:

"Your attitude isn't very good."
"You seemed hostile."
"You don't have a caring spirit."
"It seems as though you want to hurt me."
"I was offended by your thoughtless remarks."

All these have in common a lack of any concrete material.
Not a single actual event is cited, and there are no quotations.
If you are like me, you are left guessing, puzzling, and wondering about what in the world you have done to cause that
person to say such things.

But it rarely stops your reflexive defensiveness from leaping
up like a startled watchdog to growl, "Well, I certainly didn't
mean to offend you!" or, "I think I'm as caring as you are!" or,
"You're too sensitive. You think everybody's trying to hurt you!"
or, "Aw, you're always getting offended at *something!*"

Such responses are untruthful and unloving. Furthermore
they are about as effective in stopping criticism as gasoline is
in putting out fires. Your defensiveness only convinces the critic
that he was absolutely right in his negative judgments about
you. These responses give an answer before one has listened to
the details of the critique! Of this penchant for quick retorts,
the Word of God says, "If one gives answer before he hears, it
is his folly and shame" (Prov. 18:13).

The most effective possible response to a vague, judgmental
generalization is a question such as, "What is there about my
behavior that makes you say my attitude isn't good?" or, "What
did I actually do that seemed hostile to you?" or, "What actions
of mine made you feel I don't care about you?" or, "What did I
say or do that made you believe I want to hurt you?" or, "Can
you tell me what I said that offended you?"

Once you have obtained a concrete response, do not argue
and defend. Instead, agree as much as you can. If you've been
criticized for speaking harshly, you might respond with, "I guess
that does sound a little hostile, now that you say it back to me,"
or, "I can understand why that might sound to you as though I
don't care about you," or, "I can see why that might make you
think I wanted to hurt you."

Then ask for more: "Is there anything else I did that hurt
you?" or, "What else did I do to make you feel uncared for?"
And so forth.

After hearing all that the other person has to say, try asking
him if he would like to hear how you felt at the time, how your
behavior appeared to you, or what you hoped your actions would
convey: "I can really understand and appreciate how my actions

287

upset you. Would you like to hear what I was actually feeling at the time and what I was hoping my actions would mean to you?"

You can then give him your perspective. Rarely do people fail to reach a new level of understanding when personal criticisms are handled in this way.

JENNY DEALS WITH CRITICISM

Jenny's next appointment was quite eventful. She had done her homework very carefully, so her diary contained an explicit account of each interaction with Carl and his criticisms. When I asked her how the week went, her smile told me she had already put some of her learning into practice.

Especially interesting was the change in frequency of Carl's critical comments. The first day Jenny logged seven! Over the week Carl's criticisms diminished notably. On the day before our appointment, though it was a Sunday and normally a day punctuated by Carl's faultfinding, Jenny had nothing to log into her diary! Evidently, Carl had learned as fast as Jenny. I cautioned her, however, that Carl's transformation might not be permanent. Old habits tend to reassert themselves. She could expect critical comments occasionally, at least for a time. Therefore it would be vital for Jenny to practice and polish her newly-acquired skills so as to have them ready when needed.

Jenny's diary showed how successfully she had employed truthful, loving, nondefensive responses to criticism: agreeing with the criticism, adding to the criticism, and asking for more. Here are some examples from her diary.

Thursday night, when Carl tasted his coffee at dinner, the expression on his face told me what was coming. Here is our conversation as accurately as I can recall it:

Carl: What did you do to this coffee? Do you stay up nights trying to figure out how to ruin coffee? It's weak enough to die of exhaustion!

Jenny: Yes, it is weaker than we like it. [Agreeing!] Not only that, it looks pale. [Adding to the criticism.] I don't like it much either.

Carl:	Uh-huh, well, I guess it isn't easy to get everything right all the time.
Jenny:	Would you like me to throw this potful out and try again?
Carl:	No, I guess not—unless you'd rather have some stronger coffee. I'll just put a little instant powder in mine—that oughta do it.

Saturday noon I saw an unusual bird at our feeding station outside the kitchen window. I called to Carl who was in the living room reading the paper:

Jenny:	Look, honey, there's a new bird at the feeding station. I think it's a chickadee. Come and look!
Carl:	What's wrong with you? That's a wren. Don't you know the first thing about birds yet? We've had that feeder for three years!
Jenny:	You're right. I don't know how to identify birds. Except for blue jays and robins I'm pretty much stuck.
Carl:	Maybe you'd like to use my bird book. If you want it I could bring it home. I think I have it at the office now.
Jenny:	Thanks. Maybe I could use it to identify some of the birds using our feeder. That would be fun.

One of the most dreadful of all occasions is the day each month when Carl reviews our financial situation. We usually get into a hassle that can last two days. This time, it went very differently.

Carl:	(Looking through the cancelled checks) What's this check to Gregory's for $139.95 about?
Jenny:	You already know about that. It's for the new dress. Remember?
Carl:	Oh. You didn't tell me it was going to cost a fortune. Of course, I don't think you care. You don't care how much overtime I have to put in or how hard I work, do you? You never even consider that I'd like to save up enough money to retire some day, do you?
Jenny:	That's true, I don't give a great deal of thought to your retirement and the difficulty of your job.

289

Carl: Well, you should think about it. I have some rights, too, you know.

Jenny: Yes, you do have rights. And you might have a point saying that I should pay more attention to your job difficulties and plans for the future.

Carl: If you did, you wouldn't throw money around as if it were free!

Jenny: That's true, I wouldn't.

Carl: Then you admit you are careless with our money!

Jenny: You're right. I am sometimes careless with our money. I'm sometimes guilty of leaving lights on or running the car engine needlessly, too. Is there anything else you've noticed me being wasteful with?

Carl: No, nothing else I can think of. I guess we both have our faults. I don't want you to feel too bad about the dress. After all, you do look good in it.

I couldn't believe it was my husband talking. He was almost ready to urge me to go and buy another dress! From this point on, his criticisms really tapered off.

Jenny's diary included some more interactions with Carl. She had not been assigned the duty of logging criticisms of others, but she was so interested in what was taking place that she included a few interactions with other critical persons in her life. In each case Jenny applied the techniques of *agreeing with the criticism, adding to the criticism, and asking for more*. Below is an example from these interactions.

Jenny had bought some slacks, worn them once, and found that they failed to hold their color when washed. She brought the faded slacks back to the person from whom she had bought them. The interaction went like this:

THE CRITICAL SALESPERSON

Jenny: I'd like to have a refund for these slacks. As you can see, they faded when I washed them.

Salesperson: Looks as if you washed them in hot water. You are supposed to wash this type of material in cold water only.

Jenny: That's true, I did wash them in hot water; and it
                may be true that cold water would work better. I
                would like to have my money refunded, however,
                because the slacks are useless to me. And there
                is no tag attached to them saying they should be
                washed in cold water only.

Salesperson: You can't expect to get your money back, espe-
                cially when you are responsible for damaging the
                slacks. It seems to me you should have known
                that this material will not stand up to hot water.
                The best I can do is give you a new pair.

Jenny: You're right, I damaged the slacks by washing
                them in hot water when I should have used cold
                water. And I probably should have known that
                cold water is best for this type of material. But I
                didn't, and I would like to get my money back. I
                don't want clothes that need to be washed in cold
                water only.

Salesperson: Ma'am you're really being unreasonable. We can't
                give everybody who ruins a pair of slacks her
                money back!

Jenny: I'm sure it seems unreasonable to you, and you
                certainly can't give everybody a refund, but I
                would like my money returned. I can't use slacks
                that must be washed in cold water only.

Salesperson: Well, I'll have to check with my supervisor. I'll be
                right back.
                (Talks with supervisor and returns.)
                Will you please fill out this form? I'm authorized
                to give you a refund. But we can't do this all the
                time.

Jenny: You absolutely can't do this all the time. And I
                do appreciate your help with it. Thank you.

Please notice how often Jenny simply repeats her request
for a refund. Remember the rule: When the criticism is directed
at you by someone who is trying to talk you out of a goal you
know is right for you, *stick to your point.* Each new criticism is
simply an opportunity to agree insofar as possible, express understanding, and reiterate your request.

STICKING TO YOUR POINT

Nancy, too, had a critical spouse. But, unlike Carl, Jon was critical mostly when Nancy had a request he didn't like to consider. So Nancy learned the tactic Jenny used with the salesperson. She learned to stick to her point, as well as to agree with the criticisms. This tactic of sticking to her original point led to some real progress in her relationship with Jon.

One day Nancy decided to try once again to convince Jon they should have a joint checking account. He had steadfastly resisted this suggestion in the past. Notice how Nancy deals with the criticisms and how she returns to her request without anger or sarcasm.

Nancy: I'd like to discuss something important with you. Is this a good time?

Jon: I guess so.

Nancy: I would like you to go to the bank with me and sign the forms for a joint checking account so I can write checks when I need to.

Jon: You know how I feel about that. I don't see why you keep bringing it up.

Nancy: Yes, I know you have some negative feelings about it, and that you can't understand why I keep bringing it up. But it is really important to me to be able to use the checkbook.

Jon: You wouldn't keep the checkbook straight. In no time our finances would be in chaos.

Nancy: You're probably right. I would forget to complete the check stubs occasionally, and our finances might be in chaos sometimes. But I still want to be able to write checks on our bank account. Will you please go to the bank with me tomorrow and work it out?

Jon: You don't need to write checks. You have all those credit cards. You're never satisfied with anything I provide for you!

Nancy: I'm sure it seems to you that with credit cards I never need to write checks, and I know you feel I'm never satisfied. But I'd like you to go to the bank with me tomorrow anyway.

292

Jon: You're trying to take over and run things, and if you get to write checks, it'll be even worse.

Nancy: I'm sure it seems to you that if I get to write checks I'll be running our lives, and I'm sure that worries you, but I would still like for you to see that I have a checkbook of my own. Will you go with me to the bank tomorrow?

Jon: You just won't listen to anything I say, will you?

Nancy: You're right, there are times when I don't pay close attention. And I don't always agree with you. Even so, I want you to go with me tomorrow.

Jon: Well, if you insist. What else can I do?

Nancy: You've got a point. What else can you do?

Nancy and Jon did go to the bank together where they completed the forms for a joint checking account. But even more important was the increased freedom Nancy began to feel in her relationship with Jon. Both of them appreciated the new peace they began to enjoy in their life together. The negotiation you just read was a first. Never before had Nancy and Jon been able to even discuss the notion of her having checking privileges without a fight and a subsequent long period of hostility. Soon the couple learned to deal similarly with other sensitive issues.

Anyone can, as Nancy did, become adept at disarming criticism and thus avoiding hostility. Without hostility the original question can be discussed and brought to a conclusion.

FOR REVIEW, PRAYER AND DISCUSSION

1. Why does criticism usually hurt?
2. How do most people believe they should handle criticism?
3. Give some examples of everyday criticisms.
4. Is the critic usually wrong? Explain.
5. How might criticism be good for us?
6. Give examples of truthful agreement in response to criticisms you invented in answer to question #3.
7. Ask someone to criticize you, and practice handling each criticism by truthful agreement. Use Jenny as a model.
8. Give some examples of adding to criticism and of asking for more.

9. Ask someone else to criticize you and respond by agreeing, adding to criticism, and asking for more.
10. Give an example of sticking to your point when someone criticizes you to avoid dealing with a request of yours.

CHAPTER EIGHT

How Matthew 18:15 Keeps You from Blowing Up

"If your brother sins against you, go and tell him his fault, between you and him alone. If he listens to you, you have gained your brother" (Matt. 18:15, RSV).

Which of Jesus' commands is more widely disregarded than any other? (Among Christians, that is.) I mean blatantly disregarded, overlooked, and violated. Not the first commandment. Most Christians aren't regularly praying to Zeus. Hardly the fifth commandment, the one against killing. Not the one against stealing, or adultery, or bearing false witness. Many believers break them all, of course, at times. But they don't disregard them.

I don't claim to have made a scientific survey to determine the answer to my question. But I have concluded, from professional experience, that the most widely disregarded of Jesus' many instructions to His people is this: If another person does something wrong, go tell him his fault.

Instead, most people try other, less constructive remedies for a brother's trespass. Take the Rev. Yack More, for instance. When he knows somebody has done wrong, he preaches against the evil. It's easier for him than going and telling his brother—alone.

Then there's Brother Gab Fest. He raises a fuss in the congregational meeting about the dark doings in the church, all the while "not mentioning any names." But everybody knows whom he means. He sees to that.

Everybody knows Sister Suzy Tellall. She reads Jesus' words as if they say, "Go and tell someone else between you and her alone. And tell her not to tell anyone."

There was backbiting in the apostolic church, so it isn't a recent invention (Galatians 5:15). Maybe some of the first-generation church folks had already invented what I call "gossip through prayer": "We must pray for Brother Off-The-Track. He's really been walking in sin lately. Let me tell you what he did . . . so you can pray for him, of course." Maybe they had already begun the practice of going to church leaders with other people's sins: "I think, Pastor Sheepshearer, you would do well to talk to Minestrone. He's been keeping company with a woman from the office. His poor wife! The church ought to do something."

Maybe some of the Galatian believers handled wrongdoing by trying to forget about it. Others may have handled it by refusing to speak to the one who had caused hurt. Still others may have adopted a calculated program to get even. All these tactics pointedly ignore Jesus' directions on how to handle someone's wrong behavior.

What do you do? None of the above? Perhaps you keep your brother's offense very quiet. Maybe you tell no one and instead let it fester inside you until you can hardly look the offender in the eye. You bite your tongue, pinch your lips, and try to smile as a joyful, carefree Christian.

Some who try to stifle their feelings know it isn't working because they can feel the blood rushing to their faces when they have to be around the one who has hurt them. Others, alas, won't read this book. They are so out of touch with their own feelings, so hardened with denial of what's actually going on, so accustomed to telling themselves everything but the truth about their own feelings, they will chirp the usual spiritual-sounding platitudes and go nonchalantly on their way, acting out the anger they can't even feel.

All these behaviors directly contradict what Jesus taught: Go to the person who has done something you believe is wrong and tell him about the situation. In families this divinely ordered tactic can replace nagging with marvelous results. In friendships it can do away with "the silent treatment" and thus prevent the collapse of precious relationships. In the Body of Christ it can protect the unity and community of small groups and large congregations. Because, as Jesus taught, the objective is to "gain your brother."

HOW TO DO IT

We are going to work through specific directions about how to "go and tell" someone who has done something to hurt you. And, in addition, you will learn how to respond when another person admonishes you.

BEFORE YOU BEGIN

Settle three issues in your mind before you actually open your mouth to speak. It is most desirable, though not under your control, for the other person to have settled these three preliminary issues as well. When I begin working with two people whose relationship is in trouble, as in marital or family conflict, I will insist they each agree to these premises and commit themselves to applying them rigorously:

1. The past is past. Forgive the other person now for all that has gone before. Unless you do, you will be burdened by the weight of all the offenses you have stored up against him. There will be no such thing as working together to resolve the one thing your brother has done to hurt you because you will be dragging in everything you didn't like since day one of your relationship.

Couples are often in trouble because one or both persons will not release the past. Their attempts to resolve an issue then become inevitably entangled in a rehearsal of unforgiven past hurts. For example:

Wayne: Sorry I'm late, honey.
Jane: Are you?
Wayne: Of course. Don't you remember, I told you I might be late?
Jane: I should remember. You've done this to me ever since we started going together. I remember our first date.

And do you know what I remember it for? Not for the lovely time we had, because it wasn't lovely. You made me wait on the corner for you and you were an hour and a half late! Do you realize that? An hour and a half late! I was so humiliated. And you've continued to make me wait for you ever since!

Jane has treasured up the past in her mind like Fort Knox hoarding gold. She keeps it where she can tap it for immediate recall. And its presence in each argument prevents any progress she and her husband might hope to make toward solutions for their problems.

Unless you forgive the past, every effort to deal with the present will become crushed under the dead weight of the past. And once you have forgiven, it is contradictory to keep resuscitating past hurts. The past is past. Forgive it in Jesus' name and get to work on the present.

2. Both persons are equal in value and in the validity of their needs, desires, wishes, and feelings. As strange as it may seem, some of my Christian clients deny the equality of persons, confusing it with the issue of authority in the home or in other structures. Notice I am not saying you must believe all persons are equal with respect to everything. That isn't true. Some people have more physical size than others; some have more intelligence, more hair, more money, more musical talent, etc. And God has ordered that some have authority over others.

But though the policeman directing traffic has authority over me, he is not superior to me in personal worth. Though the judge has authority to sentence the criminal to a prison term, the judge's needs are not more significant than those of the criminal. The parent is equal in worth to the child; the baby in the womb of the commoner is equal in human worth to the Queen of England.

If you don't believe your needs are important, equally important with those of others, you will have no basis to "go and tell him his fault" when someone in authority harms you.

Letitia, for example, believed that, as a submissive wife, she could not speak forthrightly to her husband when he rode roughshod over her needs. Instead, she pinched her lips and

298

kept silent, though seething inside. Over time, she found her feelings hardening, and at last, in spite of exerting all her will, she was overwhelmed by hate.

When I tried to teach this poor woman to practice Jesus' own instruction to her ("go and tell him . . ."), she informed me sadly that she could not tell her husband what to do since that would be unsubmissive.

"Letitia," I replied, "do you remember who is held up as the prime Old Testament example of a submissive wife by Peter in his first letter?"

"Sarah, of course," she responded. Letitia knew her Bible.

"Correct. And what did Sarah do after she became edgy about the possibility that Ishmael, Abraham's son by another woman, might grow up to compete for first place with Isaac, Sarah's own boy?"

Letitia couldn't recall, so I told her. "She said, in effect, 'Abraham, I want you to get Ishmael out of this house. I don't want him growing up to take over what belongs rightfully to my son, Isaac.' And Abraham, perplexed, sought the Lord. God told Abraham to do exactly as Sarah had demanded. Sarah, on this occasion, had the Word of the Lord, and it was up to her husband to carry it out. Sad, but obedient to God, and respectful of the wishes of his wife, Abraham sent Ishmael and his mother away. Was Sarah being unsubmissive? Not according to the Word of God (Gen. 21:9–14)."

If you have neglected speaking to someone over you who injures you (because you believe to do so is not properly submissive), now is the time to realize that submission and authority in a relationship do not cancel Jesus' own guidelines on how to settle differences. Even a child may, and should, learn to speak and be heard when another person, whoever that person might be, is wronging him. With regard to intrinsic worth, all are equal.

3. You must be willing to make some changes yourself. Remember, you are not going to speak to your brother to vent your wrath. You are seeking change in his behavior. You want him to start acting in a different way from the way that has hurt you. But change may not proceed only in one direction. There is a chance that your brother will want you to change something, too.

An attitude of willingness to change does not imply you will thoughtlessly agree to do whatever anyone else demands. It does imply that you are willing to change behavior that is harmful to others, and you are going to remain open to change while you speak to the other person about his fault.

WHEN TO GO AND TELL

Timing is important. For instance, you almost certainly will doom your effort to get someone to change if you broach the matter in the middle of a hot argument! But many stalwart would-be admonishers sit on their peeves until a devastating argument occurs. Then, when they are "good and mad," they let the other person have it. This is not the scene Jesus envisioned when He instructed believers to tell the other person his fault. If what the other person has done makes you angry, cool off before you try to deal with his sin.

It's amazing how poor some peoples' sense of timing is. Some parents will come storming out of a child's room, yelling all the way downstairs, and interrupt what the child is doing with, "Go straighten up that room! It's terrible!" They then wonder why that child is resentful. When a person is raging mad he is unlikely to elicit anything from the other person except anger in return.

If you want to work out something with another person, cool off first and then ask for a convenient time to talk: "There's something I want to talk with you about. Would this be a good time? No? Okay, what about later this evening? You'll be free after supper? Great. Let's talk then."

DON'T

- Try to "tell him his fault" while your brother is watching the Superbowl on TV or playing "Moonlight Sonata" on the piano.
- Bring up something you consider a sin against you just as she is falling asleep in bed at night.
- Seek to practice Matthew 18:15 when either of you is

yelling, snarling, or growling. "The anger of man does not work the righteousness of God" (James 1:20, RSV).

DO

- Respect the other person's needs, desires, and ongoing activities.
- Make sure that you and the other person are both in a reasonably calm and controlled frame of mind when you "go and tell."

HOW TO TELL

"I've already told him how I feel. He knows what I don't like." This is the most common response of people to whom I suggest a program of learning to deal directly with another person's hurtful behavior. Often, they believe they have already carried out the command to "go and tell" or that it really doesn't need to be done because the other person "knows he's wrong" or "knows how I feel."

After that response I usually ask them for an example of what they have said to tell the other person his fault. And most often what they have done is wrong. Below are some examples of the prevailing behaviors my clients have imagined to be adequate, of ways many people have of "admonishing" others. Remember, all these people really thought they had done it correctly!

- "Don't you think it's about time you started getting up without having to be called?" (A question instead of a statement. Note, too, the implied exasperation.)
- "Why don't you ever think of someone besides yourself? You need to realize how hard I work around here. You ought to at least rake a few leaves this afternoon instead of making me do everything." (A question again. And the attempt to motivate with guilt. Pay attention to the "ought to.")
- "How many times do I have to tell you to pick up after yourself? You think I'm your slave, don't you?" (Implied exasperation, questions, and again, deep, dark guilt.)

301

- "Wouldn't you like to get the garage all cleaned up today?" (A question and the ever-popular, "Wouldn't you like to. . . ?")
- "Wouldn't you rather answer your own phone calls?" Another question. (It's just like playing *Trivial Pursuit* when trying to relate to these people.)
- "Why ask me if something's wrong? You should know what you did. And you know it's wrong, too. (The old guessing game: "Squirm, you louse, until you figure out what's eating me!")

These are examples of indirect communication. Nearly all the devices for circumventing truthful speech which we discussed earlier could be cited here as examples of ineffective ways people take to deal with the faults of others.

HOW TO BEGIN

Are you avoiding dealing with the irritations and trespasses of someone because you don't know how to get started talking to him? The following example should help:

"I wanted to talk to you about something you said to me during the committee meeting. You said you doubted my sincerity. That hurt me and made me quite angry. As a result I haven't felt able to talk freely with you. I want you to stop judging me and to come and talk with me privately if something I do upsets you. Will you please do that?"

Notice the above example includes four elements:
1. The speaker tells the listener *what he has done:* "You said you doubted my sincerity."
2. He admits *how it hurt or upset him:* "That hurt me and made me quite angry."
3. He reveals *what the consequences have been:* "I haven't felt able to talk freely with you."
4. He requests *what he wants the other to do differently:* "I want you to stop judging me and to come and talk with me pri-

vately if something I do upsets you."

THE FOUR ELEMENTS IN "TELLING HIM HIS FAULT"

Tell the other person:
  (1) **What he has done**
  (2) **How it hurt or upset you**
  (3) **The consequences (if any)**
  (4) **What you want the other to change or do differently.**

Note the inclusion of these elements in the following examples of the "opener." Study them and use them for models.

- Parent to teen-age son: "I'm having some problems with your use of the car, Jerry. Last night you took it with the gas tank half full, so this morning I had to put gas in it just to get to work. Two nights ago you used about a quarter of a tank without replacing it, and again I had to get gas just to make a trip. It frustrates me to find the gas gauge low when I want to use my own car, so I would appreciate it very much if you would regularly replace whatever gas you use. Would you do that?"
- Wife to husband: "I'm bothered by the way you corrected me at the party last night. I felt put down by the abruptness of your manner. Would you please wait until we're alone when you want to correct me for something?"
- Roommate to roommate: "The dishes you leave in the sink create difficulty for me. I don't like dirty dishes lying around, but if I wash yours repeatedly I feel resentful because it's unfair. Then I become uncomfortable when we're together because of my negative feelings. I'd like to work out an agreement to work together to keep our sink free from dirty dishes. Are you willing?"
- Boss to secretary: "I didn't like the way you interrupted me in front of that customer. It irritates me to be interrupted when my mind is on making a sale, and it looks tacky when you do it. Will you kindly wait to ask me

303

questions until I've finished talking to customers?"

- Friend to friend: "You've been spending more time with Agnes than you ought to, Pete. I overheard you telling your wife you had to work late. Then you had dinner with Agnes. I'm grieved and concerned, and I'm afraid that your fine relationship with the Lord is going to suffer. I'm also concerned for Joan, and I'm going to speak to her if you keep this up. I want to ask you now to stop spending extra time with Agnes and keep your relationship with her 'strictly business.' "

Perhaps you're thinking, *Why do I have to do it this way? Why is it better than my old indirect method? At least I got results—sort of—sometimes.* I don't blame you for asking. It's very hard to change old habits, especially if they are occasionally effective. But there are good reasons for including all four of the elements.

The first and most important reason is that by including all of them you *tell the truth*, and the truth is a primary concern of Christians. By admonishing in this way you are open and frank about your own feelings and reasons for wanting a change. You aren't hiding yourself and the truth about yourself behind a wall of "shoulds" and "musts" and "don't you think you ought to's," because indirect communication always evades portions of the truth. Like Paul, speaking to the Corinthians, you "commend yourself" to others with ". . . genuine love, truthful speech . . ." Your "mouth is open to" others (2 Cor. 6:6, 7, 11).

The other reason is that by using these four elements, you *must be nonmanipulative*. Including them prevents you from trying to finagle somebody into doing something because you are forced to come right out and say what you don't want and what you do want. Furthermore, the four elements involve a direct request, leaving the decision right where it belongs: with the other person.

If you follow this prescription your manner will be nonhostile and nonthreatening. You therefore will be less likely to elicit a hostile, defensive, or threatening response.

DON'T GET PERSONAL

Frequently, when I am invited to assist two people in resolving their differences, I find I am listening to anything but the issues. Before very long, each of them is engaged in an all-out effort to convince me that the other is no good, the scum of the earth, worthless, ruthless, craven, thoughtless, inconsiderate, ill-mannered, unloving, and almost without a redeeming feature.

At the same time, each labors to convince me that he himself is kind, generous, practical, considerate, thoughtful, eminently rational, truly virtuous, and without significant flaw as regards the relationship.

True, I have exaggerated. Nobody comes right out and utters all the charges and epithets I have listed. But the impression each wishes to convey is clearly expressed by these lists.

People trying to resolve problems often make the fatal blunder of personalizing. That is, they develop the notion that the problem is the other *person* and not something in the other person's *behavior*. Each abandons the aim of resolving the original difficulty and sets out to prove that the other is bad. Generally, a list of the other person's past crimes is brought in as evidence:

"Our relationship has always been jeopardized by your inconsiderate and thoughtless attitude. The first time we planned to do something together, you forgot about it—so I was all dressed to go hiking and spent half my day off waiting for you! I don't know how many times you've been late for things we planned to do together. And remember the time we were going to go to a place *I* like for dinner (for a change) and you came up with your usual 'better suggestion' just at the last minute? You never ask me what I think about anything or what I want to do. You always forget to do anything I've requested of you. Why, even your family says you think of yourself first and others second. Your father told me. . . ."

The list of crimes goes on and on. It is resurrected at every fight. And its purpose is to *personalize*. That is, to show how bad the person is rather than to deal with the offending behavior of the moment.

305

Below are examples of personalizing, of addressing the *person* instead of the person's offending *behavior*. You may observe that much personalizing of this kind employs adverbs of over-generalization such as *always, never, ever, completely, and totally*. (In the examples I have italicized the adverbs of overgeneralization so you can't miss them.)

- "What's with you? Why on earth do you *always* act this way?"
- "Do you think I'm made of money? You *always* act as if it grows on trees."
- "You must have the IQ of a turtle to bring the car home with a dent in that spot! You *never* look where you're going!"
- "Why don't you *ever* consider anyone but yourself?"
- "Why are you *always* such a klutz?"
- "You're a pig, eating like that. Why don't you *ever* wash before dinner?"
- "You're as tight as the rest of your family. You *never* pick up the check or offer to pay for anything."

NO PUT-DOWNS

Most personalizing involves the habit of slinging put-downs at the other person when his behavior causes you difficulty. Some of you automatically react to another person's sins with an insult. The theory seems to be that if you zap your friend, wife, or child hard enough he or she will cease the offending behavior.

What usually happens, however, is that the other person is hurt or angered by your attack. Sometimes he will zap you back. And sometimes he will store up the bitterness to poison your relationship. I cannot predict how you will be made to taste the poison later on, but you will taste it. The "root of bitterness" puts out many tendrils which later "spring up and cause trouble" (Heb. 12:15, RSV).

Put-downs are usually personal, and personalizations are usually put-downs, so the verbal behavior is similar in both instances. Here are a few examples of personalizing put-downs which may be hurled at others in a misguided attempt to correct a trespass:

- "You don't have the most elementary notion of courtesy, do you?"
- "You're just like your father; he doesn't pick up after himself either."
- "John, you look like a tramp. Go clean up."
- "Motor mouth! Can't you wait until the game is over?"
- "What are you crabbing about now?"

If you are a habitual "zapper," you may find that omitting put-downs is not as much fun as including them in your conversations with others. There is a certain wicked satisfaction in verbally "creaming" the other person, especially when you are upset by his actions. Because of that, you will have to work extra hard to tell yourself the truth about personalizing and zapping—namely that, in the long run, they create trouble for the relationship *and for the zapper*. That is because God has so ordered the universe that the fruits of *zapping* come back on the *zapper's* own head.

Jesus made clear that this untruthful and unloving speech is fraught with danger to the person who indulges in it: ". . . whoever insults his brother shall be liable to the council, and whoever says, 'You fool!' shall be liable to the hell of fire" (Matt. 5:22).

If you really want to resolve the issue and "gain your brother" (have a good relationship), you must stop personalizing and using put-downs.

NO RED HERRINGS

When people begin trying to work out their problems instead of just sitting on them, they often get mired in defensive behavior. That is, they subtly and probably unintentionally nudge the discussion off the track by defending.

Defending is nearly always a red herring. "Red herring" refers to the practice of drawing a very smelly pickled and smoked fish across a trail to confuse hunting dogs. The dogs lose the true trail and begin following the strong odor of the fish. That is precisely the way defending behavior works in a problem-solving discussion. It draws the participants away from the original issue.

Study the following piece of dialogue. The woman begins by asking her husband to change something, but he replies with a defensive and somewhat attacking remark. See how the entire conversation then drifts away from her original goal.

She: I feel awfully left out because you spend so much time reading the paper and watching sports on TV. There are so many things I'd like to talk about. I'd like very much for you to set aside some time for us to talk every day. (A terrific opener—virtually flawless!)

He: Don't blame me for not talking! (Defending) You never want to talk about anything except what's wrong with *me*. (Attacking as a defense against changing.)

She: I just don't see how you can say that. The other night I tried to tell you all about my day, didn't I? I suppose you wouldn't know—you weren't listening as usual. (See how she follows the herring's trail? She has already forgotten her aim: to get him to make time for them to talk each day. She defends herself instead.)

He: I was listening! I heard you! (Defending) You're the one who doesn't listen. How many times have I asked you not to leave my underwear in the dryer? But that's where it was this morning when I was trying to get dressed for work. (Attacking for defensive purposes works well for him. She now gets pulled far away from her original aim.)

She: Well, why don't you buy some more underwear? I can't run a whole washerload for your five pairs of shorts! (Now she is into the spirit of the thing and attacks for defensive purposes. She will avoid being faulted by blaming him for his shortage of briefs.)

He: Yup, there you go. Your answer to everything is to spend money. I can't afford to buy clothes because you're always getting a new blouse or something. What was it the other day? You needed a skirt for "every day" and it cost fifty bucks. No wonder I don't have enough underwear.

She: All right. All right. I won't try to look nice for you. You don't appreciate it anyway. All you can do is criticize me, no matter what I try to do to please you.

Now the emotions will become very intense, zapping and attacking will take over, and the goal she had of increasing their communication will be totally forgotten. The couple may even wonder, later, what it was that they fought about. Notice they did *not* fight about her request. They fought in a defending-attacking-personalizing-put-down manner which effectively prevented a resolution of the original problem. No wonder these two people are utterly frustrated, blaming one another, and not seeing why.

If the woman had stuck to her point, and even used some of the principles of receiving criticism, such as agreeing with the critic, the conversation would not have turned into a nuclear showdown.

WHEN YOU ARE THE ONE BEING ADMONISHED

Some of the rules above apply to both the admonish*er* and the admonish*ee*. There are some pitfalls, however, into which the person being admonished frequently falls which will, if they are pursued, ruin communication and fellowship. They can work great harm to relationships. Here are some of the important rules for the person who is approached by another believer.

1. If someone says he's hurt—he's right! Some people meet every attempt to admonish them or request change with an attack on the admonisher for being hurt or for "making a mountain out of a molehill" or for "being too sensitive." You, too, may find that when someone else tells you how you have hurt him, your instinctive reaction is to say something like this:

"Well, heavenly days, Marigold, you shouldn't be hurt over *that*! You're just too thin-skinned. You oughta work on not getting your feelings hurt so easily. You know I'd never do anything to harm you, don't you?"

Or like this:

"Don't you know, Athanasius, that a Christian shouldn't feel that way? Now what does Paul tell us in Philippians? Doesn't he admonish us to think only of the positive? I'm sure if you give the matter more thought, you'll see that you're just being critical."

When you tell another person that you have been hurt by something he said, you expect to be believed because you and you alone know when you feel hurt. Therefore, when a person says he's hurt—he's right. He is the only one who really knows.

To tell him he isn't hurt, or shouldn't be hurt, or is wrong in feeling the way he does is a put-down, a red herring, and a subtle device for defending yourself. When your brother tells you that something you have done hurts him or angers him, it isn't your place to deny or attack his feelings. Just accept him as the authority on his reactions and feelings. When he tells you he's hurt, he's hurt. And that's that.

2. Listen! And let him know you heard. This activity of listening is so important for developing relationships which "gain the brother" that I have devoted the next chapter to the subject. Most people do not know how to listen in conversation. They may listen to others in lectures or sermons, but when they are involved in conversation, they do everything except listen to the other person. And seldom do they bother to demonstrate that they have heard what the other has had to say.

3. Express understanding in your response. On a rare occasion, even when you have taken the trouble to listen to the other person, you will simply not agree that he has his facts completely correct. In that case you can at least express understanding (rather than taking exception to what he has said).

Suppose your friend has made a perfect opening speech, letting you know he really didn't appreciate your talking to his date for the entire evening, causing him to feel left out. And suppose you distinctly recall talking to your own date a good deal of the time, not to his date all the time. You are tempted to say, "You're off your rocker. I didn't talk to your girl all evening."

Instead, however, you remember this chapter and decide to express understanding even though you don't fully agree with his sweeping generalization. You do agree with as much of it as you truthfully can, saying, "You know, I did talk to your girl

310

quite a bit. And I can understand how that might make you feel a little miffed."

Sometimes you will be able to agree, at least partially, with what the other person has told you. But even when you can't, express understanding by saying something like this: "I can understand why you might think your wishes aren't important to me, especially if you believe you told me you didn't like Mexican food before I took you to Old Mexico for dinner."

Study the following examples of understanding responses to admonition. Read them aloud. Imagine yourself responding similarly to a reproof or request for change by someone close to you:

- "You're right. I did correct you at the party in front of everyone. And I can understand why you might not feel good about that."
- "You have a point, Dad. I have used the car a lot lately without filling the tank. I was going to buy you a full tank when I get my paycheck, but I can see that you don't like always having to buy gas before you can go anywhere."
- "It's true. Joan wouldn't like it if she knew how much time I'm spending talking with Agnes at the office. And I can really understand your concern as a Christian brother, too."
- "I can see what you mean and why you don't like being interrupted when you're watching football. I don't like being interrupted when I'm into something either. You've got a legitimate complaint."
- "Yes, it must be upsetting to have to run downstairs looking for your underwear when you're already rushing to avoid being late for work."
- "You have a right to be angry with me about that. I shouldn't have done it that way."
- "You know, what you say makes sense. Nobody likes moving a stack of dirty dishes to get a drink of water."

An expression of agreement, or at least of understanding, prevents argument. It's difficult to keep up an argument with someone who doesn't call your statements into question.

4. Express your own desires. Now, only *after* you have heard

311

the other person, expressed understanding, and made certain you grasp his point without arguing, defending, or attacking, you should express your desires. This does not mean you can now show the other person why he is wrong and you are right. Simply express your wishes. Describe how you would like things to go.

Here are some examples which complement some of the expressions of agreement or understanding in the previous section.

- "I want to double date with you again. I won't overdo chatting with your girl the next time."
- "I'd really like to avoid taking you to restaurants you don't like. After this, will you please tell me before we go if you don't care for the kind of food I've chosen?"
- "I want to stop correcting you in front of others. Will you help by calling it to my attention if I ever do it again?"
- "After this I'll bring the car home with the gas tank at least as full as it was when I got it."
- "I'd like to get your agreement to buy three more sets of underwear. That would help me not to have to wash quite so often."

In some situations you don't want to agree to the other person's proposal, even though you can understand completely why he makes his request. This is the place to express your own wishes in the matter. Here are examples:

- "Although I can understand where you're coming from, I want to tell you how I feel. I like to talk to everyone when Liz and I are out with another couple. I want to feel free to talk to you and your date too, to some extent. Can we work out something?"
- "Mexican food is my favorite, so I'd like us to go to a Mexican restaurant occasionally. Maybe we could work out a plan so both of us would be satisfied with the restaurants we go to."
- "Dad, there are times when I need the car but don't have the cash to buy gas. Could we negotiate some way to work around that?"
- "I really don't like washing my dishes every time I eat a snack—it's too much hassle. And besides, just rinsing and

wiping them dry isn't very sanitary. I'd like to work out something with you that would be okay with both of us."

5. *Work toward compromise.* When your wishes conflict with those of the other person, the only solution which will keep your relationship close and intact is compromise. You cannot impose your way because of some superior feature in your position. If you do, you violate the rule we laid down earlier: Treat each other as equals. Compromise recognizes the equality of each participant and the fairness involved in each giving a little to arrive at a solution.

Every Christian recognizes, in principle, that pushing to get his own way is unfair and unloving. No reader of this book has missed hearing or reading 1 Corinthians 13, which declares, "Love does not insist on its own way" (1 Cor. 13:5, RSV).

But not every Christian practices what he knows in principle. For example, when Hananiah Smith gets home from the church meeting, though he knows 1 Corinthians 13 by heart, he insists on his own way. "Because," he thumps the table for emphasis, "I am the head of this house and the Lord speaks through me alone." Meanwhile his wife, Glorianna, who also knows how to turn a Bible passage to her advantage, winks slyly and proceeds to use what she calls her "feminine wiles" to make Hananiah think he is ruling the roost.

Polycarp Tharp argues that he should get his way because his position is rational, more rational than that of Ignatius Gracious who holds that his position is based on the evidence and should therefore carry the day.

Little Tiny Smith gets her way by having a tantrum until Glorianna gives in. And young Sharp Tharp cons Polycarp by making him believe that all the other kids get it so he should too. All these situations violate the principle that "love does not insist on its own way."

Love says, "I don't agree with you. My way is different from yours. But I respect you and therefore I respect your way. Let's work out something so we can stay together through this thing." Love seeks, not to dominate, but to gain the brother.

Note, however, that compromise to gain a brother must never compromise *God's* way. Issues God has settled in His Word are not up for negotiation. But most of the issues between us and others are far from being black and white, either/or, all right or all wrong situations. On these, compromise is not only possible but effective and powerful for resolving difficulties between people of good will.

CHRISTIAN CONCILIATION SERVICES

Many Christian psychologists, psychiatrists, social workers, and Christian counselors are trained to help people negotiate resolutions to difficult issues such as marital disagreements, arguments over property, and difficulties between partners, roommates, and others. Occasionally, clergymen are equipped for such work. Recently, under the auspices of the Christian Legal Society, such conciliation services have been formally organized in a number of cities. Staffed with trained volunteers, these organizations work with both parties to help resolve disagreements. One of their purposes is to make legal actions such as divorces or civil suits unnecessary. If you and another Christian are unable to work out your conflicts yourselves, do not hesitate to use one of these resources. Often, it is just what is needed to arrive at a practical, mutually agreeable compromise.

A REMINDER

Because of the crucial nature of the material in this chapter, here is a quick review of the principles discussed. First, before trying to work out a conflict with someone, you must agree to three stipulations: (1) Forgive the past and let the past remain a bygone; (2) both persons are equal in validity of their needs, wishes, wants, and feelings; (3) you are willing to make some changes yourself.

Once you have settled that matter, observe the following principles:

- Never begin in the heat of an argument.
- Tell the other person (1) what he has done, (2) how it hurts you, (3) what the consequences are, and (4) what you would like him to do differently.

- Keep it task-and-problem-oriented; don't get personal.
- No put-downs.
- No red herrings, no defensiveness, no attacking.
- The person who is hurt is right about being hurt—don't argue that he shouldn't be hurt.
- Learn to listen (more on this in the next chapter).
- Express understanding, or, if possible, agreement in your response to admonition.
- Tell your own wishes in response to admonition.
- Work together toward compromise.

FOR REVIEW, PRAYER AND DISCUSSION

1. Recall the three fundamental premises for successful admonition.
2. Now think of someone with whom you have had a disagreement, someone you would like to face with a request for changed behavior. Can you apply the three premises to this situation and agree to all of them? Especially, have you forgiven all past hurts and sins of the other? If not, go before God and forgive your brother now.
3. Why are children equal with their parents? In what sense are they equal?
4. Why is it bad policy to begin admonition when you and the other person are angry or arguing?
5. Recall the four parts which belong in an opening speech when one goes to admonish a brother.
6. Give some examples of "getting personal" which you can imagine occurring between you and another person. Then alter your example to make them issue-oriented instead of personal.
7. What is a "red herring"?
8. What is the aim toward which most of these discussions between people should strive?
9. What about love can make you carefully consider the truth in what the other person has to say as well as in your own wishes?

CHAPTER NINE

"If He Listens to You": The Loving Art of Listening

"If he listens to you, you have gained your brother" (Jesus, Matt. 18:15, RSV).

I once attended a class in which psychologist Dr. Val Arnold taught the importance and skills of listening. To engrave on our minds the necessity of listening, Dr. Arnold asked the members of the large group to pair off for an experiment. One member of each pair was to describe the qualities he wanted in a Christian friendship, while the other person was to give every sign of not paying attention.

Dr. Arnold instructed, "Turn away from the speaker, focus your eyes on other things, activate your body. Do everything possible to avoid listening or giving the impression of listening."

What an experience! The talking members of the pairs said they felt irritated and angry, even helpless and inadequate. Some of them stopped midway through their second or third sentence, claiming they could not keep talking to a person who was pointedly ignoring them.

The non-listening members of the pairs said they really *didn't* hear what was said, that it was nearly impossible to listen when not facing their partner, and that the things said to them just slipped away.

Dramatically, Dr. Arnold had taught us the integral part listening plays in communication, as well as the importance of using the body to demonstrate attention by such actions as facing the speaker, making eye contact, nodding, altering facial expression appropriately, or perhaps saying "uh-huh" occasionally.

"Squarely face the other person," said Dr. Arnold. "*O*pen your body position by uncrossing legs and unfolding arms. *L*ean toward the other person. *E*ye contact should be made from time to time (not steady staring). *R*elax and be comfortable. Remember: *S-O-L-E-R*, the keys to using your body for listening."

Because of Dr. Arnold's brilliant teaching, the members of that class will remember the crucial place of listening in serious communication. Jesus taught it long ago.

THE CRUCIAL SIGNIFICANCE OF LISTENING

If any effort to improve relationships in the body by communicating is to succeed, the persons involved must *listen*. "If he *listens* to you, you have gained your brother," is how Jesus put it. If Jesus' instruction to "go and tell him his fault" is unheeded, the importance He placed on listening is equally ignored. When was the last time you heard a sermon on listening?

To communicate well you must learn the skills of listening. No matter how well you talk, without listening, your effort will be vain. You are responsible to develop *your* listening skills, not someone else's. You must make yourself the best communicator you can be.

The letter of James, especially James 3, is a treatise on communication—the best in all literature. Like Jesus, James is an ardent promoter of listening: "Let every man be quick to hear, slow to speak, slow to anger...."; this hearing must be "open to reason" and should eventuate in action, not argument—"be doers of the word, not hearers only" (James 1:19; 3:17; 1:22, RSV).

Some readers of this book will devour its chapters on how to speak but neglect this chapter on how to listen. People like Quintus Schmidt. Quintus believes in communication. He's always talking. He dominates relationships. He never fails to speak loudly in church meetings. He would much rather teach

than be taught, preach than be preached to, and tell instead of
be told. He views communication as a one-way street.

Maybe you, like Quintus, believe the essence of communication is being quick to speak. Do you get jumpy and impatient
during those portions of the conversation where it's your turn
to hear? Are you so anxious to be understood that you pay no
attention to the even more important skill of understanding?

A PARTY WHERE NOBODY LISTENED

I once attended a party, a professional gathering, at which
I spent a good deal of energy and attention observing the other
guests. At the beginning of the evening there was conversation
between people in pairs and little groups. One person would
talk, the other would listen politely. Then, more or less in turn,
another would talk while those not speaking appeared to be
listening.

As the evening hours went by and the effect of alcohol on
the guests (I was the only one not drinking) became more and
more evident, the strangest thing happened, which only a non-
drinker could observe: *Nobody was listening!*

The talkers became louder, more voluble, less inclined to
pause. People soon gave up even the pretense of listening to one
another. Finally, in group after group, several people were talking at once. Speakers would look around in the hope of catching
the eye of someone, anyone, who might be listening. But failing
that, they talked anyhow. To get attention they increased their
volume, and the party became very noisy. At last, all talked.
None listened. Communication no longer existed.

This is not a diatribe against alcohol, but an example, fa-
cilitated by alcohol, of what happens when communication is
destroyed by not listening. After all, it isn't only at alcoholic
parties that listening is impaired. Non-listening is an epidemic.
When I preach in my congregation, I, like other preachers, greet
people at the door after a sermon to say "good morning." Often,
the exiting parishioners will comment on the sermon they believe they have heard. Frequently, however, the sermon they
think they heard isn't the sermon I think I've delivered!

Many preachers are astonished when the people they've

preached to talk back on what they believe the preacher said. Often the difference between the sermon preached and the sermon heard is enormous. Instead of listening, people actually create the sermon for themselves, perhaps supplying what they want to hear in place of what is being said.

The same problem occurs in relationships, such as marriage. Here is an example: "I give her a chance to talk!" said the male half of a husband-wife team I was counseling for communication problems.

"That's true," I agreed. "You give her a chance to speak— but you don't listen."

"What's the difference?" he replied.

And with that, he hit the nail on the head for most of us: We don't know the difference between giving others a turn to talk and listening to them.

WHAT WE DO INSTEAD

What do we do when we are supposed to be listening? Frequently, our minds are busily occupied with other projects. Here are some non-listening techniques we frequently use:

Free associating. We may hear the first few sentences. Our thoughts, however, race much faster than human speech proceeds, so we begin to associate ideas in our heads with what we hear. Now our thoughts succeed one another with lightning speed. The speaker continues traveling down his verbal highway, while we, supposedly his passengers for the journey, take off on a detour.

Occasionally, realizing what we have done, we blush with embarrassment and wrench our minds back to listen a little longer. Usually, though, when the dialogue is for some reason unimportant to us or uninteresting from our point of view, our minds wander from association to association so that we are shocked by the silence when the speaker stops or pauses.

Killing time. Some of us don't even try to listen. We kill time instead. What we have to say is the only important part of the conversation for us. Nevertheless, politeness requires that we take a break once in a while and let someone else speak. We regard this as a necessary waste of time, and proceed to employ

319

our minds at whatever we can find to think about until a moment of silence allows us to resume speaking. How can there be any real communication with such non-listeners?

Piecemeal listening. Some of us listen just to have something to react to. We hang in there with the other person just long enough to hear an idea or a word which suggests some topic on which we can discourse. We don't actually reply. We just wait breathlessly for the speaker to stop so we can utter the gem that has occurred to us. We thus don't converse; we react piecemeal to scattered portions of what is said to us.

Waiting to argue. When the dialogue is important to us, as in an argument, we are apt to tune in with a sense of frustration, showing our haste for the other to end his speaking. We impatiently shift our gaze to the corners of the room, our posture demonstrating we are ready. At the slightest opportunity, we suck in a quick breath and dive into the discussion with our side of the argument. This is not the listening which makes for communication.

Listening to judge. Many of us listen only in order to judge others. We spend our listening time thinking, *He's too lazy . . . too greedy . . . too proud . . . too hostile,* or, *She's vain . . . self-centered . . . arrogant . . . egotistical.* As judge-listeners we imagine we can discern negative motives in others, and thus supply our judgments freely. We are unable to discriminate what we actually observe with our senses from what we construct with our minds. The following situation exemplifies judgmental listening:

Scott asked Georgia to go to a party.

She replied, "Thank you so much for inviting me, Scott, but I would rather go to church that night. I find I really need that fellowship, and I end up regretting it whenever I don't get it."

Scott later reported to his roommate: "Georgia is self-righteous. What a prude! She thinks she's too good to go to a party with me and uses church for an excuse. That's hypocritical, for sure."

Scott felt rejected by Georgia (though he hadn't been rejected), and to make up for the hurt he felt she'd caused him, he constructed judgments. Had he really listened instead, he might easily have made a date with Georgia for the next evening.

A CLINICAL EXAMPLE

Mitch and Link were good friends who had formed a business partnership. Their new racket club, under construction, promised to thrive as soon as the courts opened. Lately, however, they found themselves frequently disagreeing. Mitch, for example, wanted to add another court large enough to accommodate local volleyball teams. Link was certain the extra court would never pay for itself. Here is their discussion:

Mitch: Link, that volleyball court will bring people into our place who have never played racketball. They'll see the game and want to try it. Presto! New customers!

Link: Just how many new customers is it going to bring in, Mitch? You don't have the faintest idea. Only one thing we know for certain: It's gonna cost more—a lot more. The changes we'd need to make in design will come to at least ten bucks extra per square foot. And that's not conjecture.

Mitch: I think we should take a chance. It's bound to pay off.

Link: And I think we ought to use our heads. You don't seem to appreciate that business costs are very real.

Mitch: What you really mean is that you can't stand not running the whole show. I'm a partner too, you know.

Link: You're an airhead, man, trying to play it your way even if it bankrupts us.

Mitch and Link came to the clinic to get some help with their negotiations. They were right in concluding that they didn't communicate well. What they didn't realize is that the problem they had was actually a failure to *listen* to each other.

When an argument began, each would listen only to judge the other. Notice Mitch's last speech ("You can't stand not running the whole show."), and Link's final judgmental attack ("You're an airhead . . ."). Both judged the other person's intentions and motives unfavorably. In such statements the imputed motives are always negative.

It is impossible to guess another person's inner thoughts and motivations. It is hard enough to know your own motives. The person who listens only in order to judge another cannot be walking in the truth.

321

WHAT HAPPENS INSIDE THE NON-LISTENER'S BRAIN?

Imagine a friend is telling you about the trouble she and her husband are having with their teen-age son. The boy has just been arrested on a robbery charge. What goes on in your head? What is your internal monologue like? Might it be something like this?

> Thank God, I'm not in her shoes. I wonder what she and her husband did to that kid. Maybe it isn't the way they raised him; maybe it's all in the genes. Wow! They have to go to court with him! The thought makes my stomach flip-flop. What would I do in their shoes? How would I feel? How does she keep smiling? Oh, I'd probably manage too. Am I glad we raised ours right. Or at least picked out the right gene pool. It really is pretty dumb of them not to see that it's good for the kid to get caught. Even if he has to go to an institution for a while, it's probably the best way.

Perhaps you let your associations run on freely while your friend is talking. You let your mind wander to related thoughts, thinking about things you have read or heard. Your own notions speed through your head.

Instead of empathetically putting yourself into your friend's situation, you may give yourself a relieved pat on the back for being clever enough not to be there too. Or you might pass judgment on your friend. Or if your friend is merely dull and boring, you might be thinking of a way to turn the conversation around so it interests you.

In any case you wonder how you can recapture the limelight. And you spend some time planning your response. What you *don't* do is listen!

THE ELEMENTS OF GOOD HEARING

"Let every man be quick to hear . . ." implies that hearing is something done with energy and effort. It isn't a process of passive absorption.

Here are the activities you must learn to perform to be a good, loving, truthful, "quick" hearer: *attending; active reason-*

322

ing; creative empathizing; intuiting; letting the Spirit enlighten; facilitating; and giving feedback.

Attending. To be a good listener you must learn to attend. Attending is a response. In everyday speech, the word "attend" means little more than getting your body there, as in "I attend church every Sunday, but I sleep through the service." The true meaning of the word, however, involves an action of your mind.

Most people think of listening as passive, like being a cup someone else is filling up or a recording tape on which a magnetic head is rearranging the molecules. But your mind is not a cup or a tape. It isn't a blotter, passively soaking up drops of speech. You must use your will and direct your mind to what the speaker is saying.

In order to practice attending, imagine you are taking notes while the other person speaks. Picture a tablet you are writing on. Since you can think much faster than the other person can talk, dir~ct your mind to recall and note down on your imaginary tablet the points the speaker has been making. Lectures, sermons, and speeches are opportunities to practice active attending. Of course, this tactic is valuable in conversation as well. When you have successfully rehearsed in your mind the things the other person has been saying, reward yourself with mental praise and satisfaction.

Active reasoning. How fast can you think? Psychologists have attempted to answer that question in the laboratory. The speed of thought is much greater than that of the fastest speaker on earth. Because thoughts flash like electric currents through the mind, you can accomplish much thinking while you're listening.

To exploit your mind's capacity to think so fast, verbalize the speaker's rationale or reasoning process (not just the points he is making). Make his case for him in your mind. Rehearse his reasons for believing and saying what he is saying, as Rod is doing in the following example.

Imagine Janet is explaining her desire to take some college course at night. While she talks, Rod, who is learning how to listen, actively reasons with her, verbalizing (in his mind) her rationale, in this manner:

"She believes I am being challenged daily in my work,

323

while she has stagnated. She would like to feed her mind too. Besides, she seems to think I might be more interested in conversation with her if she had some college level material on her mind to talk about."

Reread Rod's thoughts and notice he follows Janet's reasoning process as closely as possible. He purposely avoids planning how he will argue with her, passing judgment on her motives or reasons, or thinking about what his answer will be. He employs all his mental faculties to enter the train of her thinking and to grasp how she is reasoning. This is probably what James means by being "open to reason" (James 3:17).

Creative empathizing. With empathy we tune into another person's feelings. We imagine what they are like. We enter creatively into the experiences of the speaker. We think, *If I were you, in your location, squeezed by the pressures now squeezing you, thinking and believing as you think and believe, reacting biochemically the way you are reacting, I would be feeling as you feel. I will make an effort to imagine what it would be like to experience your feelings.*

Sometimes when I am treating a patient, there is a moment of near-perfect empathy. The patient's woes are mine. His impaired ability to cope with life is mine. His sense of stark hopelessness is mine. The pain in his heart and tears in his eyes are mine. This is truthful listening. This is what the Bible means by "rejoice with those who rejoice, weep with those who weep" (Rom. 12:15, RSV).

Cultivate and develop the habit of empathetic listening. Learn to ask yourself, as the other person is speaking, questions such as these:

- How does he feel?
- What is he telling himself now?
- What would it be like if I were experiencing and believing the things he is experiencing and believing?
- Can I imagine coming from where he is coming from right now? Can I assume his role for a moment?

Then you will be able to give him answers, rather than just talk to him.

Intuiting. If your mind is attuned only to what the other

person is saying, or to what you are going to say when he stops talking, you may be ignoring an important element in listening: *your own feelings.* Notice how June makes this mistake in the following example.

June hardly noticed that she frequently developed a knot in her stomach when Robert was talking. She worked at listening to her husband, always attempting to fabricate a response, but totally ignored her own feelings.

At last, June visited her physician, complaining of burning sensations in the abdomen. He diagnosed an ulcer.

Had June paid more attention to what is commonly called "gut-feelings" she might have been able to sense the painful anger that accompanied her dialogues with Robert. She would have realized that her interpretations of her husband's speech "made her mad." She and Robert might then have worked out ways to resolve the problem of her aroused anger. But as long as June ignored her feelings, she was able to pay attention only to the things Robert said, and was forced to ignore her own emotions.

Intuition includes something called "recipathy." Different from sympathy and empathy, recipathy is one's own feeling, experienced in response to another person's behavior. It requires thinking, not, *How is he feeling right now?* but *How am I feeling when he is speaking?*

You may be surprised at the range of emotions others can elicit in you. Joy, yearning, sadness, love, anger, hatred, fear, anxiety, apprehension, frustration, irritation, fury, poignancy—all are possible. At various times you may have the desire to touch the other person, hold him, wipe his tears, hit him, or push him away from you. Sometimes you may want to yell at him. Pay attention to your intuitions, and to the feelings you are experiencing as a result of them.

Letting the Spirit enlighten. Christians will vary in the amount of experience they have had with this dimension. Every believer has been enlightened by the Holy Spirit. Most Christians have occasionally noticed the Spirit's communication of truth about current experiences (e.g., conviction of sin during a sermon on the subject). But not everyone, when interacting with another person, listens for the Spirit's whispers. A person can, by praying for sensitivity and practicing awareness, learn to be open to the Spirit's speaking.

Very often, while listening to a patient, I find I must rely on the voice of the Holy Spirit from within to give me understanding of what is happening. A psychologist, contrary to what many people think, cannot see through his patient. My scientific training prepares me to make inferences on the basis of your behavior, inferences which may seem miraculous. But they are not miraculous. Therefore, as I perform psychotherapy, I often need to be guided to deeper knowledge by the Holy Spirit. By the Spirit I am enabled to know some things which are not communicated through the senses. This supernaturally given material is sometimes referred to as a "word of knowledge."

In the very same way, you can pray for the enlightenment of the Holy Spirit in conversation. Sometimes the Spirit will moderate your listening and thus change the response you would have given. Here are some examples of the thoughts He might place in your mind:

> "Your husband truly loves you, even though right now you are aware only of the fury you feel at him."

> "Easy does it. You can blow your top now and get angry. You can tell yourself you've been provoked and you have a good blowout coming. Or you can control yourself, calm down, and suggest that both of you cool off and continue a little later when you aren't so upset. That will work out much better, you know."

> "What you are believing now doesn't have to make you hopeless if you will put hope in Me. I am your Rock. What that person is saying now cannot take away the firm foothold you have when you take your stand on Me."

> "The things he is saying are false. He doesn't understand his own motives and has conned himself into believing what he is telling you. But they are not so."

> "Stop telling yourself misbeliefs about what you're hearing. You know very well nothing that person says can make you inferior or inadequate. So instead of singing that sad song to yourself, tell yourself the truth."

Listen to the Spirit. He will help you to tell yourself the

326

truth, moderate your reactions, and give you skills for loving listening.

Facilitating. Surely you have had the experience of trying to talk to someone who did everything but make the conversation easy. Remember? He didn't really look at you. His eyes kept searching the room. It seemed as though he was looking for someone else who might interest him more. He responded with the most rudimentary grunts to what you were saying. When he did say something, it was so unrelated to what you were talking about you knew he hadn't heard you.

How did you feel? Like ending the conversation as fast as you could? Like crawling in a hole? Like asking yourself what was so dull and uninteresting about you that you couldn't keep the other person's attention? For certain, you didn't enjoy the experience, did you?

Perhaps you learned something though. And it might help now if you did. You could have learned how *not* to do it if you want to be a good facilitator in communication with another. And if you didn't learn, here are tips on how to be a good facilitator:

A good facilitator turns and inclines himself toward the speaker, not rotating around the points of the compass looking for other things to do.

A good facilitator keeps eye contact. This doesn't mean he must maintain a constant, unblinking gaze at the other person. But he should look into the eyes of the speaker most of the time he is talking. He may look away occasionally, but should return his gaze to the speaker's eyes.

A good facilitator constructs comments which draw the speaker out. "Yes, I understand." "Tell me more about that." "Can you expand a little bit on how you felt?" "I would really like to hear more about your thoughts on this. Could you fill me in?" Notice how open-ended such questions and remarks are. They encourage the speaker to talk and give him the feeling that he has the listener's full attention.

Giving feedback. This is the most critical element of good communication. Feedback is vital, especially on sensitive or very important issues. Giving the other person a sense of what you have heard him say is the best way to verify what has actually been communicated.

Giving feedback means telling the other person what you have heard him say, what reasoning you have understood him to be using, what feelings you have perceived in him, and what feelings have been elicited in you. Sometimes, but not always, feedback may include what you have heard the Holy Spirit say.

It is best to intersperse feedback comments throughout the dialogue rather than make a long feedback speech at the end. Feedback is easier to give when the speaker has not gone on so long the listener's memory is unable to retain what has been said.

In giving feedback, paraphrase what the speaker has told you. Don't merely repeat back the exact words spoken to you, but try to capture the sense in your own words. Below are some examples of feedback. Study the examples and use them for practice so as to develop the skill of feedback by paraphrase. You will need to use it in the negotiation process you studied in chapter 7. The first group contains examples of feedback which conveys the speaker's thought content as heard by the listener—a simple paraphrase.

Joan and Elroy:

Joan: I would like to landscape our backyard, put some paving stones around the beds, and run a little stream through the center of the yard ending up in a pool over by the cedars. We have plenty of water in the pond, so all we would need is a pump to get the stream started.

Elroy: You'd like to do some paving in the backyard and to run a stream through it using water from the pond. Sounds good to me.

Andy and Clarice:

Andy: I know you want to get an evening job to help with our expenses, but I don't want you to. I come home at night tired. I want a good dinner ready for me, and then I want to relax rather than help with housework and put the kids to bed. I know that if you worked we would end up with more stresses than the earnings you bring home could offset.

Clarice: You feel that my getting a job wouldn't be worth the extra trouble it would make for you. Also, you don't want to come home, fix dinner, clean house, and put the kids to bed after you've worked hard all day. You'd much rather rest in the evening and have me do the household duties. You believe we'd end up with more stress and not much more money if I worked in the evenings.

Doris and Jane:

Doris: Jane, I want to talk with you about cleaning the apartment. I haven't liked your clothes lying around the living room. Also you frequently leave your popcorn popper on the table and dishes in the sink. For the last three Saturdays you've gone out, and I have mopped the floors, cleaned the bathroom, and scrubbed the kitchen sink. I want you to pick up after yourself and share the cleaning tasks on an equal basis.

Jane: I understand what you're saying. You feel it isn't fair that I haven't done any hard cleaning for the last three weeks, and you don't like my clothes and dishes left out after I'm through with them. You want to divide the cleaning chores up evenly between us.

Here are some examples of feedback conveying the speaker's feelings as discerned by the listener.

Jonathan and Miriam:

Jonathan: I don't like the idea of going to visit your parents this weekend. It's my only chance to watch football and do some things around the house, and I don't want to spend my time sitting around talking to your dad about his store.

Miriam· You're feeling aggravated about going to visit my parents for a whole weekend. Even the thought of it makes you feel frustrated and bored.

Janice to Joel:

Janice: As I was listening to you talk about your boss, I got the feeling that if I were in your shoes, telling myself

what you are telling yourself, I'd have a sense of hopelessness. Is that what you're expressing to me?

THE SATISFYING SKILL OF GIVING FEEDBACK

The skill of giving feedback is the most satisfying commu-
nications skill a person can acquire. It is satisfying to you when
you are giving the feedback, because it relieves you of the responsibility of planning an answer and frees you to truly listen.
When you learn to do it you acquire the habit of taking responsibility for hearing, understanding, and feeling what another
person is saying and meaning. Listening in this way feels good
because it is loving and respectful.

Your feedback-giving habit is also satisfying to the speaker.
How many times you've experienced speaking up, only to feel
ignored or unheard by the other person! When another person
gives evidence that he has carefully and empathically listened,
you feel harmony, peace, and trust in the relationship.

THERE IS NO SUBSTITUTE FOR FEEDBACK

A small sailing boat was disabled about seventy miles off
the California coast. A storm had broken its mast and disabled
its ship-to-shore radio. Now the two men aboard had only a
small citizen's band radio on which to broadcast their cry for
help.

Far away in Minnesota, a visiting friend turned on his hosts'
CB radio out of curiosity—the startled family heard the distress
call being broadcast from the Pacific! Such long-distance communication with a CB radio is an anomaly called "skip." There
is no way to return such a signal. Nonetheless, the listeners
could take steps to help the troubled sailors.

The Minnesotan called his local sheriff, who called the Coast
Guard; the two men were rescued, and their crippled boat was
towed to shore. All this took several hours.

Meanwhile, however, though the sailors had communicated
their distress and position truthfully and precisely, they had no
way of knowing they had been heard until they saw their res-
cuers approaching. Until that moment their misery was una-

bated because they had no idea their cry had been received by someone and help was on the way.

That incident illustrates well the importance of feedback. Feedback lets the speaker know he is being heard. A good listener, therefore, is one who gives appropriate and frequent feedback.

ANALYZING YOUR LISTENING HABITS

You have just read about how to solve one of the most distressing problems in communication: not listening. Sometimes, people don't listen because they are too anxious and tense to hear well. They concentrate on their nervousness and miss what the other person has to say.

In our clinic we teach social skills to anxious people. That is, we try to train them in appropriate social behavior and speech. Usually I model a piece of verbal behavior by doing it for the client. Then the client imitates it. After I state the response, I try to get the client to do it just as I did.

Amazingly, the client rarely plays the speech back correctly. Even short responses of a few words are, at first, repeated wrong. Do you know why? It is because a client rarely hears what he is supposed to say. And that is because the thought of trying that new response arouses great anxiety.

I then try to get such a person to calm down, get his mind off his own performance fears, and work at the process of active listening and attending.

Getting anxious and nervous about what you are going to say; focusing attention on formulating your response; judging, condemning and forming negative opinions about the speaker; or simply letting your thoughts wander because you are sitting passively like a piece of blotting paper instead of listening actively—these are the major barriers to effective listening.

On the next page is a checklist you can use to improve your listening skills. You might want to memorize and keep it in your mind during conversations. Then check through the written list after any serious or important conversation you may find yourself in. Active listening is not vital in banter or small-talk, although it helps a good deal in some ordinary social talk

331

to at least pay attention to what is being said. But active listening becomes extremely important in serious discussions between people trying to resolve difficulties and disagreements.

After each such conversation, check yourself according to this list:

_____ I actively attended to the other person by mentally repeating what he was saying.

_____ I actively verbalized in my mind the speaker's rationale and worked through his reasoning. I was able to state his case effectively to myself.

_____ I put myself in the speaker's shoes and creatively tried to feel his emotions.

_____ I paid attention to my own feelings. I exercised recipathy and made myself notice the emotions aroused in me as I listened.

_____ I tuned in to hear the Holy Spirit's voice in my heart.

_____ I used eye contact, bodily posture, and encouraging phrases to facilitate the other person's speaking.

_____ I gave the person feedback by paraphrasing what I heard, telling what I felt, and saying what I thought he felt.

FOR REVIEW, PRAYER AND DISCUSSION

1. What single skill is most critical for good communication? (Without it there is no communication at all.)
2. Give a New Testament passage which urges this skill on us.
3. Most people erroneously believe the main thing in communication is being quick to _____.
4. What are some of the things people do instead of listening while others are speaking?
5. Describe the person who listens just to have something to react to.
6. Give an example of listening to judge.
7. List seven skills which are involved in good hearing.
8. Tell how attending can change you into an active listener rather than a passive blotter.
9. What is empathy? What does it have to do with hearing?

10. What is recipathy? What does it have to do with hearing?
11. Give some examples of facilitating.
12. Make up some examples of feedback. Include some thought feedback and some feeling feedback.

CHAPTER TEN

Wrapping the Truth in Love

"Mr. Blaine, I was wondering if you would give me time off work to take that assertiveness course they're offering at the community college." Walter had finally built up the courage to make his request.

"No way!" replied Tom Blaine, owner of the auto parts store where Walter worked as a clerk. "My wife took that course, and ever since she learned all that stuff, she's been impossible to live with!"

Maybe Tom Blaine was only revealing his need to dominate others. Perhaps he was one of those who think they have a right to push other people around. It's possible that he meant only to surround himself with human doormats on whom he could wipe his feet.

Maybe not. Consider that the assertiveness class in question might have taught Mrs. Blaine little more than how to be obnoxious. Perhaps the "communication" she learned conveyed to others nothing but fleshly selfishness. She actually may have become "impossible to live with." Such programs offered by some worldly "trainers" are little more than formalized exercises in "looking out for Number One."

What's the problem? Why do training programs, meant to help people communicate, become twisted? Why are the products of these programs sometimes graduated as outspoken creeps? What's wrong when knowledge puffs up people rather than building bridges between them?

LOVE, THE MIGHTIEST POWER IN THE UNIVERSE

Again, we will look to the fourth chapter of Ephesians. Here Paul offers a wealth of Spirit-inspired guidance for communication. Thus far we have concentrated on his injunction to "speak the truth." But in verse 15 Paul adds the words "in love." If we have tried speaking the truth and it has only made others wary of us, the problem could be that we haven't made the effort to speak truth *in love*.

The greatest power in the universe and the most potent force available to man is love. Not assertiveness. Not "standing up for my rights." Not telling other people off. Not blowing up whole nations with nuclear bombs. Not scientific research. Not technology. The greatest power ever known is the power of love.

Love brought the world into being. Love moved God to send His Son to identify with the fallen race of men and yield up His life for our salvation. Love broke the stranglehold of sin, of death, and of the forces of evil.

KNOWLEDGE MAKES ARROGANT

"Knowledge makes arrogant, but love edifies" (1 Cor. 8:1, NASB). Learn all the lessons this book holds, except the lesson of love, and you will have no more than educated arrogance.

Knowledge of psychology can unlock powerful resources. Knowing all there is to know about what makes people tick can bestow awesome power over others. The ability to predict and control human behavior can mean almost unlimited possibilities for getting your will done. C. S. Lewis, in his great novel, *That Hideous Strength*, makes this point; he imaginatively portrays global disaster that results from a vast increase in scientific knowledge, unmixed with love of God or man.

Many people try to learn more about human behavior so they can effectively manipulate others. For example, when I teach social skills and communication courses, someone often engages me in a dialogue like this:

"Well, I tried what you taught me with my husband and it didn't work."

"What do you mean, 'It didn't work'?"

"He didn't do what I wanted him to."

You may be tempted to read this book as a manual on how to get your way. You may even practice its methods to get power over people. You may, unconsciously, lengthen its title to read, *Telling Each Other the Truth (So As to Make Others Shape Up According to Your Specifications)*. This is what Paul means when he writes, "Knowledge makes arrogant."

Knowledge without love leads to manipulation. Any program to acquire knowledge and skills can go sour if knowledge is amassed without love. Such loveless knowledge promotes manipulation, the underhanded control of others. Manipulation often tries to make the other person feel guilty, anxious, depressed, or helpless in order to pressure him into doing what he may not want to do. Using knowledge to exploit a person rather than caring for him comes from learning *tactics* while failing to learn *love*.

This statement is an example of loveless manipulation: "I don't understand why you never come shopping with me the way other wives shop with their husbands. I feel like you don't care even slightly about my needs."

This statement is not manipulation, but a loving, truthful request: "Will you please come with me and help me pick out a new shirt at the shopping center?"

Knowledge without love leads to dictation. I have often seen people who have learned something about the teachings of Scripture on authority in the home use their new knowledge to abuse others. They take what they have learned and put it to work for themselves, issuing orders right and left or hinting around manipulatively. They issue dictatorial statements: "Get that garbage out!" "Hurry up!" "Where's dinner? I'm the head of this house and I'm home now."

In the arrogant dictator you can see knowledge puffing up. Every word coming out of his mouth says, "I'm big stuff around here."

Knowledge without love leads to abrasive behavior. The abrasive behavior of some who have taken worldly assertiveness training courses furnishes an example of knowledge without love. Much of their speech with others is filled with selfish demands coated over with supposedly assertive phraseology: "I want you to . . . I don't like . . . I feel angry about . . . I'm not going to do that for you, and I have a right to refuse . . . I have a right to expect you to . . ."

They cease doing anything others ask them to under the rubric of their newfound "rights." They begin badgering others with their new vocabulary of wants and wishes. Nothing kind or thoughtful comes out of their mouths. They believe that by thinking of themselves first, last, and always, they are "really communicating," or "healthfully fulfilling themselves," or "creatively self-actualizing." The only connection in which they think of "love" is in juxtaposition with "self," as in "self-love."

Pleased with their newfound self-love, they may or may not notice that others avoid them. If they do, they ascribe it to the fact that their friends only want to use them anyway, so let them go. They will find new friends who are as "into" self-actualization as they themselves are.

Without love, all you have learned in this book can become hideous, self-aggrandizing knowledge. Do your words puff *you* up or build *others* up ("edify" means to build up)? Does your speech enhance your own "big stuff" image, or does it make others glow with the importance God declares they actually have? Evaluate your use of what you have learned so far to determine whether it puffs you up or builds you and others up, and study to make your speech not only true, but loving.

LOVE BUILDS UP

Unfortunately, few words are more bandied about than "love." It often means anything the speaker wants it to mean— and therefore it means almost nothing.

The following is a list of ideas the word "love" is apt to evoke in our culture. A quick reading will demonstrate why it might be hard for us to think concretely about the love that builds up:

> Love may make you think of romance, feelings, friendship, attraction, sexual acts, heart palpitations, warmth, closeness, perversions, pining in sadness, affairs, high emotional arousal, desire, enjoyment, affection, savoring, benevolence, harmony, fondness, beauty, pleasantness, passion, ardor, adoration, tenderness, idolization, regard, popularity, charity, lust, fervor, admiration, fancying, yearning, libido, infatuation, ecstasy, rapture, enchantment, spiritual coupling, flirtation, hanky-panky, self-sacrifice, service.

So what does "love" really mean? When the writers of Scripture mention love, it may occasionally carry some of the meanings in the box above, for the Bible recognizes the full range of human feelings. Uniquely, however, the biblical authors speak of a love unlike the usual human emotions. Most often, their use of "love" has no relation to vague feelings, friendship, or attraction. Instead, the Scriptures tell us we are to love especially those who fail to attract us—our enemies. Therefore, the word must mean something besides positive feelings about other people. And it does.

Love means acting in the other person's best interests. If I love you, I speak the truth to you, not only for my benefit, but for yours. I seek the best not only for myself or for those to whom I feel drawn and attracted, but for all those with whom I associate. In all my actions, including my speech, I am to work for the other person's highest good.

But doesn't love mean I have to do what the other person wants, regardless of my feelings or desires? Doesn't love mean I give up my own judgments, thoughts, feelings, and wishes, and simply perform whatever another person requests of me? Not at all! Such "love" might even serve evil purposes, since it would make me an obedient servant of the other person's whims, whether good, bad, or indifferent. Such "love" might conceivably turn the other person into a whining, demanding, spoiled brat, as in the case of ill-informed parents trying to give their child misconceived "love" which grants all wishes. He becomes a monstrous little creature, intolerable to others, impossible with peers, and dominated by the misbelief that the universe exists to cater to him.

Obviously, I do not advocate saying and doing whatever the other person thinks is in his best interest. Loving another means discerning, saying, and doing what *really* is in his best interest.

Don't, therefore, in the guise of loving others, simply say what sounds good to them. Rather, speak the truth that *is* good for them. Don't merely bandy pleasantries and spray compliments around, but consider what is both true and good before you speak. Not merely, "What would Merilee like to hear me say?" but, "What is true and good for Merilee to hear?"

This kind of love requires sacrifice—you may, after all, risk your friendship by telling the other person the truth *in love.* But the love that ultimately lays down life for the other person is the love you want to incorporate into your truthful communication.

CHARACTERISTICS OF LOVING SPEECH

Since this is a book about speech, we will concentrate our attention on loving *speech,* rather than on the entire spectrum of loving behavior. First Corinthians 13 details a number of characteristics of the love we're discussing. These qualities mark all loving behavior, but are wholly applicable to the matter of loving speech. The rest of this chapter details principles drawn from this passage of scripture.

Loving speech doesn't put down. Instead of put-downs, loving speech will contain positive, rewarding phrases and words. Paul writes that love is "kind," that "it does not rejoice in wrong." Name-calling, put-downs, and zaps, on the other hand, are attempts to hurt others, or to revel in wrong, in another's sin. Pay attention to that unloving quality as you read the following examples:

"You stupid idiot! How could you be so dumb?" (Here the rejoicing is in the pain inflicted on the other person.)

339

"The only reason you brought me these flowers is to get your way again, isn't it?" (Here the other's motive is judged and put down.)

"Well, Genius, why all the C's on this report card? Teacher persecuting you again?" (Sarcasm is rarely loving. Rather, it is painful humbling of the victim.)

"Wait till I tell you what I heard up at church! Is it juicy!" (Gossip uses the misfortune and misbehaviors of others for one's own aggrandizement.)

"Hey, everybody, Sam's just asked a girl to go out with him—and, guess what! She told him to go jump in the lake!" (In front of Sam, giving occasion for Sam to make himself feel mortified and develop further his belief that he is worthless and unloved.)

Loving speech rewards others. "Love . . . rejoices in the right." It will make positive statements, reinforcing the good in others. The psychological law of reinforcement assures that whenever an action is followed by a positive event, the person is more likely to do that action again. If you, for instance, told me that this book was helpful to you, I would be more likely to write another book, since your statement was pleasant and rewarding for me.

Think how often you miss opportunities to put this principle to work. Instead of clobbering other people with zaps and attacks, gossip and put-downs, you could reward their positive behavior with love in your language. You could practice love talk instead of guilt talk, instead of hurtful talk, instead of sarcastic talk, instead of threatening talk, instead of condemning talk, instead of insulting, humbling, punishing, demeaning talk.

When your spouse does something to please you, don't take it for granted; show your love by saying something rewarding. When your child tries hard to achieve something, but fails, show your love by saying something rewarding; don't merely find fault and punish. Positive speech, not threats and criticism, undergirds good discipline.

The components of love talk, of rewarding speech, include: praise, thanks, smiles, bragging about the other person—rehearsing in front of others the good things he has done. Love talk will often include nonverbal expressions such as hugging, kissing, patting, squeezing, giving attention and showing interest in the other, doing things for the other, cookies, candies, flowers, money, favors.

But whatever you do, *don't hide hornets in your reinforcers!* My youngest daughter, Debbie, was chilly, so she went to her closet and wriggled into her warm exercise suit. Thirty seconds later her left hip felt as if it were on fire. A hornet had hidden in a fold of the suit, so instead of snug warmth, Debbie had put on a sizzling, white-hot jab in the hip. A source of comfort had become a source of agony.

The same can happen in speech if love is tainted. In the process of giving a reward, of saying something loving and positive, many people think, *But the act I'm rewarding wasn't quite perfect, and I wouldn't want to reward the imperfect part, so I'd better include a qualifier.* The result is the hornet in the reinforcer. The person receiving it feels at first as though he is being loved and ends up feeling the jab of the stinger. Some people are so accustomed to including zaps in their reinforcers that they almost never truly reinforce anyone.

Here the zapper tries to reinforce her little girl who has just dried the dishes for the first time in her young life: "Thank you for doing the dishes, Emily. That was so nice of you. And they are lovely. But look at the water marks you left on the glasses. You must do better next time, darling."

What little Emily gets out of this is a painful message: You didn't do a good job. If the zapper zaps routinely, this little girl will likely grow up with a full set of perfectionist misbeliefs, constantly bugging her with the notion that nothing she does is really good enough.

Some people seem always to include the hornet with their reinforcers:

> "It was nice of you to think about cooking dinner, but you forgot I don't like garlic on my meat."
> "That was a fine sermon, but I don't agree with your interpretation of the passage you used for a text."
> "Thanks for taking me to lunch. But I shouldn't have wasted so much time with you."

"You played a great game, except for the fly ball you missed in the third inning."

Notice the following examples of rewarding, loving speech—no hornets. See if you don't feel better as you read them than you did reading the zapping "reinforcers" above.

"I really appreciate you."

"I love you."

"I like you."

"I care about our relationship, and that's why I want to work this out with you."

"I really enjoy being with you."

"What can I do for you to show you I appreciate you?"

"You were great tonight."

"You did a marvelous job."

"Wow! Wearing this shirt you gave me made me a celebrity! I was the center of attention all day at work. Everybody stopped to admire it."

"Thank you for what you did for me."

"Thank you for washing and ironing my clothes."

"Thank you for working so hard to support all of us."

"You are wonderful! I'm so pleased you thought of me and invited me."

"You paid a lot of attention to me at the party. I really appreciate that!"

A note of caution: Beware of the perverse habit of bestowing reinforcers on others when the relationship is in trouble.

Ronson, for example, told me with great self-satisfaction that he had given his wife, Lena, some flowers: "They did the trick, too," he crowed.

"Just what 'trick' were they supposed to do, Ronson?" I asked, pretty sure I already knew.

"Well, we got ourselves into a hassle and Lena wouldn't talk to me. It went on for hours. And, believe me, it can actually continue for days at our house. But this time, I said to myself, 'I'm going to put a stop to it right now.' And I went right out, bought a dozen roses, handed them to Lena, and she put her arms around me. Something pretty great happened next. Flowers'll do it every time!"

I said, "Not such a hot idea, in my opinion!"

"Worked better than some of your ideas," Ronson replied, miffed. "What's wrong with it, I'd like to know."

"Nothing, if you're trying to train Lena to pout and frown silently whenever she's upset with your behavior. Is that what you want to do?"

"Huh? Of course not. I want her to discuss her problem so we can work it out."

"You must remember, Ronson, that whatever behavior you reward is the behavior most likely to occur every time similar circumstances arise. If you give Lena flowers when she pouts, she will develop the pouting habit into a real art."

Ronson, like many other people, feels strongly that no one should be rewarded for doing good—they're only behaving as he expects they should. So, unfortunately, he waits until others behave in ways that hurt him. Then he gives them the attention and love they would like to get from him when they do well.

Are you one of those who fawns over others when they cause you trouble and ignores those who are supportive, loving, and helpful to you? Like Ronson, you are probably rewarding behavior which is the opposite of what you would like others to be and do.

If you don't learn another thing from this chapter, learn to bring home flowers, fix special meals, bestow extra attentiveness, and offer positive reactions to others *when they have done things you like and appreciate*, and *not* when they are angry or giving opposition.

Loving speech admits faults. "Love does not insist on its own way." Open to criticism, willing to listen, and willing to admit faults, loving speech does not engage in defending and attacking. (See chapter 3.) Loving speech is not defensive or aggressive, even under provocation.

Here are some examples of loving speech, paired with their defensive counterparts. Wouldn't you rather learn love talk?

Loving Speech	*Unloving Speech*
Have I done something to hurt you?	What's the matter with you? Can't you ever be happy?

I see I've upset you. I think I've said something that hurt. I'm sorry.

What have I said this time? Are you ever sensitive!

You've made me see I've hurt you. Is there any way I can make up for my stupidity?

Now I've done it again. Whatever I try to do, you aren't able to accept it without getting your feelings hurt. Would it help if I stood on my head?

You're right. It wasn't very kind of me to do all the talking and exclude you.

I didn't do *all* the talking. Besides, you never say anything anyway.

You have a point. And now that you mention it, I agree that I could have been more thoughtful than I was.

I'm as thoughtful as you. What about the time you forgot even to visit me in the hospital?

You've got a point. I should do a better job of taking care of our lawn than I do.

I do as good a job as any other guy in the neighborhood!

You know, I haven't paid as much attention as I could to dressing neatly. Thanks for calling to my attention the mismatch between my shirt and tie.

I'll dress the way I want to. You wouldn't know when things match and when they don't anyhow.

As you say, it was careless of me to overlook putting gas in the car.

I'm always putting gas in your car. Once in a while I'd like to use some of it.

LOVING SPEECH AVOIDS ANGER.

Love "is not easily provoked." To be hard to provoke means to be irenic, seeking solutions and compromises. In his own eyes a great hero, in God's eyes an unloving bully, the man who never seeks compromise, but makes each of his wishes a matter of principle on which he firmly plants his big unmoving feet, is not speaking truth in love. Love attempts to avoid anger and conflict.[1]

---

[1] You can learn more about avoiding anger from the book *Telling Yourself the Truth* by William Backus and Marie Chapian. Here you can observe that dealing with anger requires that you learn to speak to others in truth and

344

"I care. Let's work it out. I don't want to give up on our relationship. I'd like to find a way for the two of us to solve this." That's a free sample of peacemaking speech. It makes a great substitute for: "Drop dead! I don't care if I never see you again. So there."

You will find that peaceful speech is nearly impossible unless you have first, quietly, under the impulse and direction of the Holy Spirit, talked to yourself in a manner like this: "Now, cool it, Ginny. He's just pushing your buttons. You can keep yourself from getting angry, and you'll be able to handle this just fine if you do. Try a soft answer."

Practice controlling your own self-talk when you feel that someone else is getting under your skin.

LOVE IS LONG-SUFFERING

You have finished reading this book. You have practiced hard, kept logs, and changed your speech. You now know how to request change, and you are very effective at it. You have done all you can. You have offered to change yourself. You have spoken positive, reinforcing truths.

Question: Now what if the other person continues the same old patterns of undesirable, offensive, unwanted behavior? He won't change, no matter how hard you try. What then?

Answer: Put up with it.

The biblical bottom line is this: live through it. If nothing you say to the troublemaker helps, no matter how scientifically and psychologically potent it is, no matter how grounded in the Word and truth of God it may be, then God's Word to you is "Hang in there."

If you live with a husband who is difficult, a wife who's impossible, parents who are utterly beyond belief, or children who remain incorrigible, *put up* with them. If you face a roommate who won't negotiate, a pastor who won't minister to you, a boss who makes irrational demands, associates who violate

---

love, as well as that you learn to change how you speak to yourself. Further discussion of the art of managing anger is offered in *Telling the Truth to Troubled People* by William Backus. Both of these books are published by Bethany House Publishers.

your expectations right and left, *put up with them*—for as long as the Lord leaves them in your life. Love is long-suffering.

One of our most dogged misbeliefs is the notion that we should not have to put up with any fault or failing in anyone else. We should be expected to relate only to perfect people. We should live in a universe where others always treat us fairly, squarely, nicely, positively, and lovingly. And if, perchance, we come across someone violating our norms, it is our right to get upset, to scream and yell, to end the relationship, to stage a protest, to walk away with our marbles and refuse to continue the game. We have, most of us, grown up believing it is awful if someone does not treat us precisely the way we want to be treated.

The truth you must tell yourself to learn long-suffering is this: *God has not given me a contract guaranteeing I will always be surrounded by people who do nothing but right, good, true, and fair things*. God has never promised a universe where the behavior of other people will be sinless toward you. When you stop being shocked at the sinful behavior of other people, you will find your angry outrage replaced by patient long-suffering.

Maybe you have been telling yourself, "How outrageous that he should treat me this way. I never would treat him so. I shouldn't have to take this. It's just terrible that I'm being subjected to it. Furthermore, I can't stand it any longer. I have every right to yell and object and get myself good and angry— maybe even do something drastic!"

Try this instead: "I have no reason to expect that so-and-so will be perfect. I don't like his behavior, and I don't have to like it. I don't approve of what he is doing, and I don't have to approve of it. But I have known since I was a tot in Sunday school that human beings sin. So I am neither surprised nor outraged that I haven't been able to make so-and-so change in the way I want him to. I am disappointed, especially since I worked so hard at it, but I can handle it. I don't have to upset myself. I can keep my cool, and I can go about my life without relying on him to change right now. Perhaps at some other time the change I want will occur. Meanwhile I can pray for him, love, and reward him for any small positive actions I like and appreciate. I can hang in there and keep myself in control."

WHEN LOVE MUST INFLICT PAIN

Sometimes love inflicts pain. God is pure love, yet He willed the suffering of Jesus, His only-begotten Son! Even when Jesus pleaded, "Father, if thou be willing, remove this cup from me," the Father, strong in love, ordered His Son to drink.

I love my children. Yet I deliberately inflicted pain on all of them at various times. Spanking three-year-old Christa when she went into the street was an act of love. Temporarily depriving sixteen-year-old Annie of the use of the car when she drove dangerously was an act of love. Martin and Debbie too could tell you of similar acts of love which, when they occurred, seemed painful.

At age ten, Christa grasped this principle so well she decorated a special stick, lettered it with the label, "The Rod of God," and contributed it for loving application by her parents!

Rarely does the world understand the sort of love which loves enough to hurt, to deny requests, and to minister frustrations and corrections. But such love is the love of God and of the people of God.

Sometimes it is necessary to address someone with truthful speech which hurts. A loving parent may have to say truthful words to a child though the child would rather not hear them: "I haven't liked your behavior this afternoon, especially when you yelled at me in the store. So I'm not going to give you a cookie."

A spouse speaking the truth in love may have some things to say which the other spouse finds painful: "I didn't like the way you talked to David today; it seemed flirtatious to me."

The point is that we cannot measure love solely by whether or not what we say hurts someone's feelings. The fact that another person may not like what we have spoken does not automatically mean we have done wrong.

Nellie, for instance, was nearly at her wits' end. She did not want to go out with Glen. But Glen kept asking her despite her excuses. One time she told him, "I can't go to the movies with you because I have to study." Another time, "I have to visit my sick aunt in the hospital." At other times, "I'm too tired." "I may be out of town." "I have to wash my hair." "I think I'm having company that night." Nellie tried all the time-worn, barely truthful excuses she could think of, but Glen kept calling.

"Why don't you tell him you don't want to go out with him and you would like him not to call you?" I asked her. "Wouldn't that be the precise truth, Nellie?"

"Sure, but that would hurt his feelings!" she responded, her tone implying that I had suggested something akin to assassinating Glen.

"Probably it would hurt Glen some. But what do you think you're doing now? Your thin excuses are telling Glen not only that you don't want to see him, but also that you don't think enough of him to level with him about it. Talking straight to Glen might hurt at first, but not as much as any other alternative you can think of."

"I guess you're right. Stringing Glen along isn't loving him. I think I'm probably just trying to make it easy for myself. And what I'm doing isn't easy after all. I'm beginning to feel like a creep. I think I'll tell Glen not to call anymore. It'll be hard, but it's the best way in the long run."

Nellie finally told Glen straight-out that she didn't want to date him. Glen's reaction surprised her. He thanked her for her openness, and suggested she keep her options open and give him a call if she ever did feel like seeing him again. Then Glen offered to have coffee with Nellie and to share openly with her how he had felt while she was putting him off with her excuses.

Eventually Nellie became curious. She called Glen and they did get together for coffee. After a little small talk, Glen explained his reaction to Nellie's excuse-making tactics.

"It wasn't easy," he confided. "I knew you intended to put me off, especially after the second or third call. But I wasn't completely certain of your reason. You might have been just shy—or you could have had some other reason for turning me down that you didn't want to tell me. Of course, I realized the most likely explanation was that you didn't want to see me. It's always been hard for me to risk any kind of rejection, but I was so strongly attracted to you I decided to force myself to keep calling until you either dated me or told me truthfully you didn't want to." Glen was open and straightforward as he divulged all this to Nellie.

Nellie began to realize there was a lot to this young man, and that her first impressions had been based on superficial evidence. She offered to see Glen again if he still wanted to get together. The last time I saw her, Nellie was dating Glen exclusively and they were beginning to wonder whether the Lord had perhaps meant them for one another.

This example of Nellie and Glen is probably more typical than it appears to you if you are unaccustomed to straightforward speech. It offers a graphic illustration of the truth that loving speech may, in the long run, mean choosing to say what hurts rather than what seems easy. And it certainly illustrates the benefits of truthful, loving speech!

THE SOURCE OF LOVE IN YOUR SPEECH

The well out of which the water of love must be drawn is the love that glues the universe together: the love of God. Infinite and incomprehensible, all-embracing and self-giving beyond any human model, God's love sets a pattern for us to follow which both encourages and discourages. God's love encourages us because the Creator and Father of us all commands us to do nothing He has not already done himself. It can discourage us, too, because we can never achieve the perfection and oceanic depth of His love. By the Spirit's power we can imitate but we cannot duplicate His love.

In fact, those who do not truly know God cannot even begin to love with His love. That is because they stand outside the realm in which they could experience His love. God loves them but they haven't yet recognized or become aware of that love.

There is, according to Jesus, one way to the Father and His love. That is Jesus Christ himself (John 14:6). If you have not yet traveled that way, you can do so right now. You can turn from your sin, your disobedience. You can believe that He died for your sins and because of that, your Father forgives them all and receives you fully into the circle of fellowship with himself and all the children of God who really experience His love in Jesus.

You can say, right now, in your internal monologue (or self-talk), "Lord Jesus, You are *my* Savior from sin and death, my

Savior from deceit and lovelessness, too. I believe this and I thank you for this gift. I choose to follow your example of love by the power of the Holy Spirit whom you send into my heart now as your Gift of Life. Amen."

Now comes into your psyche the divine power without which none of the love of God could direct your own behavior and speech, the power of the Holy Spirit dwelling within you. Now you can love with the love of God, as well as be loved by the love of God.

FOR REVIEW, PRAYER AND DISCUSSION

1. What is the sorry result of some worldly training programs in "assertiveness"?
2. What is the mightiest power on earth? Give some reasons for your answer.
3. What, according to 1 Corinthians 8:1, may be the result of truth (knowledge) without love?
4. What temptation could beset people who are working through this book without giving careful attention to the goal of this teaching?
5. What can knowledge without love lead to in relationships?
6. Give some examples illustrating your answer to question 5.
7. How can the concept of "rights" be misused?
8. Give a few of the multitude of ideas evoked in our culture by the word "love."
9. In Scripture usage, the word love most often means _____ _____.
10. Why is it important not to interpret the word "love" as meaning "Give the other person whatever he wants"?
11. Give some examples of speech which "rejoices at wrong."
12. Love in our language should ordinarily be rewarding to other people. What kind of things do we often do instead?
13. What is the mainstay of good discipline?
14. What are "hornets in your reinforcers"?
15. Give some examples of reinforcing speech.
16. Loving speech admits _____.
17. Give some examples of your answer to #16.

18. Loving speech is not easily _____.
19. Give some examples of peaceful speech.
20. Tell about some self-instruction you will need to give your-self to control anger and exhibit peaceful speech.
21. What does "long-suffering" mean in plain English?
22. Give some examples of loving speech which might inflict pain and still be loving.
23. Where must you begin if you wish to learn to love others?

CHAPTER ELEVEN

Telling the Truth in Social Talk—Small Talk

Helen was seeking psychological help, but not for the usual reasons. She was not suffering great anguish. She was not plagued by jumpy, anxious feelings. She was not ridden with unwanted habits too tenacious to break. In fact, Helen was considered a success by all who knew her. Excellent progress in her graduate studies at a prestigious university portended a bright employment future. She wasn't beautiful, but she wasn't ugly or repulsive either. All-in-all, things looked good for Helen.

Except for one thing. Helen had no friends. She had relatives back home and acquaintances on campus, but not a soul she could properly call a friend.

Here is an excerpt from our first conversation:

Backus: What do you mean by a "friend"?
Helen: Someone I can talk to and be close to. I don't feel free to phone anybody just to talk. And there's nobody I can open up to.
Backus: Do you have any theories about why?
Helen: No, I don't. I try to be pleasant to people. I greet them and observe all the amenities. I don't get it.
Backus: Do you join organizations, go to parties, work at meeting people and chatting with them?
Helen: I hate those things. Sitting around, trying to think of something significant to say, having to listen to chit-chat turns me off!

Backus: What is there about socializing that bothers you?
Helen: Well, I can never think of anything to say. And I don't think people are interested anyway. I know I'm not enthralled with what others are saying. It all seems to be "much ado about nothing."
Backus: You don't like small talk?
Helen: I certainly don't. And I see no sense in it.

Is it difficult for you to socialize? Do you find it unpleasant and uninteresting to engage in what is often called "chit-chat"? We will refer to this sort of speech as "small talk" because it is talk about small matters, generally indulged in with no great sense of gravity or importance.

Anyone may have trouble with small talk. He may be the brilliant intellectual who cannot let go of his heavy thoughts and just chat about anything and everything. Or perhaps he is the hard-driving type "A" business person whose one-track mind breaks its restless mulling over job-related matters only to grab a few hours' sleep. Again, he might be the shy, anxious, jumpy type who glues himself timidly to the wall in the darkest corner he can find when other people gather for social talk.

Such people usually have one thing in common: they have never learned to indulge in casual conversation. They haven't acquired the skills of small talk.

Chattering, getting acquainted, socializing, shooting the breeze—did Jesus occasionally "let down" and participate in purely social conversation? Some people think not. They can't envision Jesus smiling or playing. They never let themselves imagine He could have engaged in the random palaver of ordinary human beings at social gatherings.

The Bible certainly cautions us against indulging in coarse joking and foolish chatter with immoral content (Ephesians 5:4 condemns such vain speech). But I find nothing in Scripture that forbids moderate social discourse. Nowhere does it say, specifically, whether Jesus and the apostles practiced small talk or not. We can only conjecture.

In my opinion, they did. We know they observed other social amenities appropriate to their culture, and occasionally this would include attending a party or a dinner. They went fishing or hiking when they needed a break. More than likely their camaraderie included more than just formal teaching and learning. The picture I have of their mealtimes, for instance, is not that of a monastic refectory where all remain silent at the table while one reads from an appointed text. Rather, I envision men and women in relaxed desultory conversation, recounting their experiences, expressing their feelings, likes, and dislikes, and discussing together the events of their day.

Perhaps some of those who cannot imagine Jesus indulging in companionable small talk are unable to get the hang of it themselves. A common deficit among workaholics, introverts, and blue-nosed legalists suspicious of any pleasure, the inability to make small talk can be remedied by those willing to work at it. Those who are very shy, to the point where they become tongue-tied in nearly any social situation, especially where interaction is with more than one person at a time, will need to practice the skills offered in this chapter.

Some people, however, though not particularly shy, have obtained what reinforcing attention they get from others by speaking of deep, serious subjects. Consequently, they attempt to retain a little place in the limelight by uttering weighty speech on every occasion. Like people who are inhibited by shyness, these heavies feel lost in sociable contexts where the conversation is light and given to rambling. Preachers, professors, doctors, psychologists, and business people often remain nose-to-the-grindstone types because they are lost for something light to say in a circle of chatting acquaintances.

"WHATEVER IT TAKES, I DON'T HAVE IT"

"But I can never think of anything to say," Helen told me when we got to the subject of hobnobbing with others.

"It's not easy for you to participate in group verbal behavior?" I suggested.

"Oh, I'm fine when I'm giving a report to the class or discussing an assignment with someone. But where I have trouble is in social groups. I walk up to people standing together in the halls and feel like a fifth wheel."

"Like a fifth wheel?" I wanted her to go on.

"Yes, 'I don't belong here,' I keep telling myself. They are talking about football and I don't know a thing about football—or, for that matter, any other sport. And when they discuss politics, religion, or horseback riding, it's just as bad. What I know somehow doesn't seem to fit in, so I don't come up with anything to toss into the conversation pot."

"Do you ever try to chime in?"

"Not very often. When I do, nobody pays much attention. I might ask a question and not even get an answer, it's that bad. Whatever it takes, I don't seem to have it."

Helen's case is not unusual. The experiences of varied types of people deficient in the skills appropriate to small talk are very similar. Note these statements that crop up frequently in counseling sessions:

- "No one talks to me."
- "I can never think of anything to talk about."
- "People don't notice me at all."
- "I feel out of place."
- "I try to say something, but nobody responds."
- "They're always talking about subjects on which I'm uninformed."
- "I tried to break in by asking a question, but nobody answered it. It was as if I wasn't even there."

DOES SMALL TALK SERVE A GOOD PURPOSE?

Very frequently, such people exhibit a defensive disdain (or even raise "spiritual" objections) to small talk. "I can't see any purpose in it," they complain. "It's just a waste of time."

You have, perhaps, consoled yourself for your deficiencies by telling yourself that whatever it is you can't do very well isn't important anyhow. You may have handled your awkwardness with social talk by doing some of the same things Helen did.

When I suggested she learn sociable chatting, Helen objected: "It's boring, and I never enjoy it. Why learn it? Besides, I can't see that it serves any purpose. It seems to me people would be better off if they talked about serious matters. There are so many problems in the world, so many significant issues in human life, so many burning spiritual topics, I don't see why I should waste time and energy on chewing the fat!"

Are you puzzled about the purpose of what you might call "idle chatter"? Do you, like Helen, mildly resent that you are, evidently, expected by others to engage in light, insignificant banter about nothing in particular when your head is full of serious issues? Or are you, perhaps, anxious and tense at the very thought of participating freely in the recreational conversation of a group? "Why should I make myself so nervous?" you want to know.

"Helen," I suggested, "social conversation does serve some purposes. Let's take a look at some of them."

"Go on." Helen was not one to waste time.

"Well, to begin with, what may look like aimless chatter provides a setting for two people to meet each other and perhaps begin a friendship."

"But couldn't people get to know each other just as well if they discussed the theory of electromagnetism or something else *interesting*?" Helen was becoming impatient with me.

"Not very likely, Helen. In fact, your suggestion illustrates my point. How many people are you likely to meet in a social setting who are proficient in your technical, scholarly pursuits? As a matter of fact, one of the primary purposes of small talk is to give people a chance to know a little about each other and about each other's interests and experiences. After the discovery of mutual interests, conversation can pursue a path both people find exciting. Or else—and this is equally valuable— two people can discover they have few common interests and move on to get acquainted with others."

"I see," said Helen. "In other words, small talk conveys some important information, tiny bits at a time, so people don't come on to each other all at once." Helen was getting into the spirit of the thing so she continued. "I remember meeting a guy at a party once who told me in the first sentence or two of our brief conversation some intimate details about his personal life. It was too much for me to handle, all of a sudden, and I remember feeling it was inappropriate for him to reveal so much so soon."

Helen's rather exceptional experience made a point perfectly. Namely, that small talk enables people to get acquainted a little at a time. Total openness and intimate self-revelation from someone one has just met creates problems very difficult for most people to handle.

Here is a summary of the purposes of small talk as I outlined them for Helen: Small talk enables people to (1) start relationships and, in some cases, begin to build friendships; (2) get to know and be known a little at a time, meanwhile testing the waters of a new acquaintanceship; (3) pass the time pleasantly and entertainingly.

HOW TO SMALL TALK

Make your questions interesting. Most people think they would be wisest to ask questions of the other person when they find themselves in the untested waters of a new acquaintanceship. For example: "What did you think of tonight's speaker?" "How do you think the election's going to come out?" "Where are you from?" "How long have you been a member here?" "Have you known the Smiths for some time?" These all might be openers for a small talk conversation with one person. In a pinch.

Questions, however, can be dull and prosaic. If they are the same old questions everyone asks, social conversation can develop the automatic, monotonous sameness Helen complained about.

I tried to show Helen, however, that even questions can be made interesting. I suggested, "Helen, see if you can improve on some of the more routine, get-acquainted questions by asking them in ways that provoke thought." She was equal to the task.

Instead of "What did you think of tonight's speaker?" as an opener, Helen came up with, "Tell me what, for you, was the most important point tonight's speaker was making?"

Instead of, "How did you like your visit to Israel?" she suggested, "What did you find on your trip to Israel that would especially interest me? What should I make a point of trying to see or do?"

Rather than, "How long have you been a member here?" Helen thought more interest might be sparked by a question such as "What about this organization made you want to join it?"

Spend some time thinking about how you can improve your small talk questions to elicit interest and responsive enthusiasm from other people. Practice inventing questions you believe will make the other person think.

A note of caution: Don't fire questions one after the other as if you were holding an interrogation or conducting an employment interview. Remember to intersperse your questions with statements offering your own point of view, background, interests, and feelings. And give the other person a chance to initiate topics or ask questions too.

Learn to tell stories. Spend some time listening to the social chit-chat of others, carefully noting the tactics of those who skillfully gain attention in a group. If you do this you will probably discover that the best social talkers are those who tell stories well.

Questions are not enough. If you try to break into a group with a question, you may discover that no one responds. Or the response will be perfunctory and you will be as lost as before. What you must learn to do is tell stories. Experiences. Your own or those of someone else. Perhaps something you have read or heard in the media. Occasionally a joke.

The person who avoids small talk with a shudder has very likely never learned to narrate. If you have a problem with social talk, get-acquainted talk, hob-nobbing-with-new-people talk, the chances are excellent that you haven't mastered the art of telling stories.

Jesus was a master storyteller. He rarely talked without stories. He must have learned to file away the things He saw and experienced in such a way that He could recall and share them with others. After all, it need not matter if the stories are fresh or old—they only need to provide interesting conversation.

Helen argued again when I tried to convince her of the need to work at learning to narrate: "I don't see why I should have to work at this as if it were an examination in physics. I thought socializing was supposed to be fun!"

"And I suppose you want your skills at small talk to come naturally—" I replied—"as if they were encoded in your genes?"

"Well, yes. I don't want to be putting on a show I've rehearsed in advance when I'm trying to be myself. It's dishonest!"

Helen finally agreed it is sensible to work at acquiring any new skill, and that no behavior becomes second nature without practice. She went home and wrote out three stories she could conceivably tell in most social settings. She was to memorize her stories, practice telling them in front of a mirror, and tell them to me at our next session just as if we were participating together in a social conversation.

Helen's stories, like most things she did, were quite adequate. All of them were based on personal experiences.

I made her tell me her stories several times because she was tense and uncomfortable doing the unfamiliar. Finally, Helen was able to relax and feel quite comfortable as she rehearsed her material.

Helen's next assignment was to tell someone else her stories.

"That ought to work out pretty well," she said, showing a bit of tentative enthusiasm. "I'm going to an open house tonight, and I don't know most of the other guests. I'll try my stories on some of them."

Helen came to her next session beaming. For once she had felt good about a social occasion in which she was forced to talk to strangers. She reported enthusiastically that others listened to her stories, chimed in with their own, and gave every evidence of enjoying chatting with her. She had felt included in a social gathering of which she had previously known only three of the eighteen people present.

Perhaps you are having difficulty imagining how all this worked. You're thinking, What about the fact that Helen's stories were all prepared in advance? How could she be sure they would fit in? What if her stories were about—say, animals, and the others were talking about something else—baseball, or kamikaze pilots, for instance?

I had worked on this point with Helen before the party. In small talk, unlike some other forms of conversation we have studied, it is perfectly all right to tie your story loosely to the flow of things and proceed with it. This sort of talk is often desultory anyway. It frequently rambles along from subject to subject with no more to tie topics together than loose associations.

To introduce the experience you want to recount, simply say, "That reminds me of something I saw today over at the shopping center. . ." or, "For some reason, what you just described makes me think of what my doctor told me yesterday. . ." That's all the introduction you need to launch into your story.

If you bear in mind that, in small talk, you have a right to change the subject if you feel like it, you will solve the problem posed by shy, introverted people: "I can't think of anything to say on the subject others are discussing."

How do I answer that objection? "Well, then, change the subject. Nobody will mind."

Please note that such license to change the subject applies only to small talk. In other kinds of talk, you must follow more rigid rules.

Here are some stories Helen wrote out, memorized and later used satisfactorily at a party. They are reproduced approximately the way Helen told them to the group.

#1

"Al, what you said about the crime wave reminds me of my parents' effort to protect their home. When they moved to their place in the country, my dad said, 'We should get some dogs. This house is quite a distance from the watchful eye of our nearest neighbor.' So we got a pair of German Shepherd puppies. At two years old, they looked big and fierce enough to scare off any intruder.

"Well, the other day I was at my folks' house alone. I had been in the backyard, came into the house, and thought for sure I heard someone at the front door. I went and looked, and sure enough, a delivery man had the door ajar and was putting parcels inside into the hall.

"And the dogs? What were they doing? Our two fierce-looking watchdogs were on the scene all right, wagging their tails and licking the man's hands as if he were a relative. Such watchdogs!"

#2

"Tom, your earthquake experience makes me think of the day last spring when my friend and I were watching a fascinating movie in the shopping center theater. Suddenly, the projector shut off, the lights went on, and the manager stepped forward. 'Please leave the theater,' he announced. Not another word, no explanation, just, 'Please, everyone, leave the building.'

"What was it all about? A fire? We joined an orderly line and stepped out into the parking lot.

"The sky was dark brownish yellow. The crowd was excited. People were pointing to the western sky where a huge, black funnel cloud was racing toward the spot on which we stood. No one had told us we were directly in the path of a tornado! And no one had directed us to shelter. We made for a roadway with a ditch alongside. My friend had taken her shoes off in the theater and was having trouble getting them on again.

" 'Come on, Jo!' I shouted, 'hurry up and get those shoes on. We have to run. It's worth a little effort to hurry.' But the tornado was bearing down on us so we changed our course and headed for the shopping center.

" 'Maybe we can find shelter inside,' she said. Still the storm seemed determined to follow us.

"Finally I pointed my finger straight at the racing funnel and yelled, 'I command you, in Jesus' name, turn away!' I thought to myself, *You sound quite presumptuous!* Nevertheless, for whatever reason, the monster changed directions, veered off to the north, and the entire shopping center was left untouched by the storm!"

#3

"Speaking of babies, I'd like to tell you about an experience I had in the woods the other day. I was going for a walk, and I came upon a quiet little pond, nestled among the trees.

"*Keep hidden,* I thought to myself, *maybe there will be geese or ducks on the surface of that clear, lovely water.*

"I approached stealthily, keeping my feet off branches and twigs. Soon I spotted a female mallard with a brood of newly hatched ducklings swimming after her. She was alert for danger and soon became aware of my presence. Softly and swiftly she gave her babies a command, and instantly they turned their little heads down and their tails up and disappeared beneath the water, little rippling circles marking their dives.

"Almost as quickly, the mother took to the air. She made no effort to hide herself. On the contrary, she quacked loudly and flapped noisily, circling around me until she was sure I saw her. Then she flew in circles ever farther from the spot where her little ones had disappeared.

"*What a woman!* I mused. *She's offering herself and her life for her babies.* You know, she could teach something to the rest of us about unselfishness. What a contrast between the self-giving love of this mother duck and the selfish uncaring of some human mothers who sacrifice their unborn babies' lives for their own convenience!"

Self-revelation—the name of the game. Because you are a child of God, and because His very nature leads Him to reveal himself, you as a Christian must also practice openness. The things you say and do may either hide or reveal who you really are. Developing closer relationships involves revealing more and more of yourself to other people. A truly close relationship is one in which both persons practice total truthfulness. Even in small talk, you must reveal small doses of yourself to give others something to relate to.

Helen's stories are not perfect models of brilliant, sparkling small talk. However, these stories exemplify some of the functions of small talk. They are therefore included so you can learn from them.

Notice in each of these stories how Helen has revealed small bits of her inner self. Below is a list of some of the things a total stranger could learn about Helen by hearing her stories:

1. Helen's parents live nearby in the country. She probably doesn't live with them.

2. She attends the theater with her girlfriend. Helen is likely not married.
3. Helen used the name of Jesus seriously. She must be a Christian.
4. One of the issues Helen seems to care passionately about is the sacredness of human life. Moral issues seem important to her.
5. Helen enjoys walking in the woods and attending good movies.

All of that from three simple little stories!

HUMOR

The examples we have given from Helen's small talk include no jokes. Nonetheless, jokes have a place in small talk, although many Christians shy away from telling them for several reasons: First, jokes are often told at someone's expense. If your speech embarrasses or hurts another person just to gain a few moments in the social limelight, the price is too high. If the story you want to tell makes fun of some racial or cultural subgroup, make certain you don't rub a raw nerve or massage salt into an open wound. People who are battling feelings of religious, cultural, or racial inferiority in themselves, and genuine prejudice in others, are not likely to find as much humor in such stories as those of an "established" cultural group. You can usually get away with making fun of Norwegians among Norwegians. But be careful of jokes told at the expense of blacks, hispanics, or Indians. They have suffered true discrimination, and can justifiably be hurt by degrading remarks.

Second, much humor these days is immoral. I need not dwell at length on the fact that, among Christians, filthy, off-color stories have no place.

Finally, many ordinary, garden variety jokes used as small talk leave little room for self-revelation. When you tell a story you heard or read, you are telling very little about who and how you yourself are.

Humor, however, can ripple through stories of your own experiences. You do not need a punch line to get people smiling.

363

Notice again Helen's story of the two dogs. Her audience smiled as she pictured two huge canine oafs, acquired for their reputation as fierce watchdogs, fawning over the stranger who had calmly opened the front door and set packages inside. Such humor in personal experiences can serve as a vehicle to give others bits of information about the inner you. Such stories are a valid example of "telling each other the truth"—the truth about yourself.

PRACTICING

Satisfied with your own social talk? Or do you want to improve your skills? If you desire to change your small talk habits, to acquire the ability to ask interesting questions and to tell stories when you are socializing, you will have to work at change. As with other skills taught in this book, little will be gained by merely reading what I have written. By contrast, much can be done through practicing what you have read.

Helen practiced her small talk skills assiduously. As a result, she found her fear of group gatherings markedly reduced. In fact, at times she sought out get-togethers and found a good deal of satisfaction in just chatting with people she didn't know very well.

The most valuable result for Helen was an increase in friendships. This is not a chapter on the subject of making friends, but I can tell you briefly what Helen did. She found opportunities to talk at greater length with some of those who small talked with her. She discovered that her interests and values were shared by a few of them. Likewise, others discovered much in Helen to like and seek out. They exchanged phone numbers. Helen had lunch and coffee with people she wanted to know better. She made a point of initiating additional contacts—something she had feared doing because someone might reject her. In a very short time, Helen had developed a number of meaningful friendships, some of which were progressing toward closeness.

If you decide you want to practice small talk skills, remember to tell yourself the truth that small talk is *not* a trivial waste of time. Rather, it is a necessary social activity which gives people a chance to know each other gradually and without great threat.

Practice devising interesting questions and use them. Practice telling stories from your experiences and use them. You might feel a bit forced when you first try new social behavior. That feeling will occur often as you apply the teachings you find in this book. But as you continue to practice, what at first felt stiff and abnormal will eventually feel as much a part of you as the habits you have developed up to this point.

Practice devising questions. Write out a list of ordinary questions you might hear wherever two people who don't know each other very well are chatting. Here are some examples:

1. What do you think of the weather we've been having lately? Hot enough (or cold enough or wet enough or dry enough) for you?
2. Where do you live?
3. Were you born here?
4. Do you have a family?
5. Did you have a nice vacation?

These questions, asked over and over in everyday social contexts, are not likely to evoke much interest. So see if you can rework them or invent others which might provoke a bit more thought in the respondent. Here are some examples to get you started:

1. Do you think weather affects people's moods and personalities? What do you think the weather we've been having might do to most people's moods? [Weather is the old standby. People *are* interested in it. Might as well make it interesting.]
2. If you had your choice of any area of the country [city, state, world—if you like], where would you choose to live?
3. Do you think any special traits are particularly characteristic of people who were born here? How about yourself? Do you have these traits? Why or why not?
4. In your opinion, what is the ideal size for a family? Why do you think so? Is your family that size?
5. I understand you went to France for your vacation. Tell me,

what would you recommend I should under no circumstances miss if I would visit France?

Now you work out some additional revamping of common small talk questions. Memorize them carefully before the next occasion comes to strike up a conversation. Then go for it. Give your questions, or some of them, a try. You will very likely not have to use more than one or two. The conversation will likely take care of itself after one or two of your deftly crafted openers.

Practice telling stories. Chances are, you will find it easier to ask questions than to devise and tell good stories. That is why I recommend you give storytelling much more practice than questioning. Seek out opportunities and settings where you can tell your stories. Do as Helen did: Write out your stories at first. Unless you are already a skilled storyteller you will find it much easier to work out interesting stories from a written draft which you revise until you are satisfied.

Then memorize your stories.

I know, you'd like it all to be spontaneous. And if you are one of those fortunate folks already skilled at narrative, you can skip this hard work. But just wishing it would all come naturally doesn't make it so. That is why you should, at first, write out and memorize narratives.

Then get out and use what you have created. Remember, in the usual small talk setting, you don't need much of an excuse to change the subject. Not much more is necessary than to say, "Speaking of . . ." or "That reminds me of the time . . ." Your story will remind someone else of one and the conversation will follow on your new track for a while.

Don't fail to include small and tasteful truths about your inner self in your small talk. Reveal yourself to others. Give them something to like. There is nothing wrong with letting others know that you like to ski, that you never miss prayer meetings, or that you love good books.

Do you wish the old radio shows would come back? Are you looking for someone to go fishing with? Do you develop, enlarge, and print your own photographs? Tell people. Do winter days make you sad? Are you feeling considerable loss since your last child went off to college? Do your angel food cakes fall when

366

you try to make them from scratch? Open up. Let people know you.

Most people don't need a caution here, but some do: Don't reveal too much of yourself too soon. There are many things appropriately reserved for relationships which have been tested a bit. Usually, good judgment will tell you what they are. Pray for guidance in the matter of what to reveal to whom and when.

FOR REVIEW, PRAYER AND DISCUSSION

1. For what kinds of people is small talk apt to present difficulties?
2. What is the difference between the difficulties of the shy and introverted and those of the type A personality, insofar as small talk is concerned?
3. What are the reasons for learning small talk?
4. Is small talk purposeless? Give reasons for your answer— i.e., give the purposes of small talk.
5. What sort of important information is small talk meant to convey to others?
6. What is a close relationship?
7. How many very close relationships do you have? If you have none or few, you are not the only one. If you have none or a few, would you like to have more? Why do you answer as you do?
8. What two skills can you develop to improve your small talk?
9. Tell how you can go about developing each one.